BEFORE THE BLUE JAYS

HARVEY SAHKER

BEFORE THE BLUE JAYS

Professional Baseball in Toronto Prior to 1977

DUNDURN PRESS

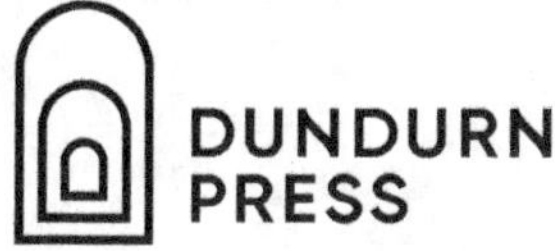

Publisher: Meghan Macdonald | Acquiring editor: Kwame Scott Fraser | Editor: Allister Thompson
Cover designer: Karen Alexiou
Cover image: Dreamwaves / Freepik

Library and Archives Canada Cataloguing in Publication

Title: Before the Blue Jays : professional baseball in Toronto prior to 1977 / Harvey Sahker.
Names: Sahker, Harvey, author
Description: Includes bibliographical references and index.
Identifiers: Canadiana (print) 20250278995 | Canadiana (ebook) 20250279002 | ISBN 9781459755642 (softcover) | ISBN 9781459755666 (PDF) | ISBN 9781459755659 (EPUB)
Subjects: LCSH: Baseball—Ontario—Toronto—History.
Classification: LCC GV863.15.T6 S24 2026 | DDC 796.35709713/541—dc23

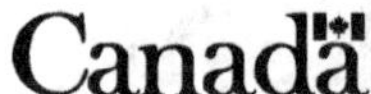

We acknowledge the support of the Canada Council for the Arts and the Ontario Arts Council for our publishing program. We also acknowledge the financial support of the Government of Ontario, through the Ontario Book Publishing Tax Credit and Ontario Creates, and the Government of Canada.

Printed and bound in Canada.

Dundurn Press
1382 Queen Street East
Toronto, Ontario, Canada M4L 1C9
dundurn.com, @dundurnpress

To my sons, David and Sam.

To the memory of my mom, who introduced me to the names Rocky Nelson and Mike Goliat.

To the memory of my dad, with whom I shivered on that snowy, damp Thursday afternoon at CNE Stadium in April of 1977.

Contents

PART V: THREE BATBOYS AND THE BOSS'S KID

PART VI: THE HOMEBREWS

PART VII: OTHER TORONTONIANS

PART VIII: TALES OF WOE

Introduction

Professional baseball leagues have been around since 1871. The first such league, the National Association, was formed that year. It was the forerunner of today's National League and consisted of a small number of teams from the American Northeast and Midwest.

The teams played scheduled games against each other, and whoever finished atop the standings was declared league champion at the end of the season.

In addition to their scheduled league games, National Association clubs played exhibition games against non-league teams.

In 1901, the American League joined the National League as professional baseball's two major leagues. The Federal League, now regarded as a third major league, was in operation in 1914 and 1915.

Apart from the major leagues, there are two types of professional baseball leagues in North America. The first, the minor leagues, consist of what are basically feeder leagues for the major leagues. Leagues are given designations that generally reflect the calibre of play: AAA, AA, A, and R (rookie league). These "classes" evolved over the years. Typically, a player signed to a contract out of high school will start in Rookie League and progress to class A, AA, and AAA before reaching the majors. Classes B, C, D, and E also existed at one time.

The other type of professional baseball is the independent leagues. These are not feeder leagues whose teams have a committed relationship with a major league club. Such leagues are sometimes referred to as "outlaw" leagues because they exist outside of the major-minor-league pyramid.

In response to the racial segregation of professional baseball from the late 1800s until Jackie Robinson's arrival in Montreal in 1946, African American leagues were formed. Referred to as the Negro Leagues, they continued to operate into the 1960s.

Professional baseball teams first visited Toronto in the early 1870s. The city got its first professional team in 1885. Toronto teams have called several ballparks home since then. Those ballparks have disappeared and are largely forgotten.

Young baseball fans in Toronto could be forgiven for thinking that professional baseball in the city started with the formation of the Blue Jays. In fact, the city's pro baseball history goes back over 140 years.

Going back to the beginnings of professional baseball, Torontonians have contributed to the pro game as players, owners, umpires, and so on. Some of these individuals were as quirky as a well-thrown knuckleball.

This book tells the stories of some of the ballparks, teams, games, and people that comprise the history of professional baseball in Toronto … before the Blue Jays.

PART I

HOME SWEET HOME

Strange Place for a Diamond

It was one of the most unique professional baseball venues ever. Anywhere. And it was in Toronto. Called the Motordrome, it was a motorcycle and bicycle racing track on Greenwood Avenue, north of Queen Street East. For a brief time, it was pencilled in as the regular home of the Toronto Beavers of the Class B Canadian League.

Construction on the Motordrome began in mid-March of 1914. In early May, it was regarded as "more than probable" that the Beavers would play their home games at the new stadium.[1] In the meantime, the Motordrome was nearing completion. The *Globe* praised the facility for its "superb accommodation for spectators."[2] Only the diamond itself "requires considerable rolling and scraping, but it can easily be made into the best ballpark in this country."[3]

According to plan, the bicycle track of the stadium was pitched at a fifteen-degree angle. Surrounding and adjacent to it was a quarter-mile motorcycle track, which was to have a sixty-degree pitch. That's steep, more vertical than horizontal. To put that into perspective, the steepest portion of Talladega Superspeedway is pitched at thirty-three degrees.

BASEBALL TO-DAY
AT MOTORDROME
AT 3.00 O'CLOCK
ERIE vs. TORONTO

Grand Stand Tickets 50c
Bleachers 25c
Children under 12 years of age...15c

Newspaper ad for a Toronto Beavers game at the Motordrome.

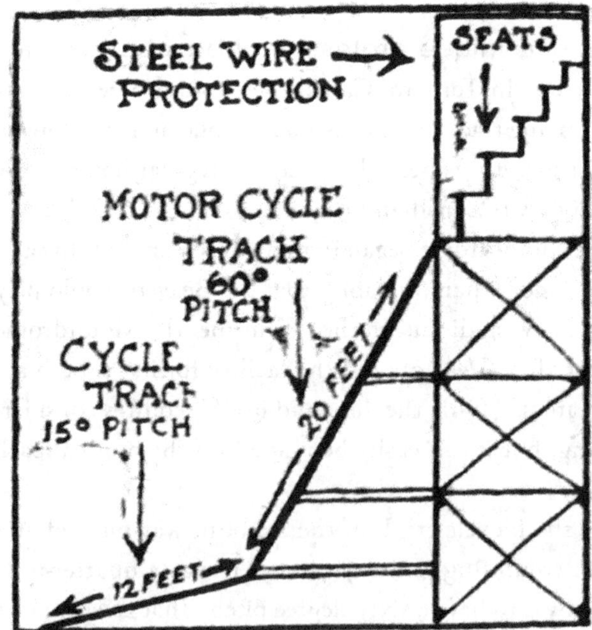

A cross-section of the Motordrome. The baseball diamond was located inside the cycle track.

The stands were positioned just above the motorcycle track. Seats in the lowest row of the stands were close to the top of the actual track. Very close. Similar facilities existed elsewhere, in Pittsburgh, St. Louis, and Cleveland, among other cities. Toronto's Motordrome was to have a capacity of 5,000.

The motorcycle races were dangerous for riders and spectators alike. In 1912, at the Newark Motordrome, a rider lost control of his bike and flew over the rail and into the stands. Eight people were killed. The track was soon closed and demolished.

Toronto's Motordrome was in the city's east end. Local baseball fans were weary of having to take a ferry to and from Island Stadium to see the International League Maple Leafs (yes, the city was home to two pro baseball teams in 1914). Getting to the Motordrome would be much faster than getting to Island Stadium. If only there could be baseball at the Motordrome. Space was certainly not a problem, since the infield of the Motordrome was big enough to hold a baseball field.

• • •

During the winter of 1913–14, there was speculation that Toronto would be granted a franchise in the new Federal League (FL). A "rebel" third major league, the FL eyed Toronto with interest. The league's president came to Toronto to gauge the viability of a Toronto club.

No fewer than five Leafs jumped to the FL that winter: third baseman Bill Bradley, catcher Drummond Brown, shortstop Ed Holly, pitcher Bert Maxwell, and outfielder Benny Meyer. Bradley, Holly, and Maxwell had all been regulars on the 1913 team.

Ultimately, the FL decided against coming to Toronto. One of the reasons was the lack of a suitable ballpark. Island Stadium was unpopular because of its remote location. The Motordrome was an alternative, but was it viable as a regular baseball venue? The FL would be competing with the Beavers and racing promoters for popular dates, like weekends and holidays. This problem would be mitigated somewhat by lights, which were part of the plan and would facilitate night racing. For some reason, the idea of playing baseball under those same lights was not seriously considered.

• • •

The Canadian League was in its fourth year of operation in 1914 and had been upgraded from Class C to Class B during the off-season. The Toronto Beavers and Erie Yankees were newcomers to the eight-team league, replacing the Berlin (now Kitchener) Busy Bees and Guelph Maple Leafs, respectively. A Toronto syndicate had bought the Berlin club for $3,000.

In mid-May, it was announced that the Beavers would begin their home schedule on the island and later move to the Motordrome. A few days later, the Cleveland Motordrome was closed permanently because of an accident that had occurred that very day. Five people were injured when a collision caused a rider and his bike to be thrown over the guardrail and into the crowd. There had been multiple fatal accidents at the track the previous year.

A panoramic photo of the new stadium was published in the Toronto *Sunday World* less than a week before the first day of racing. The structure completely dominates the image. There is a massive latticework of exposed wood beams. The stands encircle the track completely. Looking at the photo, it is easy to imagine the Motordrome as a baseball stadium. From afar, the stadium looked like a giant saucer.

Ontario premier James Whitney and some 2,500 fans watched the Beavers win their home opener 6–5 against Ottawa in late May. The game was played at Island Stadium, since the Motordrome was not ready yet. Three presidents attended: James Norris of the Beavers, J.P. Fitzgerald of the Canadian League, and J.J. McCaffery of the International League (IL). Alex Graham, a product of Toronto sandlot ball who had been recently cut by the Leafs, pitched a complete game for the Beavers. It was great to finally be home. The Beavers had started their regular season with sixteen road games, of which they won seven.

The Beavers finally made their Motordrome debut on June 13 against St. Thomas. It was the first time in several years that a Toronto pro baseball game had been played on the mainland. The attendance was 1,542. Alex

Graham started on the mound again. He allowed a pair of runs in the top of the first but threw shutout ball the rest of the way. Unfortunately for Graham and the Beavers, St. Thomas hurler Roy Wilkinson was even better and kept the Beavers off the score sheet entirely. St. Thomas won 2–0. Wilkinson went on to spend two full seasons and parts of three others in the big leagues. His pro career spanned twenty years. Graham, on the other hand, pitched in the minors for just three seasons.

A week later, the Beavers returned to the racing track. They scored in six straight innings and defeated first-place London by a score of 10–5. Charlie Isaacs, a local lad, hit a triple and had four hits overall. Bobby Auld, another Torontonian, was the winning pitcher. Auld went the distance for the Beavers.

The Beavers defeated Erie 9–7 at the Motordrome on June 27. Second baseman George Ort led Toronto with three hits. Ort, thirty-two, was near the end of an eleven-year pro career. In 1909, he played in 202 games for Portland of the Pacific Coast League. That league was well known at the time for having long schedules.

The condition of the Motordrome playing surface forced the Beavers to relocate some of their home games to Island Stadium. Their next home game at the racing track was not until August 8, when they were defeated 6–3 by Erie. Teenage pitcher Emilio Palmero entered the game in relief for the Beavers. The nineteen-year-old Cuban southpaw pitched for both of Toronto's pro teams in 1914: the Beavers and the Maple Leafs. Palmero had a long, successful pro career. He won twenty-eight games for Omaha in the Class A Western League in 1920. By the time he retired, in 1931, he had notched over 200 wins.

Palmero and five position players share the honour of playing for the Beavers at the Motordrome and the Leafs at Island Stadium. The quintet were outfielders Irvin Trout, John Sullivan, and Charles Kroy, and infielders Charlie Isaacs and Charlie Snell. The Beavers were, effectively, a farm team for the Leafs.

• • •

Emilio Palmero.

Three Beavers players made an unscheduled appearance at police court on the first Sunday of September. Pitcher Bobby Auld, second baseman George Ort, and catcher Pat Harkins were found guilty of using profane language during a game the previous day. They were fined a combined twenty-one dollars. Ort was reportedly suspended for the remainder of the season. This was presumably a symbolic gesture more than anything else. The Beavers had just one game left to play.

This was not George Ort's first brush with the authorities. In early August of 1911, while playing for Seattle in the Northwestern League, he went berserk during a game against Spokane. Ort hit the umpire, Jake Baumgarten, with a baseball. He then felled Baumgarten with a single punch. The ump was knocked unconscious. Three policemen escorted Ort from the diamond.

Ort was initially suspended indefinitely while the league figured out what to do with him. Some wanted him banned for the rest of the season. Ultimately, Ort was suspended for just over a week without pay and fined $50. In all, his behaviour cost him about $100, equivalent to roughly $3,000 today. For a minor leaguer, that's not chump change. As a condition of Ort's reinstatement, he remained on probation. If he behaved himself, he would be eligible to play.

The next year, 1912, saw Ort playing for a team in the upstart United States Baseball League (USBL). This organization should not be confused with the United States League, an African American loop that existed briefly in the mid-1940s. The USBL was in operation for less than two months before it collapsed. Ort, playing for the USBL club in Cleveland, had a memorable afternoon early in the season. Ort hit a home run and three doubles in a 13–8 victory at home against a team called the Chicago Green Sox. That is as many home runs as he hit in his full season with the Beavers.

The Toronto Beavers lasted a little longer than the USBL, but they also went bust. The club lost a reported $2,500 in 1914. That is about $75,000 today. When the Canadian League opened its 1915 ledger, its membership had shrunk from eight to six teams. One of its defunct clubs was the Toronto Beavers.

On May 22, 1915, there was a horrible accident at the Motordrome. Ernest Roberts, the track's caretaker, was struck by a motorcycle. He died of his injuries eleven days later. The Motordrome was demolished in the spring of 1917, just three years after it opened.

Toronto Ballparks and Teams

Toronto's first professional baseball team took the field in 1885. Simply known as "the Torontos," the club was based at the Jarvis Street Lacrosse Grounds at the northwest corner of Jarvis Street and Wellesley Street East. Directly across Jarvis Street was the home of Hart Almerrin Massey, the man Massey Hall is named for. The Torontos competed in the Canadian League, a loop with teams in Toronto, Guelph, London, and a pair of clubs in Hamilton. Capacity was a modest 3,000.

Professional baseball returned to Toronto in 1886, albeit in a different league and at a different venue. The Toronto Base Ball Ground (TBBG) was not quite ready when the Toronto Canucks were scheduled to play their home opener. Ultimately, the Canucks were forced to play their first few home games at Rosedale Field, which was in Rosedale Park. The first Grey Cup final was played at Rosedale Field in 1909. The attendance at that game was 3,800.

The TBBG was located on a rectangular parcel of land bordered today by Queen Street East, Broadview Avenue, Sunlight Park Road, and Baseball Place. Today's exit ramp from Adelaide Street East to the northbound Don

Valley Parkway cuts through what used to be part of deep right centre field at the TBBG.

Toronto's first dedicated baseball facility, the TBBG held 2,200 and featured a "grandstand." Almost 4,000 fans packed the house for the first game at the TBBG, on May 22, 1886. The field faced south. The Sunlight soap factory was a short distance away, and the small stadium earned an alias: "Sunlight Park." Spectators from west of the Don River had to cross that waterway to reach the TBBG. For them, going "over the Don" meant heading to the ballpark.

There was no professional baseball team based in Toronto from 1891 to 1894 inclusive. In 1895, pro ball returned to the TBBG as the Canucks joined the Eastern League, the forerunner of today's International League.

Toronto was home to a pair of professional clubs in 1897. A team in the Canadian League used the TBBG briefly, then folded in midseason, while the Eastern League team used a stadium at Hanlan's Point that was commonly known as Island Stadium. Getting there meant taking a ferry from downtown.

The Eastern League team moved from Hanlan's Point to Diamond Park in 1901. This stadium held 6,000 fans and was located at the southeast corner of Liberty Street and Fraser Avenue. The grounds of today's Lamport Stadium are on the other side of Liberty Street.

Diamond Park opened its doors on May 10, 1901. Toronto lost 6–5 to Worcester before a full house. Worcester outhit the home team 15–7. The game was preceded by a parade in which both teams participated.

The Toronto *World* correspondent had this to say about public transit for getting to and from the new stadium: "The streetcar service was totally inadequate, both going and coming, and the poor fans devoutly hope the railroad will become alive to their requirements."[4]

La plus ça change …

By this time, Toronto's Eastern League team was known as the Maple Leafs. The club kept that nickname for over sixty years.

A fire destroyed Island Stadium in September of 1903. Damage was an estimated $15,000. The baseball club was unaffected by this fire because they were using Diamond Park at the time.

Island Stadium was rebuilt and became the home of the Maple Leafs in 1908. Capacity at version two of the ballpark was 7,000.

On August 10, 1909, the ballpark burned to the ground again. The adjacent amusement park and the nearby hotel also went up in flames. A woman was killed in the blaze. Damage was an estimated $150,000 (worth around $5,500,000 as of this writing). The fire forced the baseball club to play the remainder of their 1909 home games at Diamond Park.

The third — and final — version of Island Stadium was hastily built and was ready for the beginning of the 1910 season. Capacity was 17,000. The Leafs played their home opener in front of an estimated crowd of 13,000. Many fans wore raincoats and wielded umbrellas. The Leafs fell behind 3–0 to Baltimore. Centre fielder Al Shaw hit a three-run homer in the seventh to tie the score. In the ninth, with two out and nobody aboard, Shaw doubled. He later scored the winning run.

The Eastern League was renamed the International League in 1912.

Babe Ruth hit his only minor league home run at version three of Island Stadium in 1914. It was not his only home run in Toronto.

In 1914, for the second time in the city's history, Toronto was home to two professional baseball teams. Version three of Island Stadium hosted the Maple Leafs and the Beavers of the Class B Canadian League. The Beavers also played some of their home games at the Motordrome.

The Leafs stayed at Hanlan's Point until 1926, when they moved into Maple Leaf Stadium at the foot of Bathurst Street. They played there for forty-two seasons. This ballpark held 23,500 fans.

Opening Day of 1926 was attended by some 14,000 fans, despite poor weather. The game was preceded by the playing of Canada's national anthem, which was "God Save the King" at that time. Visiting dignitaries included Judge Kenesaw Mountain Landis, the first commissioner of Major League Baseball.

In 2001, baseball historians created a list of the best hundred minor league teams to commemorate the hundredth birthday of the National Association of Professional Baseball Leagues. Five Toronto teams made the list: 1902 (#76), 1918 (#45), 1920 (#21), 1926 (#39), and 1960 (#87).

The left-field portion of the Maple Leaf Stadium grandstand. Photo taken from the roof.

The following Toronto teams played in the Little World Series, which was contested by the champions of the International League and American Association:

YEAR	FORMAT	OPPONENT	RESULT
1907	Best-of-seven	Columbus Senators	Won 4–1
1917	Best-of-seven	Indianapolis Indians	Lost 4–1
1926	Best-of-nine	Louisville Colonels	Won 5–0
1934	Best-of-nine	Columbus Red Birds	Lost 5–4
1960	Best-of-seven	Louisville Colonels	Lost 4–2

The competition was renamed the Junior World Series in 1932.

PART II

BASEBALL ROYALTY COMES TO TOWN

Overmatched: Pros vs. Amateurs

Canada was only four years old when Toronto baseball "cranks" (what fans were called in period baseball jargon) got their first look at a professional baseball team. It was back in August of 1871, when the Rockford Forest Citys came to town. That's the correct spelling, by the way: "C-I-T-Y-S."

Rockford and eight other teams comprised the National Association (NA), which was brand spanking new in 1871. The NA was the forerunner of today's National League.

The Forest Citys had recently put together a modest three-game win streak when they came to Toronto. That may not seem like much, but Rockford played only twenty-five NA regular season games that year. They finished with a 4–21 win–loss record, last in the loop.

The best-known Forest Citys player was Cap Anson, then a nineteen-year-old third baseman. Anson went on to play twenty-seven years in the big leagues. He was a member of the National League's Chicago club (not yet called the Cubs) for all but the first five of those seasons. Anson was voted into the Hall of Fame in 1939.

The Rockford lineup featured a second Hall of Famer, much less known than Anson. Bob Addy was from Port Hope, about a hundred kilometres east of Toronto. Ten years Anson's senior, Addy played second base for the Forest Citys. Addy was inducted into the Canadian Baseball Hall of Fame in 2021.

Fred Cone, a Forest Citys first sacker prior to the formation of the NA, once said the following about his Canadian teammate: "Bob Addy, our second baseman, used to practise a quick, sharp throw from his station to me at first, and I noticed that I had to make some lunges to get the sphere. One day he said that he had mastered the curve, and I believed him."[5]

The Rockford nine came to Toronto to play the Guelph Maple Leafs, one of Canada's top teams. Toronto was just a whistle stop on Rockford's 1871 tour, which included a few games against Guelph. On August 10, the clubs went toe to toe in Guelph. The tourists won handily, 26–0. The next day, in Hamilton, Rockford whipped Guelph by a score of 50–9.

The game in Toronto was scheduled for the afternoon of August 12, a Saturday. The first pitch was scheduled for three o'clock at the Cricket Ground, located near the corner of College and McCaul Streets. Admission was twenty-five cents.

It was a beautiful afternoon. The game started well for the Maple Leafs. Each team scored twice in the first inning. The second frame was scoreless. But Rockford staged a six-run rally in the third and coasted to a 38–3 victory. Half of their runs came in the ninth. Denny Mack, the Rockford first baseman, scored seven runs.

Baseball was a different game in those days. Pitchers threw underhand only. Batters could request pitches wherever they wanted them in the strike zone. Players fielded barehanded. A fly ball caught on one bounce was an out. There were no batting helmets, batting gloves, or designated hitters.

• • •

The next professional touring baseball team to visit Toronto was the Boston Red Stockings, also of the NA. They were scheduled to play an exhibition game against Toronto Dauntless on August 24, 1872. Simply

Toronto Dauntless.

known as “Dauntless” in local newspapers, the club was in only its second year of operation.

On paper, at least, the talent gap between Dauntless and Boston was huge. Dauntless was an inexperienced amateur team. The Red Stockings were in the middle of a pennant-winning campaign in which they won over 80 percent of their NA regular season games. When the Boston team embarked on their tour, they sported an astounding record of thirty wins and only three losses.

Much less is known about Toronto Dauntless. The team photo above was published in the *Globe*, some thirty years after the tussle with the Red Stockings. The collars and shield-shaped bibs were typical of that time. The stylized “D” on the bibs looks very much like the one on the home jerseys of the Detroit Tigers.

The Dauntless pitcher was William Mountain, aged twenty-two (give or take a year), who would go on to have a long and successful career. But with Consumers’ Gas, not baseball.

Boston's lineup was a veritable who's who of early professional baseball. Harry Wright, the team's thirty-seven-year-old player-manager, batted ninth against Dauntless and played centre field. A few years earlier, Harry Wright had fulfilled the same roles for the Cincinnati club. Also called the Red Stockings, Cincinnati was baseball's first professional team. They went undefeated in sixty-nine games against all comers in 1869 and 1870.

George Wright was Harry's younger brother and Boston's leadoff hitter in Toronto. He was an ambidextrous shortstop who is acknowledged as the first to play that position deep so that his range would be greater. George is regarded as the best shortstop of his time.

Hitting fifth in the Boston batting order was their pitcher, Albert Goodwill Spalding. Founder of the sporting goods empire that still bears his name, Spalding was just twenty-one years old when the Red Stockings visited Toronto. He would go on to win over 200 games for Boston in just five seasons.

The Wright brothers and Al Spalding are all enshrined at the Hall of Fame.

Dauntless did not live up to their name against Boston. The Toronto team needed confidence. They needed practice, too. They made twenty errors. In contrast, Boston booted the ball only four times. The offerings of William Mountain were hit often and hard. The Red Stockings amassed no fewer than fifty-nine hits. George Wright and second baseman Ross Barnes had nine hits each in the game. Barnes went on to hit .430 and win the 1872 NA batting crown.

When the smoke cleared, the Red Stockings won 68–0. *Sixty-eight runs.* To make matters worse, Dauntless collected just one hit off Spalding. That came off the bat of Mountain, trying to help his own cause. All but eleven of the Boston runs scored as the result of an error. The Wright brothers scored ten runs each.

That final run tally is not dissimilar from those of various games won by the Cincinnati Red Stockings during their undefeated 1869 season. That year, Cincinnati won by scores like 86–8, 80–5, 85–7, and … 103–8. Dauntless were in good company, at least.

Ross Barnes.

On August 26, two days after the Dauntless fiasco, Boston played the Independents, another amateur club, from Dundas, Ontario. The game was played at Toronto's Cricket Ground. Boston scored six runs in the first and pummelled the Independents 52–4. The *Globe* observed that it was useless for amateurs to think they could compete with professionals.

Not heeding the *Globe*, Dauntless decided to have another go with Boston in 1873. Back at the Cricket Ground, Dauntless lost, 45–10.

Dauntless player William Mountain hit a "fair foul" in the sixth inning of this game. A "fair foul" is an oxymoron today, but it was a legitimate baseball term in 1873. A "fair foul" was, simply, a batted ball that bounced fair and then went foul before it reached first or third base. A foul ball nowadays, but a fair ball then. Mountain hit a double on the play.

Later in the game, Mountain got Boston's Al Spalding out on a "foul bound." This was a foul ball caught on one bounce for an out.

Ross Barnes homered for Boston that afternoon. Home runs were a rare commodity in the 1870s. Lipman Pike of Baltimore led the NA with seven round-trippers in 1873. A total of thirty-seven dingers were hit league-wide that summer. This was partly due to deader baseballs. Indeed, that period of baseball history is referred to as the "dead ball era." The pitching was slower, too, and many batters practised what was called "scientific" hitting. That was the act of trying to place the ball, instead of trying to knock the cover off it. "Hit 'em where they ain't," as long-time major league outfielder Wee Willie Keeler said.

Actually, Keeler did not utter those words until much later. He was only a year old during the 1873 season. As it happens, his last year as a pro was with the Toronto Maple Leafs, in 1911.

"All Pro" Exhibitions

Midseason exhibition baseball games were not uncommon in Toronto throughout the pre–Blue Jays era. Most of these games pitted Toronto against a big-league club.

Here are highlights of some of the "in-season" exhibition games in which Toronto played a major league team:

SEPTEMBER 14, 1885 – The National League's Detroit Wolverines defeated the Torontos of the Canadian League 8–1 in an eight-inning game. Detroit's pitcher was Charles "Pretzels" Getzien, a twenty-one-year-old righty who had a 12–25 record for Detroit that season but completed all of his thirty-seven starts. He went 30–11 the following season. James McKinley, an early Toronto "homebrew," took the loss.

SEPTEMBER 18, 1885 – Edward "The Only" Nolan of the Philadelphia Quakers pitched a three-hitter and defeated the Torontos 5–1 at the Jarvis Street Lacrosse Grounds. Nolan, thirty, was a native of Trenton, Ontario. For losing pitcher James McKinley, it was his second loss to a National League opponent in five days.

SEPTEMBER 28, 1885 – Boston of the National League eked out a 1–0 victory over Toronto. The lone run was unearned. Toronto hurler Bill Stemmyer and Boston pitcher Jim Whitney held their opponents to just two hits each. "Grasshopper Jim" started fifty National League games for Boston in 1885. He completed them all, winning eighteen and losing thirty-two.

JULY 26, 1886 – The National League's St. Louis Maroons beat Toronto 7–5 in ten innings at Sunlight Park. An all-Canadian Toronto battery consisted of pitcher Bob Emslie (Guelph, Ontario) and catcher John Humphries (North Gower, Ontario). Emslie went on to have a long career as an umpire. He was inducted into the Canadian Baseball Hall of Fame at St. Marys, Ontario, in 1986. Humphries was a left-handed catcher.

SEPTEMBER 23, 1902 – Toronto lost 7–3 to Pittsburgh. Cooperstown Hall of Famer Honus Wagner was one of three Pittsburgh players with two hits. Deacon Phillippe, the winning pitcher, went on to defeat Cy Young in the first ever World Series game, in 1903. This game was played at Diamond Park.

AUGUST 31, 1908 – The Boston Doves (now the Atlanta Braves) defeated Toronto 7–3. Boston player-manager Joe Kelley went two-for-five. This was his last season in the big leagues. Kelley also played for (and managed) the Leafs and is a Cooperstown inductee.

SEPTEMBER 9, 1913 – Toronto lost to the New York Giants 10–3. Jim Thorpe, the famous Indigenous multisport athlete, played for the Giants and hit a home run. This game was played at Island Stadium.

JUNE 4, 1915 – The Leafs beat the Boston Braves 5–1. The Braves were the defending World Series champions. The winning pitcher was Cuba's Adolfo Luque, who held Boston to four hits and did not walk anyone. Cooperstown Hall of Famer Rabbit Maranville played shortstop and had two hits for Boston. The visitors included four ex-Leafs: Fred Mitchell, Dick Rudolph, Ted Cather, and Ed Fitzpatrick.

SEPTEMBER 1, 1916 – The Detroit Tigers defeated the Maple Leafs 6–5. Ty Cobb had two hits (a single and a double) in three at-bats and stole a base. Fellow Cooperstown inductees and teammates Harry Heilmann and Sam Crawford hit a triple and a double, respectively.

JULY 24, 1917 – Toronto lost 13–6 to the Detroit Tigers. Harry Heilmann and Bobby Veach, who went on to hit .310 in a fourteen-year major league career, homered for Detroit. Ty Cobb went one-for-five.

JULY 5, 1918 – Cincinnati pushed across the winning run in the top of the ninth in a 2–1 squeaker against the Leafs at the island. Hal Chase led the Reds with two hits. "Prince Hal" was simultaneously regarded as one of the best defensive first basemen and one of the least scrupulous players in baseball history.

AUGUST 14, 1918 – Southpaw Ferdie Schupp held Toronto to three hits as the New York Giants whitewashed the Leafs 5–0.

Ferdie Schupp.

AUGUST 27, 1919 – Fred Merkle homered for the Cubs in their 6–3 win over the Leafs. Back in 1908, Merkle had committed one of baseball's costliest baserunning mistakes.

AUGUST 17, 1920 – The Boston Braves edged the Leafs 2–1 in ten innings.

MAY 9, 1921 – Babe Ruth and Bob Meusel homered to lead the New York Yankees to a 4–3 win over the Maple Leafs. Ruth had three hits. The game was followed by an International League (IL) regular season game between Toronto and Reading. Attendance was about 10,000.

AUGUST 28, 1923 – Toronto whipped the Yankees 8–2. Ruth homered in a losing cause.

JULY 25, 1924 – The Leafs beat Detroit 6–5. Ty Cobb had this to say to Leafs owner Lol Solman about the Leafs playing on the island: "With grounds anywhere but where you are the chances of your city getting in the major league game someday will be considerably enhanced."[6] Toronto right fielder Joe Kelly had four hits, including a homer. Kelly had 680 hits in less than three and a half seasons with the Leafs.

JUNE 23, 1925 – Ty Cobb hit a homer, a double, and a pair of singles as Detroit mauled the Leafs 12–3. Cobb, then player-manager for the Tigers, put himself on the mound late in the game. This was the second game of a doubleheader. In the opener, Toronto crushed Buffalo 14–0 in a regular season IL contest.

JULY 7, 1926 – Carl Hubbell pitched a three-hitter as the Leafs eked out a 5–4 victory over Detroit at Maple Leaf Stadium. Hubbell had six strikeouts and gave up six walks.

SEPTEMBER 10, 1926 – Babe Ruth had a pair of singles and the Yankees beat the Leafs 8–2. Carl Hubbell went the distance for Toronto and was nursing a 2–1 lead after seven innings. New York then scored four times

Babe Ruth.

in the eighth and three more in the ninth. Lou Gehrig hit a double for the Yankees.

JULY 7, 1927 – The Leafs scored seven runs in the sixth inning and defeated the New York Yankees 11–7. Babe Ruth hit a double and single, and Lou Gehrig had three singles.

AUGUST 27, 1928 – Hall of Famers Rogers Hornsby and George Sisler had three hits and two hits, respectively, as the Boston Braves defeated Toronto 4–1.

SEPTEMBER 14, 1928 – Ty Cobb, forty-one, had two hits for the Philadelphia Athletics in their 3–1 win over the Leafs. Cobb had already played what would turn out to be the last regular season game of his big-league career, on September 11. Six days later, he announced that he would retire at the end of the season. This exhibition game at Maple Leaf Stadium may have been Cobb's last game in a major league uniform.

SEPTEMBER 6, 1929 – The St. Louis Browns beat the Leafs 3–0. Righty Dick Coffman pitched a one-hitter for the Browns.

JULY 11, 1930 – The Yankees defeated the Leafs 16–11 in a seven-inning game. Babe Ruth hit two homers, including a grand slam. He also doubled and drove in seven runs. New York scored eleven runs in the second inning.

MAY 31, 1939 – Robert "Red" Rolfe, Charlie "King Kong" Keller, and Tommy Henrich had two hits each as the Yankees beat the Leafs 4–1. Henrich hit the game's only homer. The losing pitcher was starter Phil Marchildon of Penetanguishene, Ontario. One of Canada's best hurlers, Marchildon went seven innings and gave up all four runs; 1939 was his first season as a pro. Less than a month before this game, Lou Gehrig had benched himself after playing a then record 2,130 consecutive games. Gehrig participated in pregame fielding practice at Maple Leaf Stadium but didn't appear in the game. Soon thereafter, he would learn that he was dying of amyotrophic lateral sclerosis.

AUGUST 13, 1951 – The Leafs blanked the St. Louis Browns, their parent club, 3–0. Satchel Paige started on the mound for the Browns and took the loss. George Armstrong of the hockey Leafs pinch-hit for Toronto in the sixth inning and played the rest of the game in right field. At the time, Armstrong was playing semipro baseball in Sudbury for the Garson Greyhounds of the Nickel Belt League.

AUGUST 18, 1952 – Toronto pushed across the tying run in the bottom of the ninth and won it in the tenth, 5–4 over the St. Louis Browns. Leafs manager Burleigh Grimes celebrated his fifty-eighth birthday on this date.

JUNE 27, 1955 – Right fielder Lew Morton and shortstop Hector Rodriguez had three hits each to lead the Leafs to a 7–3 victory over the Chicago White Sox. Morton's haul included a pair of doubles.

JUNE 17, 1957 – The Leafs scored twelve runs in the sixth inning and defeated the Detroit Tigers by a score of 16–4. The big inning featured three-run homers by Russ Rac, Stan Jok, and Lew Morton.

• • •

Occasionally, two major league teams played each other. The following four such games took place at Hanlan's Point:

MAY 31, 1917 – The Boston Braves defeated the St. Louis Browns 4–3 in a six-inning game that was called early due to rain. Burt Shotton hit a two-run homer for the Browns. Shotton hit just nine home runs in fourteen big league seasons.

AUGUST 15, 1917 – The Chicago Cubs beat Detroit 2–1 before a crowd of about 9,000. Ty Cobb had a single and a double in a losing cause.

JULY 23, 1918 – Brooklyn defeated Pittsburgh 5–2. Leafs president James McCaffery was misled into believing that this was a regular season game. "Mr. McCaffery booked the game in good faith as a National League championship fixture and had no reason to suppose that there was anything different, as the teams were scheduled to play the game and it was arranged to transfer it to Toronto," said the *Star*.[7]

JUNE 19, 1924 – The Pittsburgh Pirates nipped the Yankees 2–1. Babe Ruth hit a double. Rookie shortstop Glenn Wright hit a two-run homer and started three double plays for Pittsburgh.

• • •

Starting in the 1950s, Maple Leaf Stadium hosted games between a major league team and the International League All-Stars:

JULY 23, 1956 – The Milwaukee Braves blanked the International League All-Stars 3–0. Hank Aaron played right field for the Braves, went one-for-three, and knocked in two runs. Righty Bob Trowbridge threw a one-hitter for the Braves. Attendance was 15,028. This was the first IL All-Star Game.

JULY 28, 1958 – The Milwaukee Braves edged the International League All-Stars 3–2. Hank Aaron had a double, single, and run batted in. The winning pitcher was Gene Conley, who also played basketball in the NBA for six seasons. Attendance was 10,506.

JUNE 27, 1960 – The IL All-Stars whipped the Milwaukee Braves 7–2. Hank Aaron hit a solo home run in a losing cause. Hall of fame pitcher Warren Spahn had a pinch-hit single for Milwaukee. A lifetime .194 hitter, Spahn hit thirty-five career home runs.

JUNE 20, 1966 – The Boston Red Sox defeated the IL All-Stars 6–4. Carl Yastrzemski homered for Boston. The crowd of 2,484 was the smallest in the IL All-Star game's brief history.

The Court Jester

It would have been appropriate if some leather-lunged fan had bellowed, "Send in the clowns!" There were two bona fide clowns available to relieve Harry Kelley, a twenty-year-old who had started on the mound for the Washington Senators. The Senators were visiting Maple Leaf Stadium on an early June day in 1926.

The Toronto Maple Leafs scored four runs against Kelley in the home half of the first inning. He settled down a bit after that, but it was time to put someone else on the mound. Washington skipper Bucky Harris had lots of options. The Toronto fans wanted to see Walter Johnson pitch, but that was out of the question. "The Big Train" had recently picked up a minor injury in New York and was thirty-eight years old.

Two of the Washington coaches were baseball's best-known clowns. Both volunteered their pitching services. Both had, in fact, been pitchers. Nick Altrock, a southpaw with a rubbery face, was the Washington first base coach. He had pitched for Toronto back in 1901. That year, Altrock pitched over 380 innings. His combined win–loss record with Toronto and Los Angeles of the California League was 22–21. Al Schacht, Altrock's

Nick Altrock.

partner in comedy, had spent most of his career in the International League. He had been to Toronto many times over the years as a member of the visiting team.

It was during that 1901 season that Altrock reputedly showed early signs of marching to a different drummer. Pitching in a game for Los Angeles, he walked a batter and picked him off. He liked the experience so much that he intentionally walked a bunch of opposing hitters in the same game and picked them off as well. It is possible, of course, that seeds of his becoming a clown were sown when he was pitching for Toronto.

Altrock was called up by the American League's Boston club in 1902. He struggled in Boston and was traded to the Chicago White Sox in 1903. His career took off in Chicago. Altrock won sixty-two games between 1904 and 1906, averaging over 300 innings pitched per season. He joined Washington in 1912. From then on, he occasionally appeared on the mound. Mostly, he was a coach.

Ultimately, the Washington skipper went with Firpo Marberry, his best reliever. And why not? It was only the fifth inning. The Senators were losing 5–1, and the Leafs were not playing as if this was a mere exhibition game. Nobody was going to accuse Leafs starter Carl Hubbell of not giving his all. The twenty-two-year-old southpaw was giving the Senators fits. Hubbell was on his way up. This was his first season playing at AA, the highest level of minor league baseball at the time.

Leafs fans might have read about the on-field antics of Altrock and Schacht, but this was a rare opportunity to see them in person. They were so popular that they took their act to vaudeville, where it was a success.

This was also a chance to see a big-league team. Maple Leaf Stadium was brand spanking new, and the club had lined up several "in-season" exhibition games for the 1926 season. This early June encounter with the Washington Senators was just the first of several such games. The Leafs had played at least one game like this every year since 1912, and a few more before that. But this was their first time playing against major league opponents in their new home.

Nick Altrock and Al Schacht might have gawked at the new ballpark, but they could not let the swank stadium distract them. They had some clowning to do. Maybe they would water the first base coaching box, then sit in the puddle and use bats as oars for a stationary paddling excursion. Perhaps one of them would fall out of the invisible rowboat and flail away in the water, floundering until his partner in fun saved him. Maybe they would pretend to be tightrope walkers, each holding an umbrella to keep his balance.

Hubbell kept the Washington hitters off-balance and earned a 6–1 victory. But after the game, Walter Johnson was the player who was pestered for autographs by a swarm of kids. They had no way of knowing that Carl Hubbell was also destined for greatness.

Altrock had been clowning around in first-base coaching boxes since before the Great War. He made fun of opposing pitchers' windups. One such hurler was so amused by Altrock that he lost his concentration and gave up some hits in quick succession, allowing Washington back into the game.

Sometimes Altrock would appear on the field wearing a ridiculously oversized glove. Altrock often wore his cap sideways. This was not a custom at the time. He and Schacht sometimes impersonated famous boxers in a makeshift ring. Watching them, one got the impression that each was trying to beat the other to a pulp. This may have been true. The two men apparently hated each other.

Early in Altrock's clowning career, some had objected to his antics. All such complaints ultimately fell on deaf ears. This might be considered ironic by some, since Altrock had big ears that evoked terms like "jug-handled," "loving cup," or "elephantine."

Altrock and Schacht also did a pantomime in which one pitched and the other batted. This was done without a baseball. Once in a blue moon, Altrock got to play in a real game. Most recently, in 1924, he pitched two innings. In his only plate appearance that day, he hit a triple. He was forty-eight years old at the time. Almost a century later, he is still the oldest major league player to hit a triple.

Sunday, October 1, was the final day of the 1933 regular season. Washington had already clinched the American League pennant. They were playing at home against the Philadelphia Athletics. It was a meaningless game. With the A's ahead 3–0 and two out in the home half of the eleventh frame, Altrock entered the game as a pinch-hitter. He had recently celebrated his fifty-seventh birthday. Altrock stepped up to the plate with a dozen bats in hand. He summoned the Philadelphia outfielders into the infield and arranged them to suit his whim. Altrock hit a ground ball to pitcher Rube Walberg. But instead of dashing toward first base, he ran into the clubhouse with Walberg in pursuit.

When Altrock went into the batter's box against Walberg, a record was set. Their combined age of ninety-four (Altrock was fifty-seven and Walberg thirty-seven) was the highest of any batter-pitcher matchup in major league history. As of this writing, this record still stands.

On October 3, Altrock and the rest of the Senators faced the New York Giants in Game One of the 1933 World Series. During pregame infield practice, Washington utility infielder Bob Boken was hit in the forehead with a baseball. Dazed, Boken had to be helped off the field.

Some of the fans laughed, thinking that it was part of the Altrock-Schacht comedy routine.

The starting pitcher for the Giants was … Carl Hubbell. He scattered five Washington hits and went the distance in a 4–2 win. Hubbell was back on the mound for Game Four on October 6. The Giants won 2–1 in eleven innings. The victory gave New York a 3–1 lead in the Series. They clinched it the next day.

• • •

Nick Altrock celebrated his eightieth birthday on September 15, 1956. One of his many well-wishers was President Dwight D. Eisenhower. The president sent Altrock a telegram that was published in the Boston *Globe*, praising his achievements and congratulating Altrock on his sportsmanship and his contribution to fans' enjoyment of the game.

If major leaguers were royalty, then Nick Altrock was the court jester.

PART III

BLACK BASEBALL IN TORONTO

Nastiness at Sunlight Park

Sunlight Park was the first dedicated baseball ground in the city of Toronto, located on the south side of Queen Street East, just east of the Don River. Baseball cranks on the other side of the river ventured "over the Don" to attend games. Sunlight Park got its name from the nearby Sunlight soap company.

Toronto's population was much less diverse in the 1880s than it is today. People of colour were relatively few and far between. They were often subjected to racism. On at least two occasions, odious anti-Black incidents took place at Sunlight Park.

On May 25, 1887, Toronto hosted the Syracuse Stars. The Stars were visiting Toronto for the first time in the International Association season. The Syracuse pitcher, Robert Higgins, was making his professional debut. Higgins was African American.

What ensued that afternoon, according to the Toronto *World* newspaper, was a "most disgusting exhibition."[8] Simply stated, some of Higgins's teammates did not want to play with him. They staged what the *World* described as a boycott. They did not go AWOL. Rather, they played nonchalantly. They muffed easy plays.

When the dust settled, Syracuse made fourteen errors and lost 23–8. Amazingly, Higgins pitched the whole game. He was touched for twenty-two hits.

It is possible that the Stars were simply having a bad day in the field. The club averaged four defensive miscues a game that season. But fourteen errors in one contest was suspicious, to say the least. The *World*'s unnamed reporter saw the fielding fumbles as deliberate. According to him, some of the Syracuse players had done what they could to ensure that they lost the game.

If the Stars' mission was to get Higgins booted off the team, they failed. He pitched again on May 31, scattered eight hits, and won 10–3 at home against Oswego. Higgins spent the rest of the season with the Stars. He faced Toronto again on September 29, in Syracuse, and beat them 2–1. That's a far cry from a 23–8 defeat.

Box scores in the *Sporting Life* show that Higgins pitched in at least eighteen games that year. He had an excellent 13–4 record in those games. He also batted .294 and played some games in the outfield.

• • •

Fleetwood "Fleet" Walker, of the Newark club, was another African American playing in the International Association in 1887. Walker was a university-educated catcher who had played in the big leagues in 1884 with Toledo of the American Association. He was the last African American to play major league baseball until Jackie Robinson made his Brooklyn Dodgers debut in 1947.

Walker's 1887 Newark teammates included pitcher George Stovey. A southpaw, Stovey was also Black. Occasionally, Stovey and Walker formed an all-Black battery. This was a rare occasion, since there were few African Americans in pro ball at the time.

Stovey pitched to Walker at least once in Toronto. On June 7 of '87, Mickey Hughes was the Newark starting pitcher. When Hughes batted in the seventh inning, he was hit in the head by a pitch.

Ed "Cannonball" Crane.

The Toronto hurler, Ed Crane, threw hard and was wild. Known as "Cannonball," Crane went on to walk more than 200 batters in two straight seasons in the majors.

Hughes was hit just above his left ear, knocked to the ground, and attended to by a pair of doctors who happened to be watching the game. Hughes was taken to the team's hotel, and George Stovey pitched the rest of the game for Newark. His catcher was Fleet Walker.

Mickey Hughes made a full recovery. In fact, he had a spectacular big league rookie season in 1888. He made forty starts for Brooklyn of the American Association, completed them all, and won twenty-five.

Robert Higgins returned to Syracuse in 1888. That year, he was joined by Fleet Walker. On May 22, in Toronto, Walker and Higgins formed another all-Black battery. Walker was hit by a pitch and came around to score the only Syracuse run in a 4–1 Toronto victory.

The next day, the teams returned to Sunlight Park to continue the series. Fleet Walker was not in uniform. The Toronto manager spotted Walker and ordered him to leave the field. As Walker departed, he was baited by some unruly fans. He threatened to shoot the home team's skipper. This caught the attention of a Toronto detective, who searched Walker and found a loaded pistol on his person.

Walker was charged with disorderly conduct and carrying a gun. He spent the night "resting at Her Majesty's pleasure" — incarcerated — at Toronto's No. 4 police station on Wilton Avenue (now Dundas Street East). He was released and caught both ends of Syracuse's doubleheader in Hamilton the next day. The Stars won both games to give them an impressive 16–3 win–loss record and an early-season perch atop the league standings.

• • •

African Americans had their share of success in the International Association in the late 1880s. George Stovey won a league record thirty-five games in 1887. Buffalo second baseman Frank Grant led the league with eleven home runs in 1888. His lowest season batting average between 1886 and 1888 was .344. Grant's reward for his efforts was a steady diet of pitches thrown at his head and nasty slides that eventually forced him to move to the outfield.

Toronto fans would have seen the tactics employed against Grant when Buffalo was in town. Some of those fans would have enjoyed the sad spectacle. Indeed, some Toronto spectators greeted Grant with cries like "Kill the [n-word]." It is not unreasonable to assume that Fleet Walker acted as he did in the Syracuse game in response to similar remarks.

Black players were soon driven out of the International League altogether, and it would be over half a century before they would return. In the meantime, pro baseball in Toronto would be a segregated, whites-only endeavour.

Negro League Games

On April 7, 1977, Bill Singer (a.k.a. "The Singer Throwing Machine") of the brand spanking new Blue Jays threw a first pitch strike to Ralph "Road Runner" Garr of the visiting Chicago White Sox. It was thought that the pitch marked the beginning of the first-ever regular season major league game in Toronto.

That's not true anymore.

Here's why: In December of 2020, Major League Baseball retroactively granted major league status to various negro leagues that existed between 1920 and 1948.

As it turns out, several negro league games were played in Toronto over the years. Some of the games were played after 1948. For example, in August of 1950, Indianapolis whipped Philadelphia by a score of 9–4. In July of 1952, a doubleheader at Maple Leaf Stadium featured four teams from the Negro American League (NAL). The Chicago American Giants routed the Philadelphia Stars 7–0 in the opener. The Indianapolis Clowns then defeated the Kansas City Monarchs by the same score. Attendance for the twin bill was 3,836. The day's entertainment was not restricted to baseball;

BASEBALL
MAPLE LEAF STADIUM
Saturday, 3 and 7.15 p.m.
(Twilight)
HOMESTEAD GRAYS
World's Colored Champions
vs. CUBAN STARS
HAP WATSON and DEVIL WELLS, World's Fastest Shortstop, will entertain.

Ad for 1932 East-West League game at Maple Leaf Stadium.

Olympic champion Jesse Owens raced against a couple of baseball players. Each of the players was given a head start, and each lost.

Other games in Toronto featured African American teams that were not in the "major negro leagues." One such game was played in 1945, when two United States League (USL) games were played at Maple Leaf Stadium. The USL has not been acknowledged as major league. The Pittsburgh Crawfords (not to be confused with a more famous team of the same name) defeated Philadelphia 12–11 in early June. In mid-July, the Crawfords beat their Chicago USL counterparts 6–2.

On July 5, 1948, a regular season Negro American League game took place at Maple Leaf Stadium. The Cleveland Buckeyes beat the Indianapolis Clowns by a 5–3 score. This contest "counts" as a major league regular season game. Attendance was 3,961.

The Buckeyes were the defending NAL champs. The Clowns were the Harlem Globetrotters of baseball. They didn't just play — they played with pizzazz. One of the Clowns, Goose Tatum, also played for basketball's 'trotters. He was a star of the show, too, like Meadowlark Lemon. Tatum was a 6'3" first baseman. The Indianapolis entourage also featured Spec Bebop, a little person, and King Tut. Bebop and Tut were there strictly as entertainers.

Tickets to the game cost between seventy-five cents and a buck eighty. To put that into perspective, ticket prices for regular season Maple Leafs games were the same.

Centre fielder Sam Jethroe had three hits for Cleveland. The Buckeyes also included twenty-year-old Al Smith. Jethroe and Smith were signed by the Cleveland Indians just days after the game at Maple Leaf Stadium. Both men enjoyed success in the integrated major leagues. Jethroe integrated the Boston Braves in 1950 and was that season's National League Rookie of the Year. He led the National League in stolen bases in 1950 and 1951. Smith toiled in the integrated major leagues for twelve years, mostly with the Cleveland Indians and Chicago White Sox. He played in the World Series in 1954 and 1959.

Andy Porter started on the mound for Indianapolis. Porter, thirty-seven, was near the end of a pro career that had begun in 1932. He won twenty-one games for Nuevo Laredo of the Mexican League in 1940.

Going into the ninth inning, the Clowns were ahead 3–1. With one out, Buckeyes catcher Joe Greene singled. Up to the plate stepped Tommy Harris, a pinch-hitter. Normally a light hitter, Harris hit one over the left field fence to tie the score. An infield hit and two errors later, Cleveland had a two-run lead. The sad Clowns were held scoreless in the bottom of the inning, and the game was over.

The Buckeyes played their 1948 home games at League Park in Cleveland; the stadium was also used by the Indians. Parts of the stadium survive to this day, and sections of the exterior wall are still there. A house-sized building down the right field line that was used as club office space is intact and houses a modest baseball museum. League Park is one of the few remaining negro league venues.

The Cleveland-Indianapolis game predated the Blue Jays' debut by twenty-nine years. Was *that* the first major league regular season game in Toronto? Not by a long shot. For on June 18, 1932, the Cuban Stars and Homestead Grays went toe to toe at Maple Leaf Stadium. The Stars and Grays competed in the East-West League (EWL), which existed for just one year. The 1932 EWL "counts" as a major league, according to Major League Baseball's 2020 edict.

Major league or not, it was not a well-played game. Each team made four errors. The Cuban Stars won 5–2. Both Grays runs were unearned. The Stars had a three-run sixth inning that proved to be decisive.

The Cuban Stars were strictly a travelling team in 1932; they had no home. The Homestead Grays were based in Pittsburgh at the time.

A crowd of about a hundred people turned out to what was advance billed as a doubleheader. There is no evidence in the Toronto press that the second game was played at all. Of the city's three daily newspapers, only the *Telegram* published a summary of the lone contest. Its unnamed author wrote that the teams put on "a pitiful display of their ability."[9] The blurb was printed on the same page as a racist example of a syndicated cartoon called *Our Boarding House*.

There is no mention of the game (or games) in the Pittsburgh press.

Hall of Famers Willie Wells and Cool Papa Bell might have played in the game. In the absence of a box score and no mention of Wells or Bell in the *Telegram* story, one can only guess. Both men played for the Grays on the day before and the day after the game in Toronto.

Shortly before the Stars-Grays game, on May 24, a semipro Toronto all-star team played an exhibition game against a team called the Pittsburgh Colored Giants. There was no such team in the EWL. The game was played at Ulster Stadium, a venue at the corner of Greenwood and Gerrard that was most often used for soccer.

The game was tied 5–5 after seven innings. The Giants rallied for five runs in the top of the eighth. The semipros scored five of their own in the home half of the ninth to send the game into extra innings. The Giants scored three times in the tenth and went on to win 13–10. About a thousand fans watched the game.

The box score for this game clearly shows that the visiting team was, in fact, the Detroit Wolves of the East-West League. All twelve of the Giants who are named in the box score played for the Wolves. Their lineup at Ulster Stadium was comparable to that of an all-star team. The Giants included Willie Wells and Cool Papa Bell. Both players appeared for both the Wolves and the Homestead Grays in 1932. Wells had two homers and a double in the game. Mule Suttles, their first baseman, was one of the most feared power hitters in negro league history. Quincy Trouppe ranks among the best-ever negro league catchers. Outfielder Vic Harris, who also split the 1932 season between Detroit and the Grays, went on to play in the negro leagues for twenty-five seasons.

It is not known why the Wolves went by a pseudonym in this game.

There were earlier games in Toronto that featured African American teams. In April of 1919, the Maple Leafs hosted a team called the Pittsburgh Colored Stars of Buffalo in a pair of exhibition games at Island Stadium.

The granddaddy of all these games took place on May 18, 1897, when the Cuban Giants won 12–9 against the University of Toronto. The Giants led 12–1 after three innings. U of T made nine errors in the game. The Giants included former minor leaguer Frank Grant.

Of all these games, only the 1948 Cleveland-Indianapolis and the 1932 Cuban Stars–Homestead Grays clashes are now categorized as "major league." Unless evidence to the contrary is discovered, they were the first regular season major league games in Toronto.

Jackie Comes to Town

On October 23, 1945, Jackie Robinson signed a contract with the Montreal Royals. For the first time in over half a century, Toronto baseball fans would be able to see integrated professional baseball.

The times, they were a-changing. But slowly.

According to national census figures, Toronto's official Black population was still less than 2,000 in 1951. Unofficial estimates were three to four times that number, but that was still a small percentage of a city inhabited by over a million people.

Racism was rife. Black Canadians were shunned in places of worship. They were denied employment in many fields. Herb Carnegie was born in the north Toronto suburb of Willowdale in 1919, the same year as Jackie Robinson. And that is fitting, because Carnegie should have been the Jackie Robinson of the National Hockey League.

Carnegie was one of three Black students in his school; the other two were his siblings. He didn't ignore the taunts of his schoolmates either. He fought. Often. The school reacted by banning him from arriving until five minutes before classes began. Teachers scolded him for fighting

Jackie Robinson.

instead of simply taking the racial epithets that were frequently thrown at him.

Like so many Canadian kids, Carnegie wanted to play in the NHL. He played top-level junior hockey in Toronto. One day, after a practice at Maple Leaf Gardens, Carnegie's coach told him that Leafs owner Conn Smythe was in the stands. Smythe was obviously impressed with Carnegie's skills, but he wasn't going to approach him about playing for the Leafs. Why? Because Carnegie was Black.

Smythe is alleged to have said, "I will give $10,000 to anyone who can turn Herb Carnegie white."[10]

On October 22, the day before Robinson signed with the Royals, a play titled *Strange Fruit* opened at Toronto's Royal Alexandra Theatre, based on a novel of the same name by Lillian Smith, a white southerner. The story includes an interracial love affair between a white man and a Black woman in a small Georgia town. The woman becomes pregnant.

Her brother kills her lover. Eventually, an innocent man is lynched for the murder.

The show helped to raise some patrons' awareness of the plight of American blacks in the South. The *Telegram* noted that the novel was "shocking and disturbing." Lillian Smith was in Toronto for its debut. "People tell me that I am 'pro-Negro,'" she told the *Globe and Mail*. "I'm not pro-Negro. I am just pro-human being."[11]

It was a sentiment that Lillian Smith and Jackie Robinson shared.

On October 24, Torontonians read about an event that they knew was significant to the former residents of Little Norway, the barracks beyond the right field fence at Maple Leaf Stadium that had been used by the Norwegian Air Force in exile during the Second World War. Vidkun Quisling, the Norwegian puppet leader under the Nazis whose very name would become synonymous with collaborationist traitors, was executed by firing squad in Oslo.

The same day, the Toronto *Star* editorial page included an article titled "The White Man's Burden." It mentioned that an African American man had recently conducted an orchestra in Berlin while a Toronto club had not let its dining room be used to entertain a well-known Black singer. The story suggested that newly liberated Europe would rid itself of racism before North America.

Barely three weeks after Robinson signed with the Montreal Royals, a Toronto teenager named Harry Gairey Jr. was refused entry into the Icelandia skating rink because he was Black. Gairey's father, Harry Sr., took the matter to his local city alderman. The elder Gairey, a railway porter, was invited to tell his son's story to the city council.

Word of the incident spread. Some University of Toronto students picketed the Icelandia, which was located on Yonge Street just north of Davisville Avenue. The city eventually passed an ordinance that outlawed discrimination in places of recreation and amusement that had been licensed by the police. That was in January of 1947, and Jackie Robinson had already played his final International League game at Maple Leaf Stadium by then.

Robinson made his Montreal home debut at Delorimier Stadium on May 1, 1946. A record Opening Day of some 15,000 saw Robinson go one-for-four, score a run, and start a pair of second-to-short-to-first double plays. The Royals beat the Jersey City Giants 12–9.

That same afternoon, a crowd of similar size showed up at Maple Leaf Stadium to watch Toronto play Syracuse. Gus Bodnar of the hockey Leafs threw the ceremonial first pitch. Teammate Syl Apps was his batterymate, and mayor Robert Hood Saunders stood in the batter's box.

As usual, the Opening Day crowd featured a hefty number of kids who were playing hooky from school. One delinquent cherub made his opinions known as he mugged for a photographer from the *Globe*. "Phooey on school! We can always go to school."[12]

A lady sitting in the left field stands wore a top hat adorned with pink orchids that were in poor condition. A shameless "homer," she incongruously shouted, "Get yourself a telescope!"[13] when the home plate umpire called a strike against the Leafs. She raised her hands to the heavens and blurted "Eee!" when anything interesting happened.

Leadoff hitter and left fielder Lee Gamble gave the orchid lady reason to "go eee" in the home half of the eighth. With one out and two runners on, Gamble tripled to break a 3–3 deadlock. Toronto won 5–3.

The go-ahead run was scored by one of Toronto's newcomers. Hank Biasatti was a promising first baseman from Windsor, Ontario. "He was an extremely good fielding first baseman," recalled former Leafs batboy Ron Stead. "He was little for a first baseman, though."[14]

On Opening Day of 1946, Hank Biasatti was twenty-four years old. Like Jackie Robinson, Biasatti was a multisport athlete. He played basketball for Assumption College, which later became the University of Windsor. About six months before he made his debut for the Leafs, Biasatti turned in a memorable performance on the hardwood in an upset victory by Assumption over the Harlem Globetrotters.

On May 2, an announcement was made that certainly would have caught Biasatti's attention. Toronto was going to have a team in the United States National Basketball League. The team would be called the Huskies. They would play at Maple Leaf Gardens, starting in November.

Regardless of any aspirations that he may have had at the time, Biasatti's immediate priority was baseball. And more than anything else, he needed to work on his hitting. On May 3, he batted eighth for the Leafs and was removed for a pinch-hitter in the ninth inning of a 3–2 loss against Syracuse.

That game featured an unusual incident. In the top of the fourth, the Stars had a narrow 1–0 lead. Kermit Wahl of Syracuse hit one toward the left-field fence. Toronto left fielder Jack Houck chased after the ball but lost it. And could not find it.

Other Toronto players arrived on the scene. They looked for the ball, but it was nowhere to be found. Wahl raced around the bases, and Syracuse took what appeared to be a 4–0 lead.

Houck came into the infield to talk with the base umpire, who went out to investigate. He could not find the baseball, either, but he did find a hole in the left field wall. He ruled the hit a ground-rule double. Syracuse manager Jewel Ens protested the game, but the protest was voided by the Syracuse win.

Hank Biasatti was one of several Second World War veterans on the Leafs in that first postwar season. Biasatti had served in the Canadian Army from 1943 to 1945. Shortstop Fred Chapman and pitcher Joe Coleman had been in the United States Navy. Hurler William Connelly had been in the United States Marines.

Connelly was not merely glad to be with the Leafs in the spring of 1946. He was glad to be alive; he had been shot by a sniper at Iwo Jima. "We were advancing up a hill when suddenly I felt a numbing pain in my face," the Alberta, Virginia, native told the *Globe*. "I was stunned and didn't have any idea what happened until I found I was bleeding from my mouth. I turned and scrambled back into a foxhole."[15]

A bullet had broken the right side of his jaw, knocked out three teeth, and exited through the left side of his face. "I guess I was just awfully lucky."[16] Connelly had been optioned to Savannah of the South Atlantic League by the time Jackie Robinson made his Maple Leafs Stadium debut.

Ellis Ferguson "Cot" Deal was another returning Second World War veteran on the Toronto roster. Signed as an outfielder by the Pittsburgh Pirates in 1940, Deal had spent the previous three seasons in the US Air Force.

Deal's most vivid memory of the 1946 season was "trying to decide whether to pitch or play in the outfield. I had been an outfielder before I went into the service," he explained in an interview. "Started pitching and doing both while in the service. I liked doing both. I wanted the best chance to get to the big leagues."[17]

Cot Deal made his Maple Leaf Stadium debut in a 7–6 loss against Syracuse. He started on the mound. Deal did not figure in the decision, but he did have a reasonable outing. He was lifted in the seventh inning and gave up three runs. He also had two hits in three at-bats.

Deal was Toronto's starting pitcher when they played their first home game against Montreal, on Friday, May 17. He set down Montreal's leadoff hitter, then walked four straight batters, including Robinson. Deal was then relieved. Montreal batted around in the first and scored three runs without getting a hit. Deal and a pair of relievers issued a combined six walks in the inning.

The Leafs scored four runs in their half of the first frame, which took almost forty-five minutes to play. This prompted long-time official scorer Charlie Good to recount a pitching performance that he had once witnessed at Hanlan's Point. "A lefthander name of Bailey with the Leafs walked eight men in succession. Thought I'd never get home that day."[18]

In 1946, when he wasn't pitching, Cot Deal often played in the outfield for the Leafs. He ended up spending seventeen years in pro ball, winning ninety-six games and cranking out 847 hits.

Jackie Robinson's Maple Leaf Stadium debut sped up significantly after the first inning. Montreal tied it in the seventh and went ahead in the ninth courtesy of a bases-empty homer by shortstop Al Campanis. The home run was served up by Walt Smola, who had come into the game in the first inning. He pitched eight and a third innings in relief and gave up just two runs.

Toronto almost came back again. A single and a walk put runners on first and second with none out. One out later, Montreal third baseman Spider Jorgensen snared a line drive for the second out. He then threw to Robinson, who completed the double play before the lead runner could get back to second. Game over. Montreal won 5–4 in front of a crowd of 4,925.

Wayne Collins of the Royals was even better than Smola, throwing eight and two-thirds innings of shutout relief.

Robinson had two hits in four at-bats that day. He hit a single in the second and was thrown out trying to stretch it into a double. In the eighth, he had a bunt single. He scored one run and stole a base. But he failed to impress Toronto sportswriters. Gordon Walker of the Toronto *Star* wrote, "On the basis of what he showed last night, you couldn't pick Robinson as a man most likely to make the major grade. He was no fireball afield, didn't look real good [*sic*] as a hitter."[19]

Toronto *Telegram* columnist Ted Reeve thought that Robinson's physique was more suited for football than baseball. "Robinson's big-league chances are not so good, they say, owing to a certain stiffness of the shoulders. Football muscles as they are called in the trade."[20]

Robinson had been a standout football player at UCLA, and there were rumours that he might play CFL football in Montreal. He dispelled the rumours himself. "It's too cold up here," he told the *Star*. "I don't like this weather."[21]

During the game, Robinson threw a block while breaking up a potential double play that would have met the approval of his UCLA gridiron teammates. Toronto infielder Al Mazur was on the receiving end of the block, and he didn't like it. Reeve wrote, "Mazur said he was just going to throw the ball when everything went black in front of him."[22]

Mazur thought that Robinson's takeout was excessive. Robinson disagreed. "All he had to do was step off the base the right way," he told the *Star*, "and there wouldn't have been a collision."[23]

Some one hundred members of Detroit's Black community came to Maple Leaf Stadium to see the game. That same day, barely a mile from Maple Leaf Stadium, a team called the Colored Stars lost their Toronto Softball League season opener. And the sports pages of the Toronto *Star* included a set of horse racing cartoons, including one that depicted two Black men lounging outside a stable. The caption read, "No race track looks complete without a few southern gentlemen — they usually know hosses [*sic*] too."[24]

The Royals were supposed to play the Leafs the following day as well, but the game was rained out.

Batboy Ron Stead recalled that Robinson received more verbal abuse from his opponents than from the people in the stands. "There were a lot of white southern players and they had a hard time accepting black players. The fans were fairly good, but the players themselves made comments. And there was name-calling. Don't get me wrong. It wasn't the majority of them. But, for a lack of a better term, there were some rednecks who made some nasty remarks."[25] Please keep in mind that the "opponents" referred to by Stead were the Leafs.

During a game in Syracuse, a member of the Chiefs threw a black cat onto the field and blurted out, "Hey, Jackie, there's your cousin." Later in the game, after Robinson had doubled and scored, he shouted back, "I guess my cousin's pretty happy now."

Former baseball executive Dick Armstrong was playing college ball in 1946. He worked out with the Baltimore Orioles (then an International League team) and once travelled with them to Montreal. "I sat in the dugout during the games and was shocked how brutal the Orioles were to him. I saw and heard what they did to him. Vile obscenities. Racial slurs of the worst kind. And he had to take it. I was ashamed and embarrassed about what took place."

It wasn't just the Baltimore players who hurled racial abuse at Robinson. The Baltimore fans did as well. On one occasion, two racists were sitting behind Rachel Robinson, Jackie's wife. "As soon as we emerged on the field, they began screaming all the typical phrases such as '[n-word] son of a bitch,'" Robinson recalled. "Soon insults were coming from all over the stands. For me on the field it was not as bad as it was for Rae, forced to sit in the midst of the hostile spectators. It was almost impossible for her to keep her temper, but her dignity was more important to her than descending to the level of those ignorant bigots."

Baltimore was the only '46 IL city that was south of the Mason-Dixon Line. After one game there, a surly gathering waited for Robinson outside the visitors' clubhouse. They shouted, "Come out of there, Robinson, you [n-word] son-of-a-bitch, we'll getcha, we'll getcha." Most of the Royals, including manager Clay Hopper (himself a southerner), left Robinson to his fate. Only Spider Jorgensen and outfielders Marvin Rackley and Tom Tatum waited with him until the crowd finally left.

Montreal visited Maple Leaf Stadium again in early July. On Friday the fifth, Robinson went two-for-five with a double, a run, and a run batted in (RBI). The Royals beat the Leafs 4–0. With two out and a runner on first in the bottom of the final frame, the Toronto batter hit a ball to right field. Here's how Jim Coleman of the *Globe and Mail* described the play: "Robinson had no right to be close to the ball but he scampered out to field it. He tipped it with his glove and juggled it into the air. With the greatest grace he caught it with his bare right hand. It was a tremendous play and it ended the game."

The next day, the two teams squared off for a Saturday doubleheader. Montreal won the opener 8–5. Robinson hit another double. The second game ended as a 2–2 tie. A curfew was called after seven innings because both teams had a train to catch that would take them to Montreal. They were scheduled to play another twin bill there on the Sunday.

The teams returned to Toronto on Thursday, July 18, for another doubleheader. The Royals whitewashed the Leafs 5–0 in the first game. Toronto won the second game 2–1 in ten innings, their first home victory of the season over Montreal in six tries. Robinson had two hits that day, including yet another double. A single game was rained out the next day, and the series ended with a 9–2 Montreal win on the twentieth.

The Royals cruised into Toronto in late August for their fourth and final regular season series at Maple Leaf Stadium. By then, Montreal had clinched the IL pennant and was a whopping twenty-seven games ahead of the sixth-place Leafs.

The series opener, scheduled for August 28, was rained out. Montreal swept a doubleheader the next day. The teams played (and split) their fourth twin bill at Maple Leaf Stadium on the thirtieth. The Leafs won the opener 4–3 in eleven innings after leaving a total of twenty-one runners on base.

Robinson's last game in Toronto came on August 31. This game began the same way that his first visit had back in May. Cot Deal started on the mound for Toronto and was yanked in the top of the first frame. The Royals scored three runs in the inning. And, as Walt Smola had done in May, Herman Besse allowed two runs in eight and a third innings of relief for Toronto. Montreal won 5–4.

The Royals won nine and tied one of the twelve games that they played at Maple Leaf Stadium. Jackie Robinson played in all twelve games and had fifteen hits in forty-one at-bats, a .369 batting average. He hit five doubles, scored ten runs, knocked in two runs, and stole two bases.

Robinson would go on to hit .349 and win the IL batting title. He then led the Royals to a Junior World Series victory over Louisville.

When the 1947 season began, Jackie Robinson would be a member of the Brooklyn Dodgers. The rest, as they say, is history.

PART IV

TRAINERS

The Daly Show

Tim Daly is the only person in the 1926 Toronto Maple Leafs team photo who looks like he is late for a Danny DeVito lookalike contest. Small in stature but big in heart, Toronto's diminutive trainer had a way with words. Think Yogi Berra.

"So many malapropisms, so little time." That could have been Tim Daly's mantra.

Daly was the trainer for the hockey Leafs as well. He described his retirement from that job as follows: "It was the end of an error."[26]

An oasis of calm in a storm, Tim was. "I remain cool and collective," he once said.[27]

Early in 1955, Daly was afraid that he had an "ulster."

Once entrusted with the shipping of Conn Smythe's baggage to England, Daly complained about how slow it was: "The stuff took so long to get to England that they must have shipped it by way of the Sewage Canal."[28]

Daly is alleged to have said, "You know, when my mother came out from Ireland, she couldn't speak a word of English — she could only speak the garlic."[29]

Some of Daly's misuses of the language were related to his job as trainer. "Torn knee liniments" was a dreaded injury.[30] Older players who had lost speed suffered from "hardening of the articles."[31] In early 1950, Daly decided that he should be equipped with a thermometer. Daly thought that using a "thermidor" would help the club doctors.[32]

Daly claimed to have been a boxer in his youth. On the alleged fiftieth anniversary of his first time in the ring, he said, "Ye could say I'm celebratin' my golden jubilation in sport."[33] He added, "Yeah, it's fifty years since I had me first fight. Who cares now who won? The guy didn't kill me. Thass the main thing."[34]

"Connyism" was a political system in Russia at the time, which Daly told the hockey Leafs he had a "cure" for.[35]

Daly referred to Leafs hockey forward Joe Klukay as "Kluklux."[36]

Leafs manager Burleigh Grimes, reacting to rumours that new shortstop Antonio Ordeñana did not need an interpreter, said, "Why, the guy can even understand Tim Daly, and any guy that can keep pace with Tim's conversation is rated as an accomplished linguist on our club."[37]

Heading off to a banquet in Niagara Falls with hockey Leaf Wally Stanowski, Daly noted that Wally would speak in Polish and Daly in his own tongue.

Garth Boesch, a hockey teammate, replied, "Yeah, and they'll understand Wally's Polish better than your double talk."

Jim Proudfoot of the *Globe* once described Daly's linguistic skills as follows: "His losing battle with the English language makes Dizzy Dean sound like a professor of English."[38]

When he wasn't rewriting the dictionary, Daly was involved in all manners of hijinks.

Daly once left a stogie on a shelf in the hockey Leafs' dressing room. One of the players took it, dipped it into some iodine, and put it back on the shelf. Daly returned, put the cigar back in his mouth, and carried on with his work. He put the cigar on the shelf again. The cigar was then dipped into rubbing alcohol. Daly came back to his cigar and chewed on it, as was his habit. Coach Joe Primeau observed, "It's a sad commentary either on Tim or the quality of his cigars, but he never knew the difference. It was obvious, however, that he showed much more pep on the alcohol treatment."[39]

Jim Pattison, a pitcher for the Leafs from '34 to '36, once approached Daly in the clubhouse, held out his right arm, and requested a rubdown. Daly obliged and worked Pattison's arm for ten minutes. Pattison then explained that he was a southpaw.

According to Daly, player-manager Larry Doyle once spiked an umpire with his cleats during a game at Diamond Park. Doyle was at the tail end of a long and successful big-league career, mostly as a second baseman with the New York Giants and Chicago Cubs. For this transgression, Doyle was sentenced to fifteen days in the Don Jail. Knowing that Doyle liked chewing tobacco, Daly decided to cut some into chunks and leave them on the ground outside the jail walls. Doyle would then find them while on work duty. A guard caught Daly and asked if he would be interested in seeing the interior of the jail. Daly refused the kind offer, and Doyle had to do without "chew" for the rest of his time "inside."

Alas, there are some holes in Daly's story. Doyle was manager of the Leafs in the 1921 season only. The club was based at Island Stadium at the time — not Diamond Park. Also, no contemporary accounts of the spiking and Doyle's subsequent jailing can be found in the *Star* or the *Globe*. It seems hard to believe that such an incident would have gone unpublicized. Tim Daly told this tale in 1952, more than three decades after Larry Doyle was the Leafs' skipper. Maybe he got some of the details wrong.

One year during spring training in Macon, Georgia, Daly was charged with retrieving foul balls. After a while, the balls stopped coming back and there was no sign of Daly. Manager Joe Kelley finally found him sleeping in the grass. Kelley woke up the trainer — with his feet — and demanded to know if he was still working for the club. Daly replied, "Yes. But I hired out as a trainer, not as a marathon runner."[40]

Daly, short of cash in Chicago with the hockey Leafs, borrowed a buck from Teeder Kennedy, who then told a nearby policeman that Daly was a panhandler.

Was Daly prone to hyperbole? Most definitely. Take Leafs pitcher Lore "King" Bader, for example. Daly said of him, "They never did find out what he did to that ball. He'd throw it to the batter but it would stop just short of the plate and start back for second base."[41]

It was once reported that Daly was getting ready to warm up in the bullpen while the Leafs' pitchers were getting pummelled during a game in Baltimore. Someone other than Daly was also prone to hyperbole, or so it seems.

Tim Daly loved to tell tales. There was a strange play during a game against Jersey City. The Leafs' third baseman, Del Capes, fielded a bunt by the Jersey City pitcher and raced him to first. The batter just beat Capes to the bag. It turned out that Capes had bet the Jersey pitcher that he could beat him to first base on just such a play. A Jersey City rally followed, and the Leafs fell behind 5–4. Capes admitted in the dugout afterward that he had made a five-dollar bet with the Jersey hurler. The Leafs' pitcher, Myles Thomas, got so mad that he slugged Capes. To add insult to injury, manager Dan Howley then fined Capes fifty dollars. Capes. Not Thomas.

Then there was the time that Daly and Johnny Evers were at an entrance to the Albany ballpark. "Johnny was managing Albany. Two old men, both hobbling with canes, came in the gate. The first one handed over a ticket, but the other old bird just walked by. 'Just a minute,' says the ticket taker. 'Where's the other ticket?' 'What's that?' squeaked Old Bird Number One. 'You only gave me one ticket.' 'This is father and son night, ain't it?' 'That's right.' 'Well, stop pesterin' us then.'"[42]

Born in Pickering, Ontario, in 1884, Tim Daly's first job as trainer was in 1905 with a local lacrosse team. His career with the baseball Leafs started in 1910. After serving in the First World War, he spent the 1920 campaign as the trainer for the Detroit Tigers. That, apparently, makes him the first Canadian trainer in major league history.

Daly claimed that he left the Tigers after getting the flu, but Milt Dunnell of the *Star* wrote that he was fired for brawling. According to Dunnell, Daly liked to show off his boxing prowess. Detroit manager Hugh Jennings did not approve and told Daly that any more fighting would result in Daly's dismissal from the club. The Tigers found themselves in a Philadelphia train station waiting for a train to Washington, D.C. A stranger picked a fight with Daly, who was more than willing to reciprocate. When

Ty Cobb and Tim Daly in 1928. Cobb was then with the Philadelphia A's, who were playing an exhibition game at Maple Leaf Stadium. Cobb retired at the end of the 1928 season.

Jennings caught him in the act, Daly claimed that he was trying to teach the stranger a particular punch. While Daly was talking, he let his guard down and the stranger slugged him. Daly went tumbling down some stairs. And with that, he was fired.

The Tigers were not the only major league club to employ Tim Daly. In 1912, the New York Giants hired him as a morale booster for pitcher Jeff Tesreau during the World Series. Tesreau, who was with Daly and the Leafs in 1911, was apparently a moody chap. Giants manager John McGraw felt that Tesreau would be happier if Daly was there. "Only thing I has [*sic*] to do is sit on the bench," Daly told the Toronto *Star* many years later.[43] "Whenever Tesreau gets grumpy, I tell him a yarn an' we both laugh. Softest job I ever have. McGraw musta been happy, too. When it's all over, he hands me a nice gift."

It was not possible to work for both the baseball Leafs and hockey Leafs when their schedules overlapped. This problem had a simple solution. Daly stayed with the hockey team until the end of the season, then joined the baseball club. In his absence, someone else filled in as trainer for the baseball Leafs. In 1933, that "someone else" was pitcher Guy Cantrell.

Being a professional trainer was rather different in Daly's day. There were no related professional credentials. Some of Daly's methods were unorthodox, to say the least. For example, he applied liniment to aching limbs with a water pistol.

For some trainers, the job included keeping tabs on the off-the-field activities of the players during road trips. Daly was spared this task. "The hotel clerks allus [*sic*] done that for the Leafs," explained Daly. "One time, we wuz playin' in Montreal. Joe Kelley was manager then. An' the clerk get [*sic*] mixed up and puts the report in Bill Bradley's box 'stead of Kelley's. Happened that Bradley was among the ones who'd been out. So the report got some retouchin'."[44]

Daly became the ball club's director of public relations and press liaison in 1942. This allowed Bill Smith to take over as trainer. Jim Coleman of the *Globe* described Daly the press liaison as "the only man in the world who can carry on a thirty-minute conversation without once removing his cigar from its customary position in the centre of his mouth. He speaks with the monotonous persistence of a boll weevil eating its way through a field of cotton."[45]

By 1947, Daly was thinking of retiring. "I told Mr. [Peter, then club president] Campbell I wanted a rest after forty-two years and there was nothing for me to do now, but he said to stick around as I haven't done anything in forty-two years anyhow."[46]

Daly and the baseball Leafs finally parted company in early August of 1948. He had been with the club for thirty-eight years. "Tim Daly Night" was on August 26. Daly received many gifts that night, including a rocking chair, a pair of shoes, a set of tires, a radio, two watches, and $2,250 in cash. Goody Rosen, who had been a Leaf in '47 and was a Toronto native, gave Daly a hundred cigars and a lighter. Oh, and the team provided the cherry on top: a 3–2 win over Syracuse.

A sports fan to the end, Daly attended a Leafs-Canadiens hockey game at Maple Leaf Gardens just two days before his death. Thomas

Michael "Tim" Daly passed away at Sunnybrook Hospital on March 29, 1968, at eighty-three. Daly was one of the great characters in Canadian baseball history.

In Smitty's Time

Opening Day of the 1926 season had been called off the day before, so Bill Smith could be forgiven if he was overly excited. The curtain was going up at Maple Leaf Stadium. The new home of the International League's Toronto Maple Leafs was the pride of the minor leagues. And Bill had a job that was coveted by many: He was a batboy for the Leafs.

What a stadium it was. It had cost $750,000 and been built on land reclaimed from Lake Ontario. There were over thirty-five rows of wooden seats from foul pole to foul pole. Most of the seats were under cover. Sure, you might get stuck behind a steel support beam, but that was only if the house was full. The park held 23,500 people, and this was the minor leagues. Some gates would be big, but your chances of sitting behind a beam were remote.

If you sat high up, behind the plate, you could see the old stadium at Hanlan's Point; the club had just moved from there. The Leafs had first played at Hanlan's Point way back in 1897 and had been ever-present there since 1910. That's around the time that Bill Smith was born.

Maple Leaf Stadium was a lot more accessible than Hanlan's Point. You had to take a ferry to the old ballpark. To get to Maple Leaf Stadium, you

Sign heralding the construction of Maple Leaf Stadium.

could take the streetcar or even walk if you lived nearby. You could drive your Ford Model T there, too, and spend fifteen cents to leave your car in a lot.

The Leafs should have been pleased on that Thursday afternoon in the spring of 1926. They were one step away from the big leagues. It was spring, and all things were possible.

But when they posed for the photographer from the T. Eaton Company, only a few of them could conjure up as much as a half-smirk. Even in their button-down, wide-collared sweaters, it was cold. And damp. It rained steadily. It wasn't really baseball weather.

Tim Daly folded his arms and smiled as he knelt at the end of the front row. Toronto's trainer, Daly was conspicuous in his flat cap and dark trousers. Everyone else wore proper baseball headgear and white pants.

Bill Smith, kneeling on his own in front of the team, was not wearing a sweater. But he did sport an enthusiastic grin. In fact, if the expression on his face was any indication, then he was one of the happiest members of the Leafs at that moment. Just sixteen years old, Bill was already in a position that many people never find themselves in: He had a job that he loved.

The Leafs at their 1926 home opener. Smitty is in the white shirt, kneeling, front row centre. Tim Daly is in the front row, far left.

Perhaps he hoped that this day would never end. Maybe he hoped that his association with the Toronto Maple Leafs would go on forever.

"Smitty" was still there when the Leafs left Toronto for good. Oh, the people he would meet and the things he would see in forty-two years at the foot of Bathurst Street ...

"Fleet Street Flats" means nothing to Torontonians who are not of a certain age. But for a dwindling number of the city's sons and daughters, the term evokes images of Maple Leaf Stadium, the grand home of their city's professional baseball team.

Maple Leaf Stadium opened on April 29, 1926. Pregame ceremonies included an on-field duel between two local politicians. Thomas Foster, mayor of Toronto, pitched. Thomas Langton Church, a member of parliament and a former mayor of the city, batted. A crowd of over 12,000 people braved the inclement weather, only to see visiting Reading take a 5–0 lead into the bottom of the ninth.

With their backs firmly against the wall, the first two Toronto batters singled. Two batters later, it was 5–1 and there were two out. But each of the next five batters got hits, and the Leafs tied the score. They went on to win it 6–5 in the tenth. It was a fairy-tale ending to the first day of action in a fairy castle among minor league ballparks.

Before the season was over, Bill Smith would rub shoulders with Carl Hubbell, Babe Dye, and Lionel Conacher.

Carl Hubbell was twenty-two years old at the beginning of the 1926 season. He was still two years away from his big-league debut, which came as a member of the New York Giants. By the time he retired in 1943, he had won 253 games. Known as "The Meal Ticket" and "King Carl," the screwball-throwing southpaw played his entire major league career with the Giants. But his season with the Leafs was an inauspicious one. He had a win–loss record of 7–7 on a team that finished 109–57.

• • •

Cecil "Babe" Dye was a high-scoring forward for the Toronto St. Pats, the city's National Hockey League team that would become the Maple Leafs. Dye led the NHL in goals three times and won a Stanley Cup as a member of the St. Pats in 1922. When he hung up his skates, he had scored 202 goals in 268 games. But on Opening Day in 1926, exactly two weeks away from his twenty-eighth birthday, Dye was Toronto's leadoff hitter and centre fielder. He had two hits in five at-bats. Unfortunately for the St. Pats fans who patronized Maple Leaf Stadium, Dye would not finish the International League season in Toronto.

Lionel Conacher appeared in only three games for the Leafs. Compared with most of the other sports that he played, baseball was just not his game. In the spring of 1926, he had just finished his rookie season as a defenceman with the Pittsburgh Pirates of the NHL. He would go on to play a dozen seasons in the league, winning a Stanley Cup with the Montreal Maroons in 1935.

But Conacher was much more than a hockey and baseball player. He had won a Grey Cup in 1921 as a member of the Toronto Argonauts. He played lacrosse. He wrestled. He boxed. Eventually, he would be voted Canada's Athlete of the Half-Century. A member of parliament as well, Conacher died after suffering a heart attack while running out a triple in a softball game in Ottawa. He was only fifty-three years old.

• • •

The Leafs finished the 1926 regular season eight games ahead of second-place Baltimore, who had won the International League pennant in each of the previous seven years. In the autumn, Toronto represented the IL in the Junior World Series against the Louisville Colonels, champions of the AA American Association.

A best-of-nine affair, the Junior World Series opened at Maple Leaf Stadium on September 28. Tickets were available at the Royal Alexandra Theatre, among other places. General admission seats were a dollar, reserved seats were $1.50, and box seats cost $2.00 each.

Game One took only one hour and sixteen minutes to play. The teams combined for just eight hits. Toronto had only three, but they led to both runs in a 2–0 Leafs victory. Jesse Doyle, who had fifteen wins for Toronto during the regular season, pitched the shutout.

In Game Two, Toronto was down 2–0 going into the bottom of the ninth. The Leafs then got three hits and tied the score, sending the contest into extras. They went on to win 3–2 in eleven innings. Owen Carroll, who was the winning pitcher on opening day and led the 1926 staff with twenty-one victories, went the distance for Toronto and had thirteen strikeouts.

Game Three resulted in another extra inning victory for the Leafs. Vic Sorrell, who had a perfect 8–0 record during the regular season, threw a four-hitter and Toronto won 2–1 in ten frames.

Toronto chalked up a 4–3 victory in Game Four. Now up 4–0 in the series, the teams travelled to Louisville for Game Five.

Walter "Lefty" Stewart, who sported an 18–9 record and led the staff with six shutouts, held Louisville to five hits and the Leafs swept the series with a 7–0 win.

It was the first time that the Junior World Series had ended in a sweep. Toronto fans were not able to see the Leafs clinch it, but they did get to watch the first four games. Smitty probably missed Game Five, too. It was customary for hosting clubs to supply batboys for the visitors.

Toronto's manager in 1926 was Dan Howley. Forty years old in 1926, Howley had four separate stints as skipper of the Leafs between 1918 and 1938. The Massachusetts native had been a catcher as a player and had played briefly for the Philadelphia Phillies in 1913.

Howley's reward for guiding Toronto to the Junior World Series title was a return to the majors as manager of the St. Louis Browns in the American League. Howley was with the Browns from 1927 to 1929 and then managed Cincinnati for three years.

He came back to Toronto in 1933 and returned for the fourth and last time in 1937. When he left the dugout for good, in 1938, he had more wins than any other Leafs manager, before or since: 644.

• • •

In 1929, two years after he had returned to the Tigers, Owen Carroll was joined by two fellow ex-Leafs who had made their mark at Maple Leaf Stadium.

First baseman Dale Alexander won the Triple Crown as a member of the Leafs in 1928, leading the International League with thirty-one home runs, 144 runs batted in, and a .380 batting average. His 236 hits set a team record that would never be broken.

On the September day of '28 when the Leafs hosted the Philadelphia A's, Connie Mack offered the Leafs $60,000 for Alexander. He was turned down. Three other big-league clubs had already made a similar offer and been refused. The Leafs were in a pennant race of their own that day. They were just a half game ahead of both Rochester and Buffalo. It was hardly the right time to sell their top hitter. But Toronto faded down the stretch and lost seven of their last eight games. The Leafs ended up in third place, behind both Rochester and Buffalo.

Alexander did make his big-league debut in '29 as a member of the Detroit Tigers. He batted .343 and tied for the American League lead in hits (215) with teammate Charlie Gehringer, who had played for Toronto in 1925 when they were still based at Hanlan's Point. Gehringer, a second baseman, would eventually be voted into the Baseball Hall of Fame at Cooperstown, New York.

In 1932, Alexander led the AL with a .372 batting average as a member of the Boston Red Sox. But he lasted only five years in the big leagues, leaving a .331 lifetime batting average in his wake.

John Prudhomme was the other prominent ex-Leaf to join the Tigers in 1929. Prudhomme, a right-handed pitcher, threw two no-hitters for Toronto at Maple Leaf Stadium.

On August 23, 1927, the day after Babe Ruth socked the fortieth homer of his famous sixty-home-run season, Prudhomme held the Reading Keys hitless and the Leafs won 14–0 in Toronto. One year minus a day later, Prudhomme did it again at Fleet Street Flats. His seven-inning 5–0 victory was the second half of a doubleheader against Jersey City. With two out in the top of the seventh, Toronto's second baseman bobbled a smash and the runner made it to first safely. The official scorer first ruled it a hit, then changed his mind and charged the second-sacker with an error.

Prudhomme had a short big-league career, appearing in thirty-four games for the Tigers in 1929, completing two of his six starts. He had only one victory against six losses, his earned run average was over 6.00, and he walked more than twice as many batters as he struck out. After 1929, he never again pitched in the majors.

Lena Styles was the catcher for both of Prudhomme's no-hitters. Styles was also a member of the Leafs in 1926, and he pinch-hit for them in their Maple Stadium debut. Styles hit .313 in 1926 as a backup catcher and occasional first and third baseman. He had played his first big-league game as a teenager with the Philadelphia Athletics in 1919. He wore an A's uniform in '20 and '21, then disappeared from the majors for almost a decade. He reappeared in 1930 with the Cincinnati Reds, where his manager was Dan Howley.

• • •

In 1928 and 1929, the last two baseball seasons of a decade known best for its fast living, the International League leader in stolen bases was an aptly named Toronto outfielder named Joe Rabbitt, who pilfered forty-two bases in '28 and forty-six in '29.

A left-handed hitter who weighed less than 160 pounds, Rabbitt played just two games in the majors, with Cleveland in 1923. He had some power, too; against Baltimore in 1929, Rabbitt became just the third player in club history to hit three home runs in one game.

• • •

With the onset of the Great Depression and a new decade, the Leafs slid in the standings and at the gate. After winning one pennant and finishing second five times in the 1920s, Toronto finished as high as third only once in the dirty thirties. That was in 1934, and what a year it was.

The Leafs brought no fewer than four players from Toronto and environs to their spring training camp in Augusta, Georgia. Charles "Steamer" Lucas, a pitcher, was a Toronto native who had been out of pro baseball for three years. Earl Cook, another hurler, had joined the Leafs in '32. Cook, then twenty-five, was a farmer from Lemonville, just outside of Stouffville, Ontario. Lloyd Nourse and Bobby Porter were Toronto sandlot players who were in Augusta primarily to gain some experience.

Porter, who had played for Beaches in the Ulster Stadium League in '33, was soon summoned back to Toronto … to play junior hockey. The twenty-one-year-old played football as well. Nourse didn't make the Leafs Opening Day roster, but Cook and Lucas did.

• • •

The 1934 regular season started — somewhat bizarrely — in Albany, New York. It was a day game, and Albany's Hawkins Stadium did not have lights. After nine innings, the score was 8–8 and it was getting dark. Toronto scored five runs in the top of the tenth while the Albany manager invoked as many stalling tactics as he could in order to get the game called on account of darkness. He made player changes until the bench was empty. Albany narrowed the gap to 13–11 with two out and had a runner on first.

That's when the fans started to throw pop bottles and seat cushions onto the field. Then a bunch of kids ran onto the diamond. A dog scampered onto the field. By then the umpire had seen enough. He called the game and awarded a 9–0 forfeit victory to Toronto.

One week later, IL president Charles Knapp overturned the umpire's decision and ordered the teams to complete the game on a later date.

• • •

Night baseball came to Maple Leaf Stadium on June 28, 1934. Six light towers had been constructed at the ballpark by Canadian General Electric. Two towers, each a hundred feet high, were erected in the outfield. One was in left field, the other in right. Atop the grandstand, four sets of lights rose 105 feet above ground level. Overall, the lighting system was said to be as good as that of any other ballpark on the continent.

The game was intentionally started late to ensure that there would be no natural light when the first pitch was thrown. It was just a week after the summer solstice, so the game did not get underway until about ten o'clock. It ended after 12:30 a.m. About 16,000 fans were on hand, the largest crowd at the stadium since 1926. But the Rochester Red Wings spoiled the occasion by beating the Leafs 8–2. Ike Boone knocked in both Toronto runs with a two-run homer. Boone went two-for-three at the plate, raising his league leading batting average to a lofty .393.

Ike Boone had become Toronto's player-manager in 1934. The previous season, Boone had led the Leafs in batting and had a thirty-two-game hitting streak. He was thirty-six years old at the time. Filling out the lineup card in '34 didn't harm his batting eye, either. Boone hit .372 and won both the International League batting crown and the Most Valuable Player Award. It was his second batting title: he had topped the loop in '31 by hitting .356 as a member of the Newark Bears.

Boone had been a successful offensive player in the majors as well, hitting over .330 as a regular outfielder for the Boston Red Sox in 1924 and 1925. In fact, he boasted a career .319 batting in over 350 games. But he was slow afoot, and his glove was not as strong as his bat.

Second baseman Joe Morrissey had a six-hit game for the Leafs in 1934. He was just the fourth Toronto player to achieve that feat.

• • •

The International League had consisted of eight clubs continuously since 1895. The league introduced a new playoff system in 1933. That year, the first-place team played the second-place team and the third-place team played the fourth-place team in best-of-five semifinals. The Leafs had finished a half-game behind fourth place Buffalo, thus missing out on the postseason by the slimmest of margins. Buffalo won their series and then upset second-place Rochester in a best-of-seven final series to become league playoff champs and advance to the Junior World Series against Columbus of the American Association.

The IL playoff structure was changed in 1934; the semifinals were expanded to best-of-seven affairs. The matchups were also modified: first place played third and second played fourth. The Leafs finished third. Their reward was a semifinal berth against the first-place Newark Bears.

Newark had just finished first for the third consecutive year. The Bears would be a minor league powerhouse for most of the decade: five first-place finishes and three Junior World Series appearances, of which they won two.

The '34 Newark squad included George Selkirk, who hit .357 and made his big-league debut with the New York Yankees. "Twinkletoes" was born in Huntsville, Ontario. The left-handed-hitting outfielder would go on to play parts of nine years for the Yankees, Newark's parent club. Selkirk replaced Babe Ruth as the Bronx Bombers' right fielder. He even wore Ruth's number three jersey.

The Bears also included ex-Leaf Dale Alexander. Though he was through as a big-leaguer, Alexander was far from finished as a professional ballplayer. He batted .336 for Newark in '34 and knocked in 123 runs.

On the mound, Newark had Walter "Jumbo" Brown. The 6'4" right-hander was the only twenty-game winner in the IL in '34. He led the league in wins, winning percentage, shutouts, complete games, and earned run average.

Toronto had finished seven and a half games behind Newark in the standings. The Leafs were firm underdogs.

The series opened with two games in Newark, and the Leafs won both. Maple Leaf Stadium hosted Game Three on Thursday, September 13. About 7,500 fans were in attendance, hoping to see the Leafs take a 3–0 lead in the series. But Newark pitcher Jack LaRocca had other ideas. He held the Leafs to just three hits and the Bears won 6–0. Playing against his old team, Dale Alexander had three hits for Newark.

The next day, Toronto notched their first home playoff win. Behind 4–1 with one out in the top of the third, Boone pulled starter Walter "Whitey" Hilcher. In came Steamer Lucas, who pitched six and two-thirds innings of shutout relief while the Leafs came back to win 7–4 before a crowd of 7,200.

The Bears won Game Five 3–0 at Maple Leaf Stadium to pull to within a game of the Leafs. Then the series moved back to Newark. The home team won Game Six 3–2, and there was bad news for the Leafs. Their number-one catcher, thirty-eight-year-old John Heving, broke a finger.

Into the breach stepped Frank "Gabby" LaVeque, Toronto's back-up catcher. LaVeque singled in the first run of Game Seven, in the top of the second inning. That was all that Leafs hurler Don Brennan needed. Brennan, who had spent part of the season with the Reds in Cincinnati, had big-league stuff and kept Newark off the scoreboard. Toronto centre fielder Lincoln Blakely, who had also suited up for the Reds that year, homered in the eighth and the Leafs won 2–0.

• • •

Game One of the IL finals took place on September 19 in Toronto. Led by Fred "Sheriff" Blake, the Leafs beat the Rochester Red Wings 2–0 in front of some 8,000 fans. Blake threw a two-hitter and retired the side in order six times to defeat his former team.

Steamer Lucas got his second win of the playoffs the next day. Lucas pitched the final two innings in a 5–4 Toronto win, this time before a crowd of 10,000. John Heving, recovering from his broken finger, singled home the winning run in the home half of the eighth.

The series moved across Lake Ontario for Game Three. The Leafs won 3–2 in thirteen innings, and Don Brennan went the distance on the mound for Toronto. Brennan gave up fifteen hits in the contest but got outs when he needed them most. The Maple Leafs were one victory away from the IL title and a Junior World Series berth.

The Red Wings clobbered the Leafs 9–2 in Game Four, which was delayed a day because of rain. But Toronto clinched the series with a tight 2–1 win in Game Five. Al Hollingsworth went the distance on the mound and had twelve strikeouts. And, for the second time in five days, John Heving singled home the winning run. This time it was in the top of the ninth.

The format of the 1934 Junior World Series was the same as it had been eight years earlier when the Leafs swept Louisville. It was a best-of-nine affair with the first four games played in Toronto and the remaining games on the road at the American Association club's park.

On September 28, exactly eight years after their '26 Junior World Series opener, the Leafs hosted Game One against Columbus, the American Association champions. Columbus won 7–1. The next day, Toronto squandered a 4–1 lead in the top of the ninth and lost 7–4. The Leafs finally got on track in Game Three. Hollingsworth pitched a four-hitter and Toronto picked up a much-needed 7–2 victory. Only 3,000 people showed up for the game. Columbus blanked the Leafs 4–0 in Game Four, and Toronto fans said goodbye to their hardball heroes. Win or lose, the Leafs would play the remainder of the series in Ohio.

Columbus had won the American Association title in dramatic fashion. Behind three games to two in the finals against Minneapolis, Columbus was losing 6–2 and down to their last out in Game Six. Miraculously, they came from behind and won the game, then won Game Seven to take the series.

There was some high drama against the Leafs in the Junior World Series, too. Toronto first baseman George McQuinn stole home, and the Leafs won Game Five by a 6–4 score. The Leafs then tied the series with an emphatic 19–9 victory in Game Six. Toronto's momentum continued into Game Seven. Going into the bottom of the ninth, the Leafs were ahead 8–4 and poised to take a lead in the series for the first time. But Columbus scored five runs in the inning and won 9–8.

Game Eight was played on a Tuesday afternoon. Toronto won 5–1, forcing a ninth and final game that was played that very evening. Columbus clinched it with a 14–8 victory. It was their second consecutive Junior World Series title.

Overall, Maple Leaf Stadium hosted nine postseason games in 1934. The Leafs won only four of those games. Toronto's two series clinchers were played on the road, unseen by the hometown fans.

• • •

In terms of success, the Leafs wandered the desert for eight years after that 1934 season. In each of those years, they finished in the bottom half of the standings and out of the playoff picture. Toronto won more games than they lost in only two of those eight years. They were dead last three years in a row, from 1939 to 1941.

There were moments of brilliance, even in the lean years. Leroy Herrmann threw a ten-inning no-hitter for the Leafs against Newark on May 2, 1936. The thirty-year-old right-hander was the first Toronto pitcher to throw an extra-inning no-hitter in two decades. Urban Shocker, who won 188 games in a thirteen-year big league career, had thrown an eleven-inning no-hitter for the Leafs in 1916.

A month after Herrmann's gem, there was another no-hitter at Fleet Street Flats. This time, the Leafs were on the wrong end of it. Buffalo's Bill Harris, a thirty-six-year-old righty, threw a seven-inning perfect game. He didn't allow a single Toronto base runner. Harris also threw a nine-inning no-hitter for the Bisons in July and led the IL in strikeouts in '36.

On May 16, 1939, southpaw Billy Weir threw a no-hitter and the Leafs beat Baltimore 8–0. The game featured a player fouling a pitch into his cheek, a balk, a call of catcher's interference, and nine walks from the Baltimore pitching staff.

With the coming of the Second World War, attendance fell significantly. Almost 120,000 fans had filed into Maple Leaf Stadium in 1939. Less than 70,000 showed up in 1940, and fewer than 60,000 the following year.

Toronto's 1939 pitching staff included Phil Marchildon, a native of Penetanguishene, Ontario. Marchildon had signed his first pro contract with the Leafs the previous year, at the relatively advanced age of twenty-four, after attending a tryout camp in Barrie.

Marchildon started on the mound at Toronto's home opener in '39, only the second Canadian to do so. Steamer Lucas had been the first, losing 11–1 to Syracuse in 1935. Facing Syracuse on a cold afternoon, Marchildon had an inauspicious home debut. He gave up ten hits and walked five in front of 8,500 fans, and the Leafs lost 4–1.

• • •

The Leafs, an independent minor league club, had a farm team of their own in 1939, based in Cornwall, Ontario. They competed in the Class C Canadian-American (Can-Am) League, which was comprised of teams from eastern Ontario and upstate New York. Marchildon was sent down to Cornwall so that he could sort himself out. The demotion proved just the tonic for Marchildon's woes. He racked up six straight wins for Cornwall with a puny 1.20 earned run average (ERA) in forty-five innings. Marchildon was recalled to the Leafs in late June.

By then, future Hall of Famers Heinie Manush and Tony Lazzeri had joined the club. Manush, an outfielder, was on his way down after a long big-league career. Lazzeri, Toronto's new manager, had been the second baseman and a member of "Murderers' Row" on the 1927 New York Yankees. He hit sixty homers for Salt Lake City of the Pacific Coast League in 1925, a league record that has yet to be broken.

On July 1, Dominion Day, a crowd of 10,000 fans saw Marchildon throw a two-hitter and beat Buffalo 4–1 at Maple Leaf Stadium. It was his first win in a Toronto uniform. He would finish the season with a 5–7 record. Opposing hitters batted only .202 against him, but he was wild, giving up walks at a hefty rate of 6.4 per every nine innings.

Marchildon won ten games with the Leafs in 1940 and was called up by the Philadelphia Athletics near the end of the season. He would eventually win sixty-eight big-league games despite playing for mediocre Philadelphia teams. He was 17–14 with the '42 A's, who won fifty-five and lost ninety-nine. In 1947 he was 19–9 with a team that finished two games over the .500 mark. He also missed two and a half years due to the Second World War. A member of the RCAF, he was shot down over Germany and spent over twenty months in a POW camp.

• • •

The 1941 Leafs were atrocious; their win–loss record was 47–107. They finished thirty-eight games out of the playoffs and fifty-three games behind first-place Newark. Excluding their two top pitchers, Porter Vaughan and Dick Fowler, their record was 25–85. Lena Blackburne was Toronto's manager that season. Like Dan Howley, Blackburne had four stints as skipper of the Leafs. Blackburne had first taken the reins in 1916. But unlike Howley, Blackburne had an abysmal record as manager. His teams won less than 40 percent of their games.

In '41, Al Rubeling set the Toronto record for home runs hit at Maple Leaf Stadium in one season: nine. By then, the spacious outfield of Fleet Street Flats had earned a reputation as a pitcher's best friend.

Outfielder Frank Colman spent his first year with the Leafs that season. A native of London, Ontario, Colman had first signed with the Leafs as a pitcher in 1939. Also a Cornwall Can-Am League alumnus, Colman hurt his arm while pitching for Wilmington of the Inter-State League in 1940. He was moved to the outfield and proceeded to hit .361 for Wilmington that season. The move became permanent. Colman hit .295 in 1941 and upped his average to an even .300 the following season.

Toronto got a new general manager in 1942. Lee MacPhail was only twenty-four years old. His father, Larry, was president of the Brooklyn Dodgers. Lee had worked in Brooklyn's farm system in '41.

MacPhail hired Burleigh Grimes, one of the last spitball pitchers in the big leagues, as Toronto's new manager. The Leafs finished under .500 for the sixth straight year, but they won twenty-seven more games than they had in '41.

The '42 squad included 6'9" Johnny Gee, who had been captain of the University of Michigan basketball team and pitched for the Wolverines. Gee joined the Leafs after pitching just twenty innings in the previous two years due to arm trouble.

Then, in '43, they won the pennant for the first time since 1926. They swept Montreal in the IL semifinals but lost the finals to Syracuse in six games. Thirty-eight-year-old Luke Hamlin won twenty-one games for the Leafs. Hamlin, nicknamed "Hot Potato," was the first Toronto pitcher to win twenty or more games in one season since 1933. That year, they had a twenty-one-game winner by the name of ... Luke Hamlin.

In between his twenty-one-win seasons with the Leafs, Hamlin had spent most of his time with the Brooklyn Dodgers. In 1939, he won twenty games for them.

The Leafs made the playoffs in 1944 and 1945 but were knocked out in the first round both years.

By now, Bill Smith had been with the Toronto Maple Leafs for over twenty years. His service to the club had been broken only by a spell in the armed forces during the Second World War. He had started as a batboy, but he was now in his mid-thirties and had been the club's trainer for some time.

He had fetched bats for Charlie Gehringer and Babe Dye and Dale Alexander and Ike Boone and Frank Colman. He had seen no-hitters and Junior World Series games and so much more. In terms of baseball, he must have felt like he had seen it all at Fleet Street Flats.

But he hadn't ...

PART V

THREE BATBOYS AND THE BOSS'S KID

Ron Stead, Batboy

Soldiers didn't have to pay to get into Maple Leaf Stadium during the Second World War. It was predominantly Canadian servicemen who passed through the turnstiles at that time, but there were others for whom baseball was something new and foreign.

Just beyond the outfield fences of Maple Leaf Stadium were barracks. Housed in those barracks were members of the Royal Norwegian Air Force. Norway's air force in exile trained at the Island Airport, just across a narrow channel from the barracks. The channel led (and still leads) from Toronto's harbour to the open waters of Lake Ontario.

The Royal Norwegian Air Force relocated to Gravenhurst in 1943. The airport was then taken over by the Royal Canadian Air Force and resumed its original function as a civilian facility in 1945. The Norwegians were in their barracks long enough for the area to be christened "Little Norway." The buildings became rental accommodations for locals.

One of those locals was a little boy named Ron Stead. "Little Norway was great," recalled Stead. "It was an ideal place for a kid to grow up. The old parade ground, which was right in the centre of the complex, was our ball field in the summertime and our hockey rink in the wintertime. There was also a gymnasium there, and we had classes there all winter long: basketball, floor hockey, dances on Saturday night. It was a great community atmosphere. We lived there from about 1945 to 1954."

With so much to do in the complex, local kids didn't stray from the area. "Our parents pretty much knew where we were all the time. They just had to look out the window. I thoroughly enjoyed living there, and I've often told my own kids about what a good place it was."

The former barracks were of different sizes and shapes. "There were only four families in the building that I lived in. Some of the other buildings were H-shaped, and I'd say that there were sixteen families in those. There were two that were two storeys. One had just one apartment upstairs. The other had twelve on the bottom, I would guess, and another twelve up top."

Maple Leaf Stadium was literally a stone's throw from the Steads' apartment. "My building was in left-centre. There were doors at either end of my building, plus one at the side. If I went directly out of the side door and climbed the fence, I was probably two signboards over from the scoreboard."

To Stead and the other kids of Little Norway, the stadium was simply an extension of their play area. "We were always at the ballpark. We'd climb the fence and we were there. We did all sorts of things in the ballpark that I don't care to mention!"

One day, he spotted trainer Bill Smith. "It was an off day. The ball club wasn't there. But 'Smitty' was there. I happened to see him, and I just kind of wandered over and started talking to him. He was putting socks on some of the pipe railings that they had all around the ballpark to separate the boxes from the rest of the seats as you moved up the stairs. That's where he used to hang the sweat socks and towels."

As he and Smith chatted, Stead started to help the Leafs with the laundry. "I struck up a friendship with him. I started to go to ballgames at night. Joe Coleman, a former Philadelphia Athletics pitcher, was with the Leafs. I'd hang around the ballpark after the game and help Smitty and the batboy of the time clean the spikes and so on, and then I'd head home. Joe Coleman befriended me and promised that he would give me an autographed ball. In those days, anyone who hit a home run got a case of Wheaties. He said that

The many faces of Smitty.

he'd get me a case of cereal. I kept on going back and hanging around, and it sort of developed from there. I was nine years old."

Before long, Stead became Toronto's batboy. "I just sort of grew into it. The previous batboy, John Sylvester, was getting older, and he ended up doing more of the straight clubhouse work. Almost an assistant trainer but more of a clubhouse boy. I took over the field duties. Smitty gave me an old Toronto uniform. My mother, who did a lot of dressmaking and so on, cut it down for me. I started 'batboying' in 1946 or '47. The ball club also had a batboy for the visiting team. I just did Toronto. I never asked for the job. I just enjoyed being around the ballpark. And I loved the sport anyway. That love just grew deeper and deeper. I just wanted to be around it."

Ron Stead has fond memories of Bill Smith. For the most part. "Bill was great. Sometimes he'd try to be gruff. There was one time. I'd been there a year or two and something happened. A couple of kids from Little Norway hassled him while he was doing the clothes one Sunday. I was there, too. They were giving him a hard time, and I think they knocked the laundry off the pipes. We used to do all our own washing right in the dressing room. He had to rewash it. He kind of took it out on me. I guess I went home crying."

Stead's father came to the rescue. "My dad was very gentle, but he was a big man. He went over and had a few words with Smitty. After they had a little chat, I think that Bill realized that I had no control over the kids who had come there. I used to go there by myself when there was work to be done."

Stead has a theory as to why Smith initially took a liking to him: "When I first went there, he was childless. I have no idea how old he was. He and his wife did have a baby girl, probably after I was there three or four years. I have a feeling that I was sort of the missing child in the early years that I knew him, and that's probably why he took a liking to me."

As a batboy, Stead had several duties. "I did the on-field stuff, which was making sure that the umpires were supplied with balls. I'd clear the bat away if I thought there was a chance of a play at home. It was a judgement call on my part. But I was given very strict instructions to stay out of there, and either the catcher or the umpire or somebody else would have to worry about getting the bat out of there if I was going to get in the way. I chased foul balls and got balls coming off the screen."

Those duties extended beyond the end of the game. "When the ballplayers left the park, the clubhouse boy and I would clean the spikes, probably throw a load of towels and sweat socks in the washer." The laundry was then dried and put in the players' lockers. "So when everybody came back the next day, everything was where it belonged."

The nights could be very long. "During the summer I got home around one or one thirty in the morning, but my commute was just over the fence! And more than once, I didn't go home. We just slept on the rubdown tables in the clubhouse."

Stead remembers one elderly fan who befriended him. "There was someone called the Lady in Black. Her name was Mrs. Anderson. She was a deaf lady, and she sat right behind home plate. She never missed a ball game, and she never missed a hockey game. When I first started batboying, I was very small for my age. I think that she took pity on me. That was before Sunday ball, and they used to have Saturday doubleheaders. She used to bring a little package of fruit and cookies, and she used to have one of the ushers bring it down to the clubhouse for me. She took me to my first professional hockey game. She called me during the winter. She was well into her eighties, and she invited me to go to a game at Maple Leaf Gardens."

After he'd been batboy for a few years, Stead's responsibilities expanded to throwing batting practice. "It probably started when I was about twelve or thirteen. Some of the players used to come early, before batting practice was actually called for, to get some extra hitting in. They always used to have a player behind the batting practice pitcher to feed him balls and take throws from the players in the field. It probably started in one of those sessions. There was no one else left to pitch, so I said that I would. I'm sure I was nervous, but I always felt comfortable pitching. I really did. I just enjoyed it so much, and I'd always had so much coaching on the sidelines."

Stead was playing sandlot baseball at Stanley Park, near King and Bathurst, at the time. Ironically, he wasn't a pitcher. "My first year or two at Stanley Park I only played first base. I don't know why they put me there, I was so small. They would never let me pitch because I was so small. But I used to pitch batting practice, then jump on a streetcar to go up to Stanley Park, play a ballgame, and usually make it back by game time. I had a friend who would fill in for me if I was an inning or two late."

It's hardly surprising that after throwing to Leafs hitters and receiving ad hoc pitching lessons from Leafs pitchers Stead became a pitcher. In 1955, Stead went to spring training with the Leafs — as a combined batboy and prospect. "I went as a batboy, but I worked out with them. The deal that I had with [club owner] Jack Kent Cooke was that they wouldn't pay me, but my room and board was looked after. I still did all the clubhouse chores, but I participated in the workouts, in uniform. I chased balls in the outfield, backed up the batting practice pitcher. I got to participate in a lot of the drills. They even let me pitch to a batter or two in games. I got a ride home from one of the reporters."

At the end of that season, Stead turned professional himself. "I threw batting practice almost every night. And that did really good things for me. In 1955, I signed a contract for the 1956 season."

Stead signed with the Leafs, but not until he had worked out in Cleveland for the Indians. "I was still small for my age. I probably only weighed about 140 pounds. I was about to sign with them. I was going to the scouts' office and Hank Greenberg came by. He was the GM at Cleveland. He said, 'Well, Ron, we'd really like to have you in the organization, but unfortunately we can't give you a bonus. With your size, we're afraid that when we get you down into that hot weather you might not have the stamina.' Their judgement was that I wouldn't be able to stand up to the hot weather."

He opted to sign with Toronto instead. "I knew that, if I had a bad year after signing for no bonus, they'd drop me like a hot potato. With Toronto, I probably got about the same deal, but I thought that because of the publicity aspects they'd stick with me for an extra year or two. That was my thinking at the time, and I don't regret it."

Stead went to spring training with the Leafs as a player in 1956. Their camp was at Fort Pierce, Florida. "I probably didn't get as much of an opportunity as I would have liked, but there was no way that I was going to make the ball club unless some sort of miracle happened."

He doesn't recall how nervous he was when he first took the mound for the Leafs in Florida as a paid baseball player. "If I had the jitters and the shakes, it was because of the opportunity that I was getting. I was used to throwing batting practice. I pitched against seasoned ballplayers."

The designated hitter phenomenon was years away, which meant that Stead had to take his turn at-bat. During one game that spring, he faced the immortal Satchel Paige. "I was never much of a hitter. I don't imagine that I did too well unless he was having an off day!"

The Leafs immediately gave Stead a chance to prove the Indians wrong regarding their concerns about his ability to cope with the heat. "After I signed with Toronto, they sent me to Orlando, Florida. If I had signed with Cleveland I would have gone to Cocoa Beach." Stead was 10–17 with a fine 3.04 ERA at Orlando in 1956. He also completed twenty of his twenty-nine starts.

Stead had an even better season in 1957 for Gainesville of the Florida State League, a loop that then had a Class D designation. He had a record of 17–10 for a club that finished seventh in the eight-team league, almost twenty games under .500. He had a 2.43 earned run average, threw two shutouts, and gave up only eight home runs in 226 innings. The Florida heat was not a problem. "I started twenty-six ballgames and completed twenty-four. That always made me feel good!"

His occasional batterymate was a fellow Toronto farmhand, Jim Baker. A catcher and left fielder, Baker hit .245 for Gainesville in 116 games.

Stead played briefly in the Class C Northern League in 1958, then returned to southern Ontario. He had an outstanding career in the semipro Ontario Senior Intercounty Baseball League, winning over a hundred games despite a comparatively short season. Stead was inducted into the Canadian Baseball Hall of Fame in 2006. He passed away in 2011 at the age of seventy-five.

John Bukowski, Batboy

To be batboy for the Toronto Maple Leafs,
that was a position to be cherished.
— JOHN BUKOWSKI

John Bukowski calls them "the urchins." They were a bunch of kids who hung out beyond the outfield fences of Maple Leaf Stadium in the early 1950s, trying to get their mitts on as many stray baseballs as they could. Bukowski was one of them.

"The urchins either lived in Little Norway or on the other side of the railway tracks, as you went up Bathurst Street," recalled Bukowski. "I lived on Baldwin Avenue, in the Jewish Market. And I'm sure that some of the other urchins came from even farther away."

Growing up in "the market," Bukowski played pickup ball in Bellevue Square. "Home plate was right across the street from the synagogue on the north side of the square."

Bukowski started to chase wayward balls at "Fleet Street Flats" when he was about eight or nine years old. "We learned the trade from the ten-to-twelve-year-olds. There was a pecking order. There were twenty or thirty of us."

Getting to Maple Leaf Stadium was an adventure for Bukowski and the other urchins who lived nearby. "We'd walk. If batting practice was at five o'clock we'd leave at three. We might stop and look at the trains on the way. We'd miss a lot of suppers, but our parents knew where we were. We had mobility as kids. We never thought that anything would happen to us. It was a free environment."

The fun would start on Opening Day. "You could take the afternoon off from school to go to Opening Day, but you had to bring a note. That half-day off was a highlight of the school year. Some kids became very adept at forging their parents' signatures. The teachers knew what we were doing, but baseball was baseball."

The chances of getting a baseball have always been higher during batting practice than during a game. But there was one small problem at Maple Leaf Stadium: There were two sets of fences. The inner fences formed the boundary of the playing field. The outer fences separated the stadium from the outside world. Naturally, some balls landed between the fences.

The urchins had a tried and tested methodology for getting into the space between the fences. While a designated urchin intentionally attracted the ushers' attention, the others would literally leap into action. "We'd run like hell. Then it was one leg up, and if you landed two-thirds of the way up your momentum carried you the rest of the way. Ushers were there so that we couldn't hop the fence, and if they could beat us to a ball I'm sure that was extra pennies in their pockets."

The ushers never had a chance. "How does one person manage against twenty or thirty urchins? And we were very good at what we did, especially the art of distraction." Sometimes the urchins would play their cat-and-mouse game with the ushers even when there was no baseball at the end of their rainbow.

Right-handed pull hitters hit to left field and vice versa. This fact was not lost on the urchins, and they would position themselves accordingly once they figured out who was batting. "The regulars would come out at about five thirty or so. They never changed their order in batting practice. You could actually tell who was hitting by the sound of the ball."

Outfielder Stan Jok was a stereotypical right-handed pull hitter. "Stan Jok would hit balls from the left field foul pole to left-centre. Lou Limmer and Rocky Nelson were the opposite. They were left-handed hitters and their target seemed to be the right field pole."

The likes of Nelson and Limmer would hit balls beyond the confines of the stadium and into Little Norway. "Each building had a central hallway and you could only get in or out at the ends. Balls were expensive in those days. There were ushers outside the right field fence, too. One building was located just beyond that fence. I can't tell you how many times those ushers chased urchins through that building's central hallway after one of us got hold of a ball. It was hilarious. I don't know why the ushers were so possessive. After all, it was outside the ballpark."

Long-time Leaf Mike Goliat was a favourite of the urchins. "You could guarantee that Goliat would hit eight to ten balls over the fence. The man had enormous power. And every time he hit he would grunt. It was known as the Mike Goliat Grunt. We couldn't see who was hitting but we could hear the Grunt. And the Grunt would trigger the Goliat Shift. Any of us in centre or right would move to Goliat Alley. Mike Goliat must have hit a majority of his home runs within fifty to seventy-five feet of the left field foul pole."

Part of the urchins' booty was sold. "Over the course of a season we'd average about twenty balls apiece. You could clean up a ball with an eraser, wrap it up in wax paper so that it would have a layer of wax on it, and sell it for fifty cents or a dollar. We'd look at the kids coming out of the stadium after the game. Judging from what they were wearing, we'd decide how much we could squeeze out of their parents for a ball. It became a business."

Other balls could be reused in places like Bellevue Square or traded in to the club for a free pass to an upcoming game. "We kept some of the balls for our own games because we didn't have the money to buy them. We weren't really interested in the passes."

For a while, chasing baseballs at the foot of Bathurst Street was a way of life for Bukowski and his cronies. "We made Maple Leaf Stadium our second home. If we went there once, we went there a thousand times. There was a mystique about the ballpark itself and about being able to go to school the next day and say 'look what I got' and show off a ball."

If the urchins were inside the park legitimately, for whatever reason, they sometimes made some money down the left field line in the bleachers. "The bleachers were separated from the rest of the main grandstand by a fence that was about seven feet high. The bleachers were somewhat cheaper, and they were home to a gambling syndicate."

Wagers were made on more than just the score. "They would bet on what the next pitch would be, where the next ball would be hit. There were plainclothes officers in attendance but they got around them by using sign language for who was going to do what to who, and when, and how."

Urchins in the bleachers could make themselves available to the gamblers. "There was a concession stand underneath the bleachers, but the gamblers didn't want to miss what was going on in the game. It wasn't profitable for the vendors to make the trek to the bleachers. As a result, we urchins would run pop and ice cream bars and hot dogs and cigarettes to the gamblers."

Pursuing balls eventually gave way to peddling pop for Bukowski. "Little kids like me were carrying twenty-four bottles in a bucket filled with ice up and down the stairs. We'd empty the melted ice water out of the pail to reduce the weight. Commission was a penny a bottle, and if you really hustled you'd made sixty or ninety cents at the end of the day. That was an awful lot of money in those days."

Vendors showed up early if they wanted to ensure themselves work on any given day. "We'd line up outside the stadium, and the club would decide how many vendors they required, depending on the crowd. If you were chosen you'd run to the main concession stand. There would be pushing and shoving because you made the most money selling hot dogs or ice cream. Bigger kids — high school and university students — usually sold those."

Cecil Finkler was the head concessionaire. "He was a very heavy man, but very athletic for his weight. He'd been a handball champion. He was a hard taskmaster, but he was very committed to young people. He was a role model for us. If you worked for him, he took care of you."

• • •

Bukowski entered the club's inner sanctum when he moved on to his next job. "There was one clubhouse boy. Maybe he was a gofer or he shone shoes. He had experimented with the freezing that they spray onto players if they get hit by a ball, for example. He put some spray into a bucket and he lit it. It exploded."

Trainer Bill Smith needed a replacement immediately. "I just happened to be there. I shone shoes for a couple of years. Then I went over to the visitors' clubhouse and shone shoes over there."

Clubhouse attendants were not paid. "It was an honour to be able to shine the players' shoes. Sure, the player would tip you if you got a hot dog for them or shined their street shoes. There was always a way to make some money, but you did the job out of love for the game."

Bukowski later became batboy for the visiting team. One of his "customers" in that capacity was the immortal Satchel Paige. Officially in his early fifties — and many people believe that he was actually several years older — Paige was then pitching regularly for the Miami Marlins.

Paige sat in a rocking chair when he was in uniform and not on the mound. He had one of the largest ever repertoires of pitches, including one that was borderline legal at best. "Satchel Paige used to moisten the right side of his uniform below the belt with a mixture of resin and 7-Up. You could say that, indirectly, he was using a spitter. I'm sure that the resin and 7-Up gave him an advantage, but nobody would ever question it because he was Satchel Paige. In those days you didn't question Satchel Paige or people of his status."

The Leafs would host each of their seven International League opponents eleven times each. That was enough for Paige to make an everlasting impression on Bukowski. "He'd only show up on the days that he was supposed to pitch — or when he chose to show up. Flashy dresser. Very skinny. Lanky legs. Thin arms. There was always a group around him in the dugout, listening to his stories. He was a legend, and he was unique."

Finally, in the late 1950s, Bukowski got the job that was the most coveted by his age group: he became batboy for the Leafs. He was now on centre stage. He had constant contact with Toronto's baseball heroes; the bat rack was next to where the manager sat. Team owner Jack Kent Cooke was sitting in the box seats nearby.

Bukowski became respectfully familiar with the regular patrons of the best seats in the house. "But you couldn't get too close to them because the next thing you know they'd want a baseball, hat or they'd want you to get them autographs."

Some female fans were interested in other things. "They'd want you to pass a note to a ballplayer with a phone number on it. I can't say that I didn't run a few numbers to the players, but only to the single ones!"

On at least one occasion, Bukowski was ringside for an all-Leafs wrestling match. Catcher Tim Thompson and manager Dixie Walker went at it in the dugout one day in 1959. The club had been struggling on the field, and frustrations boiled over. Thompson and Walker patched up their differences afterward. But while the catcher was back with the club the following season, the skipper was not.

The batboy's duties included keeping count of how many baseballs the home plate umpire had in his possession at all times. "Some umpires had one satchel, and some had two. Each satchel could hold six balls. They didn't want to be calling for balls, so it was our job to make sure that they didn't have to. It may sound like a little thing, but they appreciated it."

Among the umpires, Bukowski remembers Augie Guglielmo most of all. "Augie was very short. He would interact with the crowd. His manner of calling balls and strikes involved all sorts of contortions and the fans would mimic him, especially if they felt that he had blown a call. After a while he would start playing to the crowd."

Guglielmo had plenty of experience. He reached the major leagues as an umpire in 1952 and spent the entire season there. There is a well-known photo of Jackie Robinson stealing home, deftly avoiding the tag of the opposing catcher. Guglielmo is the umpire calling him safe. That same season, Guglielmo became the first umpire to eject Robinson from a big-league game.

After the '52 season Guglielmo went back to the minors. He never umpired in the big leagues again. Toronto fans saw him work International

League games until the end of the club's penultimate season, 1966. "In a sense he was the godfather of International League umpires. He was the one that young umps like Harry Wendelstedt looked to for guidance in yesteryear."

Bukowski and the other batboys could joke with Guglielmo and other umps. "Here we are, teenagers, and we'd tell Augie that he blew a call. He'd reply, 'get out of here, you little twerp,' or something like that, but he was never vindictive. Some umps were more sensitive than others, but if you fulfilled your role they'd talk to you, protect you, and just make you feel like a person."

The umps were fed at the end of the game. "Their meal consisted of a Coke and two hot dogs each. Sometimes it was three hot dogs, depending on how well they knew the vendors. Sure, they may have stayed at the King Edward Hotel, but when you consider their salaries you can bet that they pinched every penny they could."

The batboys also pitched batting practice, if they could throw strikes. Bukowski was a pitcher for a minor baseball team at Christie Pits, so he was a natural choice. "They were always looking for someone who could put the ball over the plate. Sometimes you'd throw three or four days in a row, and it wasn't for five minutes. It was for fifteen or twenty minutes. You weren't paid extra for it, but what it did was allow you to work on your mechanics."

A small canvas screen was the batting practice pitcher's only protection. "It was waist high, just some two-by-fours with a piece of canvas nailed between them. It was mainly there to protect your legs, but proper mechanics taught you to follow through and be ready to field your position. It was either that or you died!"

Throwing to the Leafs was a learning experience. "You got to know who wanted what, and where. You had to feed their egos, too, so you'd pitch to their zones. Let's face it: Rocky Nelson could have hit a home run during batting practice almost any time he wanted to. The players were trying to work on their rhythm. You learned to change speeds, too, and if a player called for a curveball you'd throw a curveball."

There would occasionally be extra throwing duties. "If a player was having a hard time, I'd come to the ballpark at two o'clock. They'd get three or four kids from the area, and they'd chase the balls. In return, they'd get a ball or a couple of passes. That was the way to get in some extra hitting. There were no batting cages with pitching machines."

Game days were long days for batboys, and they didn't end with the final pitch. "Afterwards you'd help the clubhouse boy shine the shoes. You might be there until midnight. The batboys were paid $2.50 a game. So that was sometimes $2.50 for ten hours' work. But you didn't do it for the money. To be batboy for the Toronto Maple Leafs, that was a position to be cherished."

Labour of love or not, the batboys hung around the clubhouse after the last home game of the season. "You always made yourself available when the players were leaving. They'd always throw you a dollar, three dollars, five dollars. Tim Thompson was always good for five dollars."

The players voted to give Bukowski a share of their winnings after they captured the IL championship in 1960. "I elected to take a ring instead. In those days, it was probably worth $150 or $200, which was a lot of money then. It's an excellent ring and I still wear it today. It's my pride and joy."

The Leafs occasionally played exhibition games against teams from the semipro Ontario Senior Intercounty Baseball League. John Bukowski and Tim Thompson's son, Timmy Junior, pitched in one such contest. "It was quite an experience. Tim and I were about fifteen and there we were, pitching against twenty-five-year-olds. I pitched the first three innings. And we won! Frank Mahovlich was our centre fielder."

It wasn't unusual for a member of the hockey Leafs to be on hand for a promotion at Maple Leaf Stadium, or even to participate in an exhibition game. "Mahovlich or Dave Keon would show up in the dressing room. The hockey players took batting practice on occasion. Smitty was probably the catalyst for a lot of that, but I'm sure that Jack Kent Cooke and Conn Smythe talked, too."

Some members of the intercounty teams were hockey players. "They were keeping in shape for the summer. Some of those guys were idols, and I got to pitch to them. How many people had the opportunity to be where I was at that time?"

As a developing amateur pitcher, John Bukowski was in an ideal position. Not only did he get to work on his game by throwing batting practice to professional hitters, he was also the beneficiary of some willing tutors on the Leafs pitching staff.

Different pitchers showed him different things. "Eddie Blake taught me how to throw a curveball, even just how to hold the ball continuously so you become familiar with it. Ron Negray taught me composition — stance on the mound, rotating the hips, release point. Pat Scantlebury taught me how to hide the ball, throw from inside my body."

Bukowski was a willing pupil. Before long he was developed beyond his years and attracting the attention of big-league scouts. "In my last year as batboy Chuck Tanner offered to become my agent. The deal was this: he'd pay for what it would cost me to travel to major league tryouts, and he'd get half my signing bonus." Chuck Tanner went on to manage in the majors for nineteen years. His Pittsburgh Pirates won the World Series in 1979.

The fledgling Houston Colt .45s eventually signed John Bukowski. He was later dealt to another new club, the New York Mets, but he never made it to the majors. He pitched in the minors for four years. Long after he hung up his cleats, he pitched batting practice for yet another set of new kids on the block: the Toronto Blue Jays.

Bill Park, Batboy

Bill Park was the batboy for the Toronto Maple Leafs in 1964 and 1965. "My becoming a batboy was a combination of happenstance, pure luck, and a three-game sweep," Park said.

Park explained the happenstance: "We heard an announcement at our house on the radio. The Toronto Maple Leafs would be holding tryouts to select a batboy for the 1964 season."

Some forty wannabe batboys showed up at Maple Leaf Stadium one Saturday morning. "Bill Smith, who was the trainer of the team, and Billy Carnegie, who had been the batboy in previous years, ran us through some tryouts. After that stage, we were whittled down to a group of four. We were told that we would have to audition at a game to see who ultimately would be selected."

Park's "pure luck" kicked in at the tryout. "I got to the clubhouse so early that there was nobody else there, except for 'Smitty' and Billy. So I automatically, by default, became the Leafs' batboy for that game. The second fellow who showed up became the batboy for the visiting team."

Carnegie was a big help. "Billy showed me the ropes and how I should manage the on-deck circle, how I should deliver baseballs to the home plate umpire. The other fellow had no such coaching, so I looked pretty good. I had no idea what I was doing, but I looked good by comparison."

The Leafs won the game that served as Park's audition. "Smitty told me to come back the second night. He was very superstitious that way. The team won that game, too. Smitty then told me that I should come back for a third game of the series. I believe it was against Syracuse. That resulted in a win as well. Smitty came to my locker after the game and said, 'Billy, you're with the team. You're gonna be paid ten dollars a game.'" Park was elated. "I would have done the job for free."

By 1964, Maple Leaf Stadium was in rough shape. "It was literally falling apart," recalled Park. "You had to be careful when you made your way into the stadium to make sure that you weren't hit by a chunk of concrete. It happened a few times, that concrete fell from the ceiling. Nobody was hit, but nobody told anybody because the city would have shut the place down."

Park's two years with the club turned out to be quite different from one another. "There was a contrast between the managers of the two teams. There was a contrast between the players on those two teams. And there was a contrast between the results that those two teams had."

Even the batboy's role was different. "On the '64 team I was largely a spectator. I managed the on-deck circle. I delivered baseballs to the umpire. I collected the bats, as you'd expect."

Park's job description grew in '65. "I was invited to be more of a participant. Particularly pregame. I was able to take part in batting practice, with the pitchers. I was able to take part in fielding practice with the infielders who were not starting that particular game."

He warmed up pitchers in the bullpen a couple of times as well. This was a frightening — and potentially dangerous — task. "I was scared [bleepless]. Billy Rohr could throw hard. He's one fellow who comes to mind." Rohr, a southpaw, was barely older than Park.

Smitty was Park's boss. "He wore a few hats. He was team trainer. He was clubhouse manager. He was travelling secretary. And, perhaps most important, he was Father Confessor to a lot of the players."

In 1964, the Leafs were affiliated with both the Washington Senators and the Milwaukee Braves. "The Braves had their best players playing in

Denver, and the leftovers came to Toronto. The Senators were a woeful team, and nobody on the Leafs was going up to Washington to make a difference either." Park added, "The players played for themselves, and there was a general ennui in the clubhouse and on the field."

The manager of the Leafs was none other than Sparky Anderson, who was making his managerial debut after an eleven-year playing career that included one full season with the Philadelphia Phillies.

Bill Park remembered meeting Sparky for the first time. "On that first night, he came up to me, shook my hand. He said, 'Call me Sparky,' and, 'We're gonna have a great year!'"

Anderson had two distinct personas, depending on whether or not the game was ongoing. "Sparky was Dr. Jekyll in the clubhouse. On the field, he could be volcanic. He showed that on more than one occasion," said Park.

"Sparky also had a thing about pitchers," Park added. "He didn't trust them. If a leadoff hitter got a walk and another batter got a base hit, he would get someone warming up in the bullpen. And so the legend of 'Captain Hook' began."

Many of the Leafs were older than Anderson. Two such players had nicknames that stood out in Bill Park's mind. "J.W. Porter had freckles of various shapes and sizes all over. His nickname was 'Trout.' Marshall Bridges, not surprisingly, was called 'Sherriff.'"

Just two years earlier, Bridges had saved eighteen games for the New York Yankees on route to their World Series victory over the San Francisco Giants. "Sheriff" was an African American southpaw from Jackson, Mississippi. Bridges sported a scar on his left leg that was allegedly the remnants of a bullet wound. "I never had the nerve to ask him how he got it," admitted Park.

The Leafs got stuck in a racially charged throng in Rochester in 1964 while on their way to a game. "We came across a crowd of people who thought that we were there to see where rioting had taken place in the last few days. The bus stopped, and some people started to rock the bus. Billy Williams and Marshall Bridges got off the bus and convinced the people that we were the Toronto Maple Leafs on our way to a ballgame. They opened up the hold of the bus to show them our equipment. Eventually, we were allowed to pass."

Williams was a journeyman Black outfielder whose lone major league stint was at the tail end of his eighteen-year playing career, with the Seattle Pilots in 1969. He is not to be confused with the Billy Williams who played mostly with the Chicago Cubs and is enshrined at Cooperstown.

Several members of the 1964 Leafs stood out in Bill Park's mind. "Ron Piche, from Verdun, Quebec, was the best pitcher on the '64 team. Jim McKnight was always in a sour mood, despite the fact that he hit twenty-four home runs that year. Bob Sadowski had played the year before for the Angels. He was bitter about being sent down. He made a point of putting his Angels bag on the top of his locker so that everyone could see it."

Ken Retzer was a catcher on the team. "He had been sent down from the Senators after a four-year big-league career. Lucky for me, Ken befriended me a little bit. As a catcher, he was quite willing to share with me how he'd call a game and why he'd call a game the way he did."

Retzer was generous, kind, and not naive about his place in baseball. "He gave me a pair of cleats and some bats. I'd say that he was more resigned than bitter about being sent down to the Leafs. On one occasion, he said, 'If you can't stick with the Washington Senators, you should probably consider another line of work.'"

Bobby Del Greco was the team prankster. "If you found liniment in your underwear or Vaseline in your socks, it was probably Bobby. It was his year-long mission to persuade one of the members of the team, who was particularly well endowed, to parade around the clubhouse wearing nothing except a hot dog bun. And he was successful!"

Toronto's '64 season ended on a low note. "They went into Syracuse for a final three-game series, needing to win one game to make the playoffs. They were swept."

In 1965, the Leafs became a farm team of the Boston Red Sox. They had a new skipper, too, a fourteen-year big-league veteran who was cutting his teeth as a manager. Like Sparky Anderson, he ended up in Cooperstown.

His name was Dick Williams. His first meeting with Bill Park went something like this: "He shook my hand and said, 'Hi, I'm Dick. We're gonna [bleeping] win!'"

Park remembered Williams as the opposite of Anderson. "He was Dr. Jekyll on the field. He was collaborative. He would consult with players. In the clubhouse, he was Mr. Hyde. He had no problem singling out players and lobbing verbal abuse at them in front of their teammates. Dick Williams was a hard man to like, and I'm being generous."

Catcher Mike Ryan took over from Ken Retzer as Bill Park's pal in 1965. "He shared his perspectives of calling a game with me. Mike was a very big football fan as well. On one occasion, he brought a football to batting practice. He and Mike Andrews and I were throwing it around in the outfield. That was, until we heard Dick Williams bellow from the top step of the dugout, 'You three! Get the [bleep] in here.' We went into the office, where Dick berated us by saying, 'What is the [bleeping] matter with you guys? This is a [bleeping] baseball team! Not a [bleeping] football team! Someone could have been [bleeping] hurt.'"

Park was not able to escape Williams's wrath. "Ryan and Andrews were fined fifty dollars each. I was fined ten. Sure enough, when I picked up my next paycheque, ten dollars had been deducted. Thanks, Dick."

Like their counterparts from the previous campaign, the '65 Leafs included a couple of interesting nicknames. "Joe Foy was nicknamed 'Baby,'" said Park. Grabbing some flab around his own belly, Park explained, "He had a roll here that he dispensed with before he went up to Boston the next year." Billy Harrell, who turned thirty-seven in mid-July of that season, was "Grandpa."

The Leafs were a different club in 1965. They finished third, made the playoffs, and went on to win the Governors' Cup Championship. "It was a phenomenal experience," recalled Park.

The '65 Leafs had several players who were on their way up. Six had signed contracts that included significant bonuses.

The arrangement of lockers inside the Toronto clubhouse suggested that the players were most comfortable if they were separated into three groups: Black, white non-southern, and white southern. Bill Park's locker was pinned between Joe Foy, an African American from New York City, and Russ Gibson, a white from Massachusetts. Farthest away from the Black players were the southerners. "I asked Smitty why the clubhouse was set up this way," said Bill Park. "He said that it was because the players wanted it that way. I didn't know how to respond."

Perhaps not surprisingly, Park was exposed to chewing tobacco while he was batboy.

"A number of the players used it. It came in leaf form, plug form, and powder. I tried it once. It was okay for about five minutes. Then, after it started to work, I was in some distress. I then proceeded to barf up my breakfast, lunch, and supper. And I had not had supper yet!"

"Greenies" were close at hand, too. "After batting practice, and before the players went back on the field, a paper cup would appear in the clubhouse, and players would help themselves to greenies. These were amphetamines. The players believed that these would provide them with heightened awareness, stamina, and aggression."

Bill Park travelled with the Leafs, which enabled him to see a lot of the eastern half of the United States from the inside of a bus. Among the stadiums where the Leafs played on the road, the first pair that came to mind were War Memorial Stadium in Buffalo and Ponce de Leon Park in Atlanta.

Nicknamed "The Rockpile," War Memorial Stadium was used in the filming of the 1984 movie *The Natural*. Two decades earlier, it was in rough shape when Bill Park and the Leafs rolled into town. "It would have needed a coat of paint and a thorough clean before it could even be condemned," recalled Park. The Rockpile had been home of the Bisons since 1961, but its history as a football venue went back to 1937.

Ponce de Leon Park was a pro baseball venue for almost sixty years. It closed in 1965. The stadium had a feature that locals referred to as "The Fourth Outfielder." "That was a huge magnolia tree beyond the centre field fence. The locals called it the fourth outfielder. Sure, it had limited range, but it did catch the occasional fly ball."

Atlanta was the site of a disturbing experience for Bill Park. "After a game, I was walking along a main street, and I saw a police officer at a corner. I noticed that he was carrying what looked like an aluminum broom handle with a disk at the end of it. I asked him what it was. He said, 'Y'all ain't from around here, are you, son?' I said, 'No, I'm not.' He said, 'Well, this here's a cattle prod. If any uppity [n-word] comes along, I'll move him.' I was very shaken. I went back to the hotel, and I was sick to my stomach."

Travel was by bus. "We called the bus 'the iron lung.' Journeys were measured in time, not miles. Every bus driver was called 'Bussy' by the players. 'Hey, Bussy, can we go any slower? Hey, Bussy, are we lost again?' The gin rummy games would never end. They started as soon as the bus fired up."

The parent Red Sox came to Toronto to play a midseason exhibition game against the Leafs in 1965. The Boston Red Sox featured Carl "Yaz" Yastrzemski, the Monster (early closer Dick Radatz), Rico Petrocelli, and Tony Conigliaro. "The best part of the game for me was batting practice. The sound of the Red Sox taking batting practice was amazing. It was an explosion when the ball came off their bats. It was only batting practice, but it was impressive."

Dick Radatz threw hard. "During the course of the game, the Monster faced Joe Foy. Foy struck out looking. When he passed me in the on-deck circle, he said, 'Man, that last one sounded high.'"

The '65 Leafs defeated Columbus in the best-of-seven International League finals four games to one. "After winning the Governors' Cup, before he passed out cigars, Dick Williams said, 'This is why we play the [bleeping] game.' There was a team meeting the next day, at two o'clock. It was a 'players only' meeting. When the doors finally opened, I learned that the players had voted me a half share of playoff money. Fifty dollars. Big money, man! Big money."

Sparky Anderson and Dick Williams went head to head twice in the World Series. Dick's 1972 Oakland A's beat Sparky's Cincinnati Reds. In 1984, Sparky's Detroit Tigers defeated Dick's San Diego Padres.

Williams won two World Series in his managerial career. Anderson won three.

Bob Hunter, the Boss's Kid

Bob Hunter was a huge Leafs fan when he was growing up. "I was at the ballpark every Sunday afternoon from, oh, 1956, until it closed in 1967," Hunter said.

Going to games at Maple Leaf Stadium was a family outing for Hunter, who went with his sister and his parents. His dad, Robert, had once interviewed for the club's position of travelling secretary.

The interview was held in the early 1930s. Hunter made such a good impression that he was encouraged to … do something else. This advice came from businessman Percy Gardiner, then president of the Leafs. Gardiner told Robert Hunter that there was no future in baseball. Instead, Gardiner offered Robert Hunter a job with his Bay Street firm. Hunter ended up working there for fifty-five years as a stockbroker.

Hunter fondly recalled the route from the main stadium entrance to his family's seats on the third base side of the plate. "When you walked through the main gates, there was a large concession stand. It was about 180 feet long."

Above the concession stand was a high mural of all the Leafs greats from over the years. "When you went past that, you walked up the ramps and saw the field. The grass was so green. The billboards were freshly painted. For a child, it was amazing. It was like a major league ballpark. It must have been the best minor league facility at the time." The junior Hunter was hooked. "I fell in love with baseball. I fell in love with Maple Leaf Stadium."

The ballpark was not yet showing its age. "At that time, it was only thirty years old."

Bob Hunter remembers International League games in Buffalo, too. "Offermann Stadium was less than 300 feet down the right field line. There was a street beyond the right field fence, and there were houses beyond that road. The people who lived in those houses would take their windows out. Buffalo always had big left-handed hitters, like Luke Easter, Ed Kranepool, and Duke Carmel, because of that short right field fence."

Jack Kent Cooke owned the Maple Leafs at the time. "He made sure that there was always something going on," recalled Hunter. "They would give out roses on Mother's Day. Father's Day was always Bat Day. The first 3,000 children who went to the game with their dad would get a baseball bat. The first bat that I ever got was a 1957 Rocky Nelson bat. Sponsored by 7-Up."

Nelson, a three-time International League Triple Crown winner, was just one of the players who benefitted from Cooke's generosity. "When Mr. Cooke owned the team and they were getting massive crowds, the players were making more in AAA than they would have in the big leagues. In the season when he hit forty-three home runs, Rocky Nelson made about $12,000. When he joined Pittsburgh, his salary dropped to something like $7,500."

Steve Ridzik, a Leaf pitcher in 1950, and again from 1960 to 1963, was a cousin of Bob's mother. "He was my favourite Maple Leaf baseball player."

Ridzik threw four of the club's amazing thirty-two shutouts in 1960. He had a 44–37 record in 118 games with Toronto between 1960 and 1963.

Midway through the 1963 campaign, Ridzik was thirty-four years old. He had not pitched in the majors since 1958, but that was soon to change. "Washington had such a young staff," explained Hunter. "The Leafs were playing the Richmond Virginians. Steve hit two batters in a row. He was the sort of competitor that Washington needed. Steve joined the Senators and ended up playing for them until the end of the 1965 season."

The Hunter family's relationship with the club changed dramatically in 1964. "My father purchased the team. I was fourteen at the time."

Robert Hunter had barely settled in as team president when disaster struck on February 28. "There was a fire in the main office, which was under the grandstand down the left field line," recalled Bob. "It was so hot, it melted the trophies. They thought that it was an electrical fire. They lost a lot of the team's history. It was heartbreaking."

Not all of the contents of the main office were destroyed. "There was a big safe that had contracts and club records going back to the 1880s. The contents of the safe were saved and sold at auction after the 1967 season, along with the other contents of the stadium."

Despite his youth — or maybe because of it — Bob Hunter made an impact on the Leafs in the spring of '64. "Frank Pollock was the general manager when my father bought the club. He was an outstanding minor league general manager. He told my dad that he had the opportunity to purchase second baseman Bob Sadowski from the Los Angeles Angels."

At the time, there were four players with that surname who had played big-league ball and were still active as pros. Pollock wanted to make sure that he was pursuing the right Sadowski. "My father ran out to find me. I was doing something at the ballpark. This was in March. My dad asked me about Bob Sadowski. I said that he was a left-handed hitting second baseman, that he hit the ball well, and he was a great defensive second baseman. My father then went back to Mr. Pollock and said, 'Yes, let's purchase him.'"

Bob Hunter's involvement in the transaction made the news. "The *Globe* ran a story about how I was involved in getting Bob. They took a photo of us together."

The story was titled "Club President Credits Son, 12, with Tip to Purchase Sadowski." Gord Walker wrote, "When Robert L. Hunter undertook the job of saving professional baseball for Toronto, he didn't realize he had his own built-in talent scout in the family. He does now."

The junior Hunter was a voracious consumer of baseball information. "I read the backs of all my baseball cards. I read baseball magazines until I knew as much about some of the players as the scouts did!"

In addition to his one-off role as assistant GM, Bob had a regular job at the ballpark. "I ran the scoreboard from the press box. The scoreboard had balls, strikes, and outs. If the umpire called 'strike!' I would press the strike button, and it would light up on the scoreboard. I did that from 1964 until Labour Day of 1967."

Playing hooky from school on Opening Day was commonplace for Bob when he was growing up. "My mom's scrapbook has a letter from the principal of Richview Collegiate saying that it was improper to take your children to Maple Leaf Stadium on Opening Day." The principal went so far as to phone Robert Hunter at his office and plead his case. Bob's dad chided the principal for calling him at work over such a matter and hung up on him.

Bob Hunter recalls one particularly odious problem that confronted some of the Toronto players. "At that time, in Toronto, it was very difficult for Black people to rent an apartment. Reggie Smith, who was twenty-one at the time, came north with the Leafs in '66. He couldn't get a room. He and his wife ended up living at my house for a while."

Dick Williams took over from Sparky Anderson as Toronto's manager in 1965. Williams was a feisty guy who actually brawled with one of his players at the stadium late in the 1966 season. The fight pitted Williams against Mickey Sinks, a relief pitcher. "I was in the clubhouse when that happened," recalled Bob. "Mickey was a schoolteacher in the off-season, in Michigan. He would leave the team after Labour Day because he had to go back to school. Mickey went into Dick's office after the other players had left. He asked if he had a chance at making the Red Sox the next year."

Williams replied with an emphatic "no." Sinks then left the clubhouse. "They got into a fistfight, and Mickey kicked Dick's ass. Then Mickey quit. He was a good pitcher, too. Big, tall guy, about 6'4". A sinker-slider relief pitcher. And the Red Sox needed pitching desperately."

The next day, Dick had a meeting with the players. There, he admitted that Mickey had hit him so hard that he pooped his pants.

Even at spring training, Dick Williams had more resources to work with than Sparky Anderson did as his predecessor. "When the Leafs went to training camp at Conrad Field in Deland, Florida, he had three of Boston's best instructors. When Sparky had the team, he was almost all by himself. When you're running a camp, and you have fifty-five players, you need some help."

Not even Ted Williams — "Teddy Ballgame himself" — was going to change Dick's mind about one practice activity that was used in Deland. "Dick got the pitchers to improve their reflexes by playing volleyball during spring training. Ted Williams said that wasn't baseball. Dick replied, 'This is my team. I'm running it.'"

The prospects on Dick Williams's Leafs teams included some "bonus babies" — players who had been given large signing bonuses when leaving the amateur ranks. Bob Hunter remembers one such player who had the other Leafs scratching their heads. "This guy didn't want to come down to Toronto. When he did, he brought no luggage and no clothing. Just six baseball bats. When he took batting practice, he would not allow anybody to be on the infield because he thought he would kill them."

The player in question certainly set the bar high for himself. "If he went two-for-four in a game he would break down and cry because he thought he was that great a hitter."

Another bonus baby was gun-shy. "They put him at first base and tried Reggie Smith at shortstop. Reggie threw the ball so hard that this player wouldn't even try to catch the ball. He would let it go by him."

Robert Hunter was devastated when the Leafs picked up stakes and moved to Louisville after the 1967 season. "My father took the move as if he'd lost World War III. He worked to pay every debt that the team had. He did his best. He had only purchased the team for one reason: to keep it in Toronto."

PART VI

THE HOMEBREWS

Homebrew *noun* member of a team that is based in their hometown.

Dick Fowler and the First "No-No"

Toronto native and local sandlot product Dick Fowler made his International League debut at Maple Leaf Stadium as a nineteen-year-old. Five years later, Fowler became the first Canadian to throw a no-hitter in the major leagues.

Fowler was called up to the Leafs from Oneonta of the Can-Am League late in the 1940 season. He earned the promotion after sporting a 16–10 record for Oneonta. Unlike many young minor league hurlers of the time, the 6'4" righty had good control. He averaged just 2.8 walks per nine innings.

His first game as a Maple Leaf took place on September 4, in the second game of a doubleheader. The setting was Maple Leaf Stadium. Toronto won the first game 3–1 in a seven-inning contest. The losing pitcher for the visiting Buffalo Bisons was Earl Cook, then a thirty-one-year-old career minor-leaguer who had spent five seasons with the Leafs. Cook went five innings for Buffalo and gave up all three of Toronto's runs.

Cook was chosen to start on the mound in the second game, too. The Leafs hit him often and hard; Toronto scored three runs in each of the second and third innings. Cook was lifted in favour of a reliever with two out in the third frame. At the end of the inning, Toronto led 6–0.

Dick Fowler was pinch-hit for in the seventh inning. He surrendered ten hits in seven innings, but he got outs when he needed to. Fowler was touched for just two runs. Toronto won the game 9–3. The Leafs defence turned three double plays in the game. Dick Fowler had won his AA debut, and at home as well. Earl Cook walked away with a pair of losses.

Fowler was a good pitcher on a poor Leafs team in 1941. He had a record of 10–10 with a 3.30 ERA on a team that won forty-seven and lost 107.

Early that season, Fowler almost pitched a no-hitter for the Leafs. Toronto was playing the Orioles in Baltimore. Fowler had a no-no going through eight innings. He gave up a pair of hits in the ninth and settled for a two-hit 3–0 victory.

On May 1, Fowler became the second Canadian in three years to earn the role of starting pitcher at a Toronto home opener. The Leafs were ahead 5–4 after eight innings. The visiting Baltimore Orioles tied it in the ninth. Fowler trudged back to the mound in the tenth, but it was clear that he was out of gas. The Orioles banged out four hits in the tenth (two for extra bases) and scored three runs. Baltimore won 8–5.

Toronto's poster boy for failure in 1941 was Carl Fischer, a thirty-five-year-old southpaw. Fischer had a "perfect" 0–17 record for the Leafs and a 5.62 ERA in 125 innings. This was not a typical season for Fischer. Just the previous year, he was 10–12 with a 2.53 ERA. He went on to pitch in the pros for twenty-three years, winning forty-six games in the majors and 210 in all.

Dick Fowler was promoted to the Philadelphia Athletics, Toronto's parent club, in August of '41. He spent 1943 with the A's, then did a stint in the Canadian Armed Forces that kept him away from major league pitching mounds until 1945.

Late in the '45 campaign, Fowler was discharged and rejoined the A's. After a couple of relief appearances, he made his first start on September 9. That was in the second game of a doubleheader at Shibe Park in Philadelphia. Fowler's opponents were the St. Louis Browns.

The first game of the doubleheader was a 6–2 win for the A's. Pete Gray, an outfielder for the Browns, pinch-hit in the ninth inning. Gray had only one arm, his left. He had lost his right arm as the result of a childhood accident. He played pro ball for seven years and had a career .308 batting average in the minors.

Early in the second game of the twin bill, it was obvious that Dick Fowler had command of all his pitches. Midway through the game, members of the crowd of 16,755 cheered whenever a Browns batter was retired.

Fowler was throwing a no-hitter.

John "Ox" Miller, the Browns pitcher, was pitching almost as well. The game was scoreless at the end of the eighth. By now, the fans were cheering every Fowler pitch.

In the top of the ninth, the Browns had a runner on first and one out. Lou Finney, a former Athletics player, hit a loud foul ball to right field. On the next pitch, Finney grounded into a second-to-short-to-first double play.

In the bottom of the ninth, Hal Peck tripled for the A's. Irv Hall singled him home. Game over! No-hitter!

Fowler's accomplishment was celebrated in the sports pages of newspapers all over North America, from British Columbia to California to Florida to Quebec. "War Veteran Hurls No-Hitter for A's," read the headline of the sports section of the *Star-Tribune* of Casper, Wyoming.[47]

The Browns hit only five balls to the outfield in the game. Fowler logged six strikeouts and walked four. "I felt I was going to pitch a no-hitter," Fowler said to the United Press. "But I was worried when Lou Finney hit a long fly ball down the right field line in the ninth."[48]

"It was a wonderful feeling when we got that one run," Fowler told the Lancaster *New Era*.[49]

Fowler's no-hitter was the first in the majors since June 22, 1944. It was the first in the AL since April 16, 1940. It was the first at Shibe Park since September 7, 1923.

Buddy Rosar, the A's catcher, told Stan Baumgartner of the Philadelphia *Inquirer* that Fowler's fastball, curve, and changeup were all working for him. The fastball had some extra movement on it. "Mixed with this was a combination half fork [*sic*] and slider. I wouldn't have got a good foul if I had been batting against him."[50]

Fowler even outhit the Browns in the no-hitter. He hit a double in three at-bats.

The no-hitter also served as a bit of revenge for Fowler. "I'm certainly glad that this game came against the Browns," he explained to UP. "They beat me 1–0 in a sixteen-inning game here in 1942."[51]

Connie Mack, nearing the end of his forty-fifth season as A's manager, had this to say about Fowler's performance: "I did not have much chance to congratulate him today but I'll have a lot of nice words for him tomorrow."[52]

Ox Miller, the losing pitcher, allowed just five A's hits and went the distance for the first time in his big-league career. Miller spent parts of four seasons in the majors.

Despite the doubleheader sweep, the A's propped up the AL standings in 1945. The Browns finished third.

St. Louis finished seventh in the AL with a .249 team batting average. Still, they were no pushovers. Vern Stephens, their shortstop, led the American League in home runs in 1945.

Fowler said that his biggest regret regarding the no-hitter was that his wife and two-year-old son were not there to see it.

Alex Hardy: "Dooney"

Alex Hardy was a much better pitcher than the twenty-first century gives him credit for.

"Dooney," as Hardy was known, did not have to venture "over the Don" to go to work. He lived east of the river, less than a ten-minute walk from Sunlight Park.

Opening Day 1897 was on a Friday afternoon. Toronto was playing their first-ever game in the Canadian League against Hamilton. Dooney was Toronto's starting pitcher, making his professional debut. Dooney's entry in the 1897 Toronto city directory listed his job as "ball player." This was his chance to prove it.

For a while, it looked like the game would be called off. A steady rain fell, starting at about three o'clock and lasting for an hour. The precipitation finally stopped, and it was time to play ball.

The game started really well for the twenty-year-old southpaw. It was scoreless through five innings. Hamilton opened the scoring with a single tally in the sixth. They scored again in the seventh and twice in the eighth. All the while, Hamilton's hurler kept the home team at bay.

Alex Hardy.

Hardy was the only Toronto player to have any success at the plate. Dooney had Toronto's only two hits and scored their only run. The home team lost 4–1. Hardy allowed seven Hamilton hits.

That Opening Day defeat turned out to be one of his best performances of the Canadian League campaign. He was regularly hit hard. He was exceptionally wild, sometimes. In another game against Hamilton, he issued nine free passes. The Hams must have seen something in Dooney, though, because they acquired his services shortly after his wild outing.

So much for that dream commute.

Dooney did poorly in Hamilton, too. In a game against London on Dominion Day, Hardy gave up sixteen hits and thirteen runs.

When the sun rose on the 1898 Canadian League campaign, Alex Hardy was nowhere to be seen. But the following season, he was back. He split 1899 between the Canadian League and the Eastern League. He was much improved as a pitcher. His walks plus hits per inning pitched (WHIP) fell by more than two-thirds of a run.

Dooney pitched in Quebec in 1900. In mid-June, he pitched a two-hitter for a semipro team in front of a reported 3,500 fans. On August 1,

Hardy made his debut for Montreal's Eastern League club. He started on the mound against Springfield and surrendered six runs in seven innings. Hardy emerged with a no-decision as Montreal lost 9–8 in thirteen innings.

Back in Ontario in 1901, Hardy pitched for a team in Waterloo. His career win–loss record as a pro was only 7–14, spread over three seasons. Yes, he had pitched in the Eastern League, the game's top minor loop at the time. But he had pitched poorly at that level.

Perhaps competing at a lower level of pro ball would give Hardy a chance to work on his game and contribute to his team's success. Ultimately, that is what he did. Dooney joined Binghamton of the New York State League (NYSL) in 1902.

After a few mediocre games with Binghamton, Dooney was dealt to Troy, another NYSL club. The move proved to be just what the doctor ordered. Hardy won three straight starts for Troy, including a five-inning, one-hit shutout against Binghamton.

The streak earned Dooney a June call-up to Toronto, where he whitewashed Newark 13–0 at Diamond Park on Fraser Avenue (near today's Lamport Stadium, in the western part of Liberty Village). Hardy had four hits in the game, one more than the entire Newark squad. Dooney then returned to Troy, where he finished the NYSL season. He sported a combined 14–8 win–loss record in Binghamton, Troy, and Toronto.

Hardy was then called up by the Chicago Cubs and made his big-league debut in Brooklyn, on Thursday, September 4. His Brooklyn counterpart, Wild Bill Donovan, had won twenty-five games in 1901. Donovan was thirteen days younger than Hardy.

Dooney could not have dreamed of a debut this good. He held Brooklyn to two hits and shut them out 1–0. Chicago's lone run came in the fourth inning.

Five days after his magnificent debut, Hardy fell to earth with a thud. Pitching in Boston against the Beaneaters (forerunners of the Braves), Dooney gave up four runs in the home half of the first inning. Boston hung on to win, 7–6.

Never a pushover at the plate, Hardy helped the Cubs' cause by hitting a double against Boston. It was his first major league hit.

Dooney's third start was against Cincinnati, in the second game of a doubleheader on September 14. Once again, he was hit early. The Reds led 5–0 after three innings and went on to win 8–6.

Playing behind Hardy in this game was a Chicago double play combination that was immortalized in one of the game's best-known poems. The players in question were shortstop Joe Tinker, second baseman Johnny Evers, and first baseman Frank Chance.

The poem is titled "Baseball's Sad Lexicon" or simply "Tinker to Evers to Chance" and was written by Franklin Pierce Adams from the perspective of a New York Giants fan whose favourites have just been burned by the Cubs infielders. Ironically, Adams was a Cubs fan. He wrote it for his employer, a New York newspaper. The Cubs and the Giants were fierce rivals at the time. Tinker, Evers, and Chance broke the hearts of New York Giants fans on many occasions. Here's the poem:

> These are the saddest of possible words:
> "Tinker to Evers to Chance."
> Trio of bear cubs, and fleeter than birds,
> Tinker and Evers and Chance.
> Ruthlessly pricking our gonfalon* bubble,
> Making a Giant hit into a double** —
> Words that are heavy with nothing but trouble:
> "Tinker to Evers to Chance."

In the game against the Reds, Dooney coaxed a Cincinnati batter to hit into a "Tinker to Evers to Chance" double play (TECDP, for lack of a better acronym).

But this was not just any old TECDP. This was the *first* TECDP. The first ever.

Hardy made his final start of the season on October 5 against St. Louis. The Cubs won 11–4, and Dooney went the distance for the fourth straight time. The victory evened his record at 2–2. His win–loss record at all levels for the 1902 season was 16–10.

---

* a banner or pennant

** i.e., a double play

The 1903 season started off where 1902 had ended, with Dooney in the Chicago Cubs' starting rotation. But things went sour in a hurry for Hardy, and by mid-May he was pitching for Toronto in the Eastern League. He never made it back to the big leagues.

Dooney split '03 between Toronto and Buffalo, then played for Atlanta of the Southern Association in 1904. There, he became known as "Hard Luck Hardy." He was better than his 9–14 win–loss record indicated.

Hardy returned to Troy of the NYSL in 1905.

There, that season, he almost died.

On June 30, while walking around Troy, Dooney was shot in the back. The bullet lodged in his left lung, just inches from his heart.

News of the shooting was widely reported. Some newspapers wrote that Dooney's life hung in the balance.

Hardy had been shot by a man from Danbury, Connecticut, named Charles Thero. According to Thero, Dooney had been "paying attention" to his wife, a Troy resident. Hardy denied Thero's accusation.

Dooney recovered. Thero was charged with assault, first degree. Hardy was back on the mound for Troy in the second half of August. He finished the season at Troy and returned to that city for two more seasons.

Those two years proved to be the most productive of Hardy's pro career. However, as of this writing, Dooney's records for 1906 and 1907 are missing from the main digitized baseball stats archives on the Internet. This is true of NYSL records in general.

Alex Hardy played professional baseball for parts of ten seasons during a thirteen-year period between 1897 and 1909 inclusive. According to one digitized stats archive (www.baseball-reference.com), his career win–loss record is 31–48. Not included in those totals are his NYSL records.

It is possible to build NYSL stats from contemporary box scores in newspapers. While there is no guarantee that the resulting stats are complete, they might at least provide some insight into the effectiveness of a given player. And so, without any further ado, here are some missing wins and losses belonging to Alex "Dooney" Hardy:

YEAR	LEAGUE	TEAM	WINS	LOSSES
1900	Eastern	Montreal	0	0
1902	NYSL	Binghamton	1	1
1902	NYSL	Troy	12	7
1902	Eastern	Toronto	1	0
1905	NYSL	Troy	6	6
1906	NYSL	Troy	16	19
1907	NYSL	Troy	22	13
1909	NYSL	Scranton	8	10
1909	NYSL	Binghamton	3	3
Totals			69	59

If you add the above sixty-nine wins and fifty-nine defeats to Hardy's 31–48 record on www.baseball-reference.com, his career record improves to 100–107.

While such numbers might not be enough to get Dooney into the Canadian Baseball Hall of Fame, they do provide a fuller picture of his contributions to the teams that he played for over a century ago.

In any case, those 1907 numbers stand out. That year, Hardy pitched more than 300 innings. He threw five shutouts and completed thirty of his thirty-four starts.

One would be hard pressed to find other Toronto natives who had twenty-win seasons in the minors, Oscar Tuero, whose career is chronicled elsewhere in these pages, notwithstanding.

Dooney umpired for a while after he hung up his glove. He worked at the Gooderham and Worts distillery in Toronto for decades and died in 1940 at the age of sixty-three. Dooney was survived by his widow and eight children.

Will Jeffers: In a Fishbowl

William Wellington Jeffers was born in Georgetown, Ontario, in 1853. His father, Thomas, was a reverend. William lived most of his life at the same address on Robert Street, near the intersection of Spadina Avenue and Harbord Street, in Toronto.

On May 5, 1881, Jeffers made his debut as a National League umpire at a game played in Buffalo. The NL had a team in that city from 1879 to 1885 called the Bisons, just as they are today. James Francis "Pud" Galvin pitched the Bisons to an 8–1 win over the Detroit Wolverines in the first of a three-game series. Detroit had a National League team at the time.

Pud threw strikes. He did not walk a single Detroit batter. Over the course of his long career, he walked an average of about one batter every eight innings. Galvin usually threw a complete game. This was nineteenth-century baseball, after all. Pitchers were expected to go the distance. In 1881, Pud started fifty-three games for the Bisons; he completed forty-eight of them. In other words, he completed just over 90 percent of his starts that year. And that was nothing. In 1884, he finished all but one of his starts. His seventy-two starts.

The Buffalo *Morning Express* generally praised Jeffers for his performance in his first National League game. He was lauded for his calling of balls and strikes in particular. He got a positive review from the Detroit *Free Press*, too. Both publications found fault with a couple of perceived mistakes. These must have been inconsequential, since they were not described in any detail.

Galvin pitched against Detroit again the next day. It was a quiet afternoon for Jeffers. The Bisons staged a dramatic come-from-behind victory. Down 2–0 after eight frames, Buffalo scored three runs in the ninth and won 3–2.

Jeffers officiated on his own; that was the way umpires were deployed in those days, the one-umpire system. Players fully exploited this. For example, they cheated by rounding a base early, thus shortening the distance from first to third or second to home. This happened when a player thought that the umpire was looking elsewhere. Such antics triggered plenty of "kicking" (fussing, complaining) by the defensive team. And justifiably so.

A missed call — or perceived missed call — of any sort would result in the umpire enduring all sorts of abuse. This would be worse if the call favoured the visiting team. Spectators would hurl invectives and pop bottles. Sometimes, an umpire stayed in the dressing room after a game until the fans were gone. A policeman might have to accompany an umpire to his lodgings or to the local train station.

Assaults on umpires were commonplace. Umps were punched in the face. They were stabbed. They were beaten with bats. Eddie Burke, a Toronto outfielder for a couple of years, tried his hand at umpiring at the end of his playing career. The job was sufficiently dangerous for him to carry a gun and a knife when he was working. He was once forced to brandish both after awarding a forfeit victory to the home team during a game in Helena, Montana. He was charged with carrying concealed weapons.

Umpires worked alone, travelled alone, and when forced to fight, fought alone. Such was the life of an umpire in 1881. That life became apparent for William Jeffers on May 7. It was his third game in three days, the finale of the three-game series between Buffalo and Detroit. Detroit had lost the first two games and wanted to avoid a sweep.

The Bisons warned Jeffers that one particular Detroit player might try to intentionally round a bag early and miss it entirely. They asked the umpire to watch the runner and make sure that he touched all the bases and didn't take any shortcuts. Sure enough, the Wolverine in question went home from second without touching third. Jeffers called him out.

The Buffalo *Morning Express* reported that, in response to Jeffers's call, the Wolverines "kicked and threshed around like a lot of mules attacked by hornets. They attempted to bulldoze the umpire, to leave the grounds, etc."[53]

The behaviour of Lew Brown, the Detroit first baseman, stood out the most. "Brown particularly made himself conspicuous by his filthy language and rowdyism. Leaping into the grandstand, proceeding up the steps and swearing as he went in his hot-headed search for [manager Frank] Bancroft."[54] The Detroit skipper ordered Brown back onto the field. "Bancroft told him never again to make such a demonstration while he played under him." It's not known why Bancroft was in the grandstand or why Brown was looking for him there.

Cooler heads prevailed for the rest of the game, but the situation bubbled over again at the hotel when Jeffers attempted to collect his pay. Several of the Detroit players — and their manager — hurled a barrage of abuse at the poor umpire. Brown offered to fight him at the hotel for $15. He outweighed Jeffers by some fifty pounds. Jeffers declined the offer. The angry Wolverines then adjourned to a couple of local gin mills, where they continued to be loud and obnoxious.

The first nine games that Jeffers umpired that season were in Buffalo. Pud Galvin pitched in six of those games, winning three and losing three. One of the victories was a four-hit shutout against Boston. Galvin was in his third full big-league season in 1881. He went on to pitch over 6,000 innings in his fifteen-year career. Galvin was inducted into the Hall of Fame at Cooperstown in 1965.

Buffalo turned a triple play against Providence in the first inning of a game that Jeffers umpired. His performance in another game between the same two clubs prompted the Buffalo *Commercial* newspaper to crow, "Over the river, Jeffers!"[55] That sounds like an invitation for Jeffers to return to Canada, hastily, perhaps in response to his officiating.

The request of the *Commercial* notwithstanding, Jeffers continued to receive kind words from the press. The *Inter Ocean*, a Chicago daily, had this to say about him after a game in late May between the White Stockings and the visiting Providence Grays: "The umpiring of Mr. Jeffers gave general satisfaction. He worked hard, and, though his voice in calling balls and strikes had a far-off tone, yet, in spite of his defective technique, he was unusually successful in deciding a large number of close decisions."[56]

Jeffers went home to Toronto on May 27 after working a game in Chicago between the White Stockings and Providence. The Chicago *Morning News* noted that he had umpired twelve games that season and described it as hard work, with his weight dropping from 150 pounds to 132.

It was a whirlwind visit. Jeffers returned to action on May 30, in Troy, New York. Troy had its own major league team at the time. The following day, he worked at the Polo Grounds. The New York Metropolitans, then competing in the minor league Eastern Championship Association, hosted an exhibition game against Chicago. This was the original Polo Grounds, the first of three Gotham ballparks to use that name.

In mid-June, Jeffers was working a game in Providence between the Grays and the White Stockings. Chicago had a big lead, and the situation became threatening in the later frames. "The crowd acted like a mob of rowdies, especially in the eighth and ninth innings," according to the Boston *Globe*. Mercifully, the situation did not boil over.[57]

Some 12,000 souls assembled in Chicago on Independence Day to watch a run-fest. Boston won 13–12. This would have been one of the biggest crowds that ever saw William Jeffers work. He acquitted himself well, according to the *Inter Ocean*: "Mr. Jeffers had a number of close decisions to make, and did not altogether satisfy the crowd, but his judgements were clearly and promptly given, and probably correct."[58]

William Jeffers umpired in the National League for just over two months. His final NL game was on July 7. Thereafter, he occasionally officiated at minor league games back home in Toronto. He worked various Canadian League games at the lacrosse grounds in 1885. This venue was at the northwest corner of Jarvis and Wellesley and was the home of pro baseball in Toronto prior to the opening of Sunlight Park.

Things got ugly for Jeffers at a Canadian League game between the Hamilton Clippers and London Cockneys in early September of '85. Early in the game, he fined Hamilton second baseman Charles "Chub" Collins $5 for "back talk." Collins, the Hamilton captain, had spent part of the summer with the Detroit Wolverines.

The game continued. Joe Knight, the London pitcher, received a steady stream of cheering from someone on his bench. The source of the verbal encouragement was James McKinley, a player for the Toronto team. He was inebriated. The stage was set. London was playing Hamilton. A Toronto player was on the London bench, cheering for the London pitcher. Oh, and the Toronto player was drunk.

Collins demanded that McKinley be removed from the London bench. "Clear the field, umpire," he bellowed. Jeffers responded, "Clear the grounds yourself. I'm no police force."[59] Collins then instructed the Clippers batter, seventeen-year-old Elton "Ice Box" Chamberlain, to refrain from entering the batter's box. "I'll give this man one minute to go to bat," yelled Jeffers. Chamberlain kept his distance. Joe Knight shouted at Jeffers, imploring him to "know what he should do."

Then it happened. "Some of McKinley's friends were walking off with him to the rear as Jeffers called, 'Batter's out,' meaning Chamberlain."[60] Jeffers told Collins that he had five minutes to resume play or the game would be forfeited to London. "A gang of young men, boys and betting men, jumped the fence and grand stand [*sic*] rail, and in an instant Jeffers was being terribly hustled in the middle of a roaring, excited crowd." Chub Collins and a plainclothes police officer protected Jeffers as he escaped the scene. Ice Box Chamberlain was confronted by a thug who accused him of throwing the game.

In 1889, Jeffers was chosen as one of three emergency umpires for International League games played in Toronto. In that capacity, he worked the second game of a Dominion Day doubleheader. Syracuse, the visitors, won by a score of 5–0. It was the first time that season in which Toronto was shut out. Jeffers did the game on his own.

The 1897 edition of the Canadian League featured a mid-July game between Guelph and Hamilton, two teams that had a reputation for "unruly" behaviour. The league assigned the game to Jeffers, confident that he was best at defusing trouble.

The game was played in Hamilton and was scoreless through five innings. Hamilton scored three runs in the sixth. Roberts, the Guelph catcher, started to "chirp" at Jeffers. This continued until the eighth frame. Jeffers had heard enough. Roberts was ejected but refused to leave the field. Jeffers had no choice but to award Hamilton a 9–0 forfeit victory. The *Globe* reported that "Roberts attempted to pick a quarrel with Jeffers after the game, but he was quickly surrounded by a group of small boys, who hooted him off the grounds and nearly all the way to his hotel."[61]

Jeffers, a long-time employee of the Ontario Ministry of Education, seems to have faded from pro ball after the game in Hamilton. He died of chronic myocarditis, a heart condition, in 1936. He was eighty-three. Jeffers is buried at Prospect Cemetery in Toronto.

Knotty Lee: Not Dead Yet

George "Knotty" Lee of Toronto played and managed in pro ball for parts of six decades. His long baseball odyssey did not include any time in the majors, but he had his share of adventures in a career that started in 1898 and ended in 1940.

One of Lee's biggest "ups" — maybe the biggest of all — was his pro debut. He was pitching for the amateur Toronto Athletic Club in the summer of 1898. Toronto's pro team was in the Class A Eastern League. That loop was later renamed the International League. Class A was the highest minor league designation at the time.

It was the second week of September. The pro team gave Lee a trial, a starting assignment at home, against Ottawa. Lee responded with what turned out to be the best outing of his career, a one-hit shutout. Toronto beat Ottawa 6–0. Knotty Lee logged one strikeout, issued four walks, and hit one batter. Ottawa's lone hit came in the second inning. The score was 1–0 going into the home half of the sixth frame. Toronto rallied for five runs in their half of the inning, and that was the end of the scoring. Lee faced the minimum possible number of batters from the fifth inning onward.

Pitching debuts don't get much better than that.

Lee played in the Class C New York State League (NYSL) in 1899 and 1900, pitching for four different clubs during that time. Two of those teams moved in the middle of the season. Thus Lee had six different homes during that period.

The 1900 season was one best forgotten by Lee. He was cut by Utica in June, and with good reason. His numbers were poor. Only two Utica players were released in midseason. One of those two was at the player's request. The other was Lee. Utica won the league pennant, but by then Lee was long gone.

Lee played for Gananoque, an amateur club, in 1901. Concord, New Hampshire, was his summer home from 1902 to 1904 inclusive. The Concord Marines were in the Class B New England League.

Knotty Lee pitched in a forfeited game on Independence Day of 1903 in Lowell, Massachusetts. Concord scored a run in the top of the ninth to tie the score 3–3. Then, in the tenth, Concord rallied for three runs. In the home half of the inning, with two out, the crowd stormed the field. There were some 4,000 fans in the ballpark that afternoon. The police could not restore order. Concord was awarded a forfeit 9–0 victory.

Another unusual event took place at Lowell in late June of 1904. Concord, the visitors, had brought only one substitute player with them. Late in the game, William Diggins, the Concord catcher, was ejected. This was a problem because Concord's lone sub had already been inserted into the game.

With no players left on the bench, Concord put their "mascot" (batboy) into right field and shuffled their defence. Had they not put in the batboy, they would have forfeited the game. Knotty Lee did not pitch in this game, but he did play left field. As for the batboy, he struck out in his only at-bat and had no chances in the outfield. He is referred to in the game summary and box score as "Diggins, Jr." In fact, the batboy was George Diggins, William's son, who was ten years old at the time. George Diggins is commonly considered to be the youngest person ever to play in a professional baseball game.

And so Knotty Lee's baseball resumé includes playing pro ball with a ten-year-old.

George Diggins lived to the age of ninety-five. At the time of his death, it had been eighty-five years since he "retired" from pro ball.

• • •

Knotty Lee returned to Canada in 1905 as the player-manager of the Brantford team in a small organization that is referred to as the Canadian League and the Western Ontario Baseball League, depending on the source. Baseball stats websites use the former name. The Brantford *Expositor* and Ingersoll *Chronicle*, daily newspapers from two of the five cities in the league, used the latter name. That is what will be used in these pages. After all, "WOBL" is a colourful acronym. The other three WOBL clubs were based in St. Thomas, Woodstock, and Simcoe.

An Opening Day crowd of some 1,500 hopeful fans were on hand to see Brantford host Woodstock. The home team was up 7–0 after four innings. The wheels then didn't so much as fall off as fly off. Woodstock scored seven times in each of the fifth and seventh frames en route to a 15–8 victory.

Lee, who batted second, played right field, and had three hits in a losing cause, allayed fears that he might leave the club. "Never mind, I am here to stay," Lee told the *Expositor*. "We will get a pitcher and I'll bet a new hat we trim Woodstock on Wednesday."[62]

Wednesday was May 24. Victoria Day. The Brantford nine set off for Woodstock with the promised new pitcher in the fold. His name was Sam Cobean, an experienced minor league hurler. Woodstock spoiled his debut, breaking a 1–1 deadlock with four runs in the bottom of the eighth and hanging on to win 5–4.

It is not known who got the new hat.

Cobean had played sandlot ball in Toronto. He and Lee were not the only Torontonians on the Brantford roster; Fred Lepper and Fred Hickey were both from "Hogtown" (by 1905, "Hogtown" was already established as a Toronto nickname).

Fred Lepper was a light-hitting infielder. In twenty-five Brantford games for which box scores could be found, Lepper batted just .183 (19-for-104) with one extra base hit. He played pro ball again in 1906, hit for an even lower average, and never played pro ball again.

Fred Hickey, who pitched and played the infield, joined Brantford in midseason and proved to be a useful addition to the squad. In his Brantford pitching debut, Hickey defeated Woodstock by a 2–1 score and helped his own cause with three hits. His other accomplishments for Brantford during his brief association with the team included a two-hitter (which he lost 2–0 at Woodstock) and a four-hit game against Ingersoll.

Alfred "Doc" Sheppard was signed along with Hickey. Sheppard had played professionally as far back as the mid-1880s. In more recent years, he was part of Toronto's amateur baseball scene.

• • •

Simcoe dropped out of the WOBL in midseason. The loop finished the season with four teams. There have since been other leagues with the same name, but only the 1905 edition of the WOBL was professional.

Box scores of minor league baseball games can be found in local newspapers and, more so, in the pages of the *Sporting Life*. Published in Philadelphia, the *Sporting Life* was the bible of two sports: baseball and trap shooting. Box scores were printed for the major and top minor leagues.

Some of Knotty Lee's stats are missing from the Internet. For example, the major stats providers have no stats at all for the 1905 WOBL. Pitching stats are also missing for Lee for the years 1903, 1904, and 1906. In those three years, Lee pitched a total of at least 550 innings. This is not conjecture. It is fact, borne out by the box scores of the games in which Lee appeared. Lee's hitting stats are available on the Internet for those three years. His pitching stats are not.

Annual baseball guides also provide massive amounts of minor league stats. These are for entire seasons. When stats are not available in this form, one must compile them from individual box scores. Compiled from box scores, here are some previously missing pitching stats for Knotty Lee:

YEAR	LEAGUE	TEAM	G	GS	CG	IP	W	L	K	BB	R
1900	New York State	Utica	6	5	1	15	0	1	5	13	29
1903	New England	Concord	29	28	23	208	13	10	121	38	94
1904	New England	Concord	20	19	16	149	10	7	81	35	86
1905	WOBL	Brantford	8	7	7	61	3	4	N/A	N/A	32
1906	New England	Lawrence	27	25	21	195	12	12	146	58	89
Totals			90	84	68	628	38	34	353+	144+	330

Legend: G = games pitched; GS = games started; CG = complete games; IP = innings pitched; W = wins; L = losses; K = strikeouts; BB = bases on balls; R = total runs allowed; N/A = not available

If one adds the thirty-eight wins and thirty-four defeats noted in the above table to Lee's 35–28 record on baseball-reference.com, his career record becomes 73–62. Some statistical categories are missing: earned runs, batters hit by a pitch, and so on. Regardless, Knotty Lee pitched a lot more than is currently indicated on the primary baseball stats websites.

The last entry in the above table is for 1906. That's appropriate, because Knotty Lee died that year in a manner reminiscent of Mark Twain.

Here's what happened: Lee and his Lawrence teammates were playing a New England League away game at Worcester, on August 1. Lee was pitching. In the middle of the game, he was hit just above the heart by a scorching line drive. Somehow, he caught and held on to the ball after it struck him. He had to leave the game.

On August 4, the *Globe* published a story titled "'Knotty Lee' Is Dead."[63] A similar piece was printed in the *Star*. A Worcester daily had published the story, and it had been picked up on the wire.

As it turned out, Knotty Lee was not dead. Like Mark Twain, news of Knotty's death had been greatly exaggerated. One can only imagine the havoc that the news caused among his friends and family members.

Lee was injured on the play, but he was back on the mound later in the month. In one of his first games back in the lineup, he pitched an eleven-inning complete game against New Bedford.

In 1911, Lee was player-manager for the Hamilton team in a new circuit, the Canadian League (CL). Lee was the Hamilton skipper for three years. One of the teams in the league moved to Toronto during the 1913–14 off-season. Toronto did not have a CL team in previous years. Lee seized the chance to manage in his hometown. The team was called the Beavers, and they were a mediocre side. Off the field, they competed with the Maple Leafs of the superior International League for fans. The Beavers moved after just one season in Toronto.

Fast-forward to February of 1930, and Knotty Lee was restless. Professional baseball had been missing from Southwestern Ontario for a few years. Lee wanted to create another pro league, like the WOBL, that would attract talented players from both sides of the Canada-U.S. border. With that in mind, he travelled to cities like Guelph, London, and Brantford, drumming up support for a new pro loop. By the middle of March, the new league had teams in Brantford, Hamilton, London, and St. Catharines. Guelph and St. Thomas joined the fold soon thereafter, and the Ontario League opened for business that spring. Each team was required to have a minimum of six Canadian players on its roster.

Like the WOBL, the Ontario League signed numerous players from Toronto sandlots. Clare Hoose, a catcher, was player-manager of the Guelph Biltmores. His infielders included Rolly Connacher. Lex Rice caught for the London Tecumsehs. One Rice batterymate was Charles "Steamer" Lucas, a right-hander who later pitched for the Maple Leafs. Rice and Lucas were managed by Knotty Lee. Alf Noble, another righty pitcher, was a member of the Hamilton Tigers.

And just like the WOBL, the Ontario League failed. The Hamilton Tigers disbanded in early July. The last league game took place about three weeks later. The London Tecumsehs had the best winning percentage in the league, a bittersweet achievement.

By now, one could be excused for assuming that Knotty Lee had seen enough of founding professional baseball leagues. He had not. In 1936, he created the Canadian-American League (CAL). Called the "Can-Am League" for short, this loop had teams in cities and towns that straddled the St. Lawrence River, in Ontario and New York.

In the CAL, Knotty Lee managed the Ogdensburg Colts. The Colts were the first U.S.-based pro team that Lee managed. Ogdensburg finished fourth in the six-team league in 1936, seven games under .500 and thirteen and a half games behind first-place Perth. The top four teams made the playoffs, so the Colts played a best-of-five semifinal series against Perth. Ogdensburg lost in five games. Their season was over.

The CAL expanded to eight teams in 1937. Ogdensburg had a newcomer to the league named Maurice Van Robays. A twenty-two-year-old Detroiter, Van Robays was in his first full year in pro ball. The numbers that he put up in 1937 were jaw-dropping: a .368 batting average, forty-three homers, and 150 runs batted in. Please keep in mind that Ogdensburg played just 102 games that year. Van Robays also led the CAL in hits (159) and runs scored (135).

Ogdensburg qualified for the postseason for the second straight year. They finished the regular season in fourth place, a dozen games off the pace. Lee's crew, firm underdogs, made a proverbial statement in the series opener against first-place Perth-Cornwall, winning by a score of 21–3. Van Robays hit two homers, scored five runs, and knocked in four. The Colts won the best-of-five series in four games.

The Gloversville Glovers were Ogdensburg's opponents in the best-of-seven finals. The Glovers had finished third in the CAL standings, only three games out of first place. Gloversville hosted and won the first three games of the finals. The series then moved to Ogdensburg for Games Four and, if necessary, Five and Six.

Their backs against the stable wall, the Colts galloped back into the series. Ogdensburg won three straight 6–5 decisions. Van Robays hit a walk-off home run in Game Five and a walk-off single in Game Six.

The teams returned to Gloversville for Game Seven. There, for the first time in the series, the visiting team won. The Colts ran out 4–1 winners. Van Robays hit his third round-tripper of the series, his sixth of the postseason.

Knotty Lee, age sixty-one, had finally won a league title.

Lee was not "merely" a player, manager, and league organizer. He was business manager for the Maple Leafs in the early 1920s. He scouted for the Leafs, managed in the CAL for a few more years, and then retired from professional baseball.

Charles Lucas: "Steamer"

Charles "Steamer" Lucas is usually referred to as a Toronto native, though one newspaper article claimed that he was British-born. Regardless, Toronto is where he grew up and learned the game. Lucas played sandlot ball for the Hillcrests, then, for several years spread over a decade, he pitched in the pros.

Steamer threw hard, hence his nickname. He was also an accomplished singer. For him, making the right pitch was important whether he was on a mound or in a studio at a radio station.

As a first-year pro with Hanover of the Class D Blue Ridge League in 1927, Steamer did something extraordinary, something that was becoming increasingly rare in pro ball and is unthinkable today.

He pitched two complete game victories on the same day.

The date was August 15. Hanover was playing a twin bill against Chambersburg. In the opener, Lucas went the distance in a 7–2 win. Then, in the seven-inning second game, he threw a one-hit, 1–0 shutout. Chambersburg's lone hit was a single in the third inning.

In the big leagues, only ten hurlers have made such a remarkable

Charles "Steamer" Lucas.

achievement since 1905. The most recent of those ten occurrences was in 1926. Urban Shocker, an ex-Leaf, did it as a member of the St. Louis Browns in 1924.

One feature of Steamer's performance that day makes what he did rarer still. When he won both ends of that double dip, he had been in the pros for less than three weeks. Steamer debuted on July 30.

Steamer's stint in Hanover was a busy one. He got into thirteen games in a period of five weeks. He completed seven of his ten starts.

When Hanover's season ended, Lucas came home to Toronto and joined the Maple Leafs. He made his debut for his hometown team on September 8, pitching two innings of relief against Syracuse. He allowed no base runners. Syracuse won the game 9–4.

Steamer made his first Toronto start on September 10. He beat Buffalo 5–1 in the second game of a doubleheader. Lucas threw a complete game six-hitter, striking out four and walking three.

On September 14, Lucas started again. This time, in Syracuse, he went seven innings and left with the Leafs losing 3–1. Toronto rallied for three runs in the top of the ninth and held on for a 4–3 victory.

Lucas relieved in the first game of a twin bill at Rochester on September 17 and was tagged with the loss in a 9–8 defeat.

The next day, Lucas started the first game of a doubleheader on the final day of the regular season. Toronto won 6–2. The game was completed in one hour and twenty minutes. Steamer whiffed four Rochester batters, walked one, and pitched another complete game.

Steamer's rookie season had been a promising one.

In 1928, Lucas went to spring training with the Leafs. He did not make the team. Instead, he joined the Syracuse Stars of the Class B New York-Pennsylvania League. Steamer lasted about two months with Syracuse, starting in May. He started five games, winning two, losing three, and completing all five. He also relieved in two games. In all, Lucas pitched fifty-three innings for the Stars. He was then returned to the Leafs, who held his contract.

Lucas seemed to have ruffled management's feathers at this stage of his career. The *Globe* reported that he had returned to Toronto "and the only explanation given is that the Syracuse club is not in need of two managers."[64] The *Star* reported that Lucas was back home "not because he was shy in ability but for the reason that managers dislike opposition in their own organizations."[65]

Steamer was promoted to Springfield of the Class A Eastern League in 1929. He threw a five-hit shutout in his Springfield debut, a 1–0 win on the road at Bridgeport.

Thereafter, Lucas floundered with Springfield. He walked six batters in four-plus innings at a game in New Haven. He failed to finish the second inning at a game in Albany.

Pitching in relief in Allentown, Steamer gave up six hits and walked seven in just two thirds of an inning. He was tagged with the loss in a 17–12 slugfest. It was still May, but Lucas was finished in Springfield. In fact, after that woeful performance, he was finished for the season.

In 1930, Lucas joined the London Tecumsehs of the Class D Canadian League. Perching on the bottom rung of the professional baseball ladder may not have been Steamer's first choice, but it's hard to argue with success. Lucas was leading the league in strikeouts (eighty-four) and winning percentage (.786, arising from an 11–3 record) when that league folded in midseason. Riding on the coattails of his success in London, he found work with the Buffalo Bisons.

As a Bison, Steamer was shelled. In three relief appearances, he allowed sixteen runs in four and a third innings. Buffalo lost the games by scores of 19–7, 17–7, and 22–4.

The storied House of David barnstorming, bearded squad from Benton Harbor, Michigan, visited Buffalo on August 20. The visitors defeated Lucas and several second stringers by a 4–3 score. Steamer went the distance for the Bisons.

Lucas then took a sabbatical from pro ball and was out of the game for three years. During that time, he tried to make a go of it as a singer. As a crooner, he went by the name Charles Stainton Lucas.

Billed as "Toronto's singing baseball pitcher," Steamer performed at venues like the Uptown Theatre and the Eaton Auditorium. The latter, now called the Carlu, is a spectacular art deco venue that is still in use today.

Usually referred to as a bass and occasionally as a baritone, Lucas was a regular on Toronto's CKNC for much of 1932.

The Toronto *Star* was full of praise for the former pitcher: "We haven't heard all the bass singers on the air, but among those we have heard we nominate Charles Stainton Lucas for the hall of fame."[66] The paper added, "He faces the microphone as if he were going to strike out a 'homer' just as he did when he was 'Steamer' of the Maple Leafs." Never mind the fact that he was a pitcher. When at the mic, Lucas would take off his tie and collar and balance on his toes when hitting the high notes.

Lucas sang "ballads and semi-classic" songs. And Handel. And a song called "Indian Lover Lyrics." He was accompanied by a piano player. He battled for listeners with the likes of Rex Battle's orchestra.

Then, in 1934, Steamer gave pro ball one more chance. Not only did he get work, but he also landed a job on the pitching staff of the Toronto Maple Leafs.

Charlie Good of the *Star Weekly* was unimpressed with Lucas. "Even at his best Lucas was no Mathewson and no more than he was or is a Bing Crosby as a crooner."

Neither Mathewson nor Crosby, as a pitcher Lucas seemed more like Longfellow's little girl: "When he was good, he was very good indeed, but when he was bad he was horrid."

For example, on April 30, two weeks after Charlie Good's unkind critique, Lucas pitched four scoreless innings and got credit for a 9–5 win. Then, in late May, he had what was probably his worst outing as a Leaf. Steamer was Toronto's starting pitcher in a game at Montreal. He went seven innings, gave up fifteen hits, seven walks, and fourteen runs. He struck out nobody. Montreal whipped the Leafs 15–8.

Despite clunkers like the game against Montreal, Lucas got his share of work in the postseason. Toronto earned a berth in the best-of-seven IL semifinals against Newark. Steamer threw six scoreless innings in Game Four, a 7–4 win.

The Leafs won the series and advanced to the finals, another best-of-seven affair. In Game Two, at Maple Leaf Stadium, Rochester was down 4–3 after seven innings. Enter Steamer Lucas. Rochester tied the game in the top of the eighth, but Toronto scored a run in their half of the frame. Steamer pitched a shutout ninth and the Leafs prevailed 5–4.

Toronto dispatched Rochester, which gave them a place in the Little World Series against Columbus of the American Association. This was a best-of-nine series, with the first four games in Toronto and the rest in Columbus.

Lucas started on the mound in Game Four and lost 4–0. This gave Columbus a three-games-to-one advantage. Worse still, the remainder of the series would be in Columbus.

Steamer returned to the mound in Game Six as a reliever. He got the save in a wild 19–9 Toronto blowout. The series was now tied at three games apiece. Columbus won it in nine games. Lucas came out of the bullpen to pitch in Game Nine, which the Leafs lost 13–6.

Toronto dropped out of the playoff picture in 1935. Steamer's numbers were poorer than in the previous campaign. His earned run average increased from 4.05 to 5.57, and his WHIP grew by more than one.

Lucas was traded from Toronto to Buffalo in late June of 1936. This was good for Steamer. Though he had been banished by his hometown club, the Bisons were a much better team. Buffalo won the IL pennant and the league's playoff championship. Steamer appeared in just one post-season game, a two-inning relief outing against Baltimore in Game Four of the IL finals.

Late in Game Four, Lucas and several of his teammates charged the field when Buffalo manager Ray Schalk engaged in some fisticuffs with Baltimore hurler Cliff "Mickey Mouse" Melton.

With two out in the top of the ninth, Buffalo was behind 8–6. The Bisons had runners on second and third. Schalk was coaching third base and taunting Melton. The Baltimore pitcher ultimately snapped and threw the ball at Schalk. The combatants ran at each other.

On paper, this punch-up should have been a lopsided win for Melton. This version of Mickey Mouse stood 6'5" tall and weighed 205 pounds. Ray Schalk was 5'9", tipped the scales at 165 pounds, and was twenty years older than his opponent.

Melton landed the first punch, a left to Schalk's chin. Melton was a southpaw through and through, on the mound and in this makeshift ring. Lucas et al. then arrived, but they merely pushed their skipper on top of Melton. The fight was finally broken up by members of the local constabulary.

By winning the IL championship, Steamer and the rest of the Bisons earned a berth in the Little World Series. Their opponents were the Milwaukee Brewers, champions of the American Association. Milwaukee won the series in five games.

Steamer Lucas did not pitch against the Brewers. In fact, his Game Four appearance against Baltimore turned out to be the last of Steamer's pro career.

Lucas got married at the end of the 1936 season. He later coached senior ball in Nova Scotia, then played in Oshawa.

Steamer still belted 'em out from behind the mic at weddings and home and school council meetings. He managed a theatre and later worked for Bulova, the watchmakers.

Lucas died of a heart attack in New York City on January 3, 1958. He was only fifty-two. Steamer left his wife, Gertrude, and a son, Ray.

James McKinley, Homesick Hurler

Toronto native James McKinley first picked up a baseball at the age of five. Once he grew up, he played senior amateur ball and was playing at that level by 1880. His 1880 team, the Toronto Clippers, played their home games at the Toronto Cricket Ground. McKinley's teammates included Will Jeffers, who had become a top-notch umpire by 1885. In fact, this was the same Will Jeffers who was umpiring the 1885 game at which McKinley was drunk and disorderly.

Not much is known about McKinley's baseball career in the early 1880s. His name appears sporadically in the local press, mostly in box scores. Those box scores are not complete.

One newsworthy highlight of McKinley's early career was a 1–0 shutout of Guelph on August 15, 1882. By then, he was pitching for a team called the Torontos. The baseball correspondent for the Toronto *World* wrote that spectators were "treated to one of the most brilliant games ever played in Canada, and probably the shortest played game on record."[67] The game took only one hour and five minutes to play. Three double plays were made by the Torontos.

On August 19, the Torontos faced Guelph again. The score was 5–5 after nine innings. In the eleventh inning, Toronto scored four runs. Guelph answered with five runs of their own to earn a come-from-behind 10–9 win. McKinley played left field and had a pair of doubles in defeat.

In 1885, Toronto joined the Canadian League, a professional loop. There were five teams in the league: the Hamilton Clippers, Hamilton Primroses, London Tecumsehs, Guelph Maple Leafs, and the Torontos.

The season did not start until June. On May 16, the Hamilton *Spectator* revealed that the Torontos had been formally organized. The club announced that 350 of 500 shares had been taken up. By May 20, over 400 shares had been sold. The team's treasurer was none other than William Mountain, who had pitched for Toronto Dauntless against the Boston Red Stockings in 1872.

The Torontos hired Harry Spence as player-manager on May 26, barely two weeks before Opening Day. Spence was a known commodity in Canadian League circles, since he had previously managed the Maple Leafs.

The *Spectator* was glad to see Spence at the helm of the Torontos: "Harry Spence, the new manager of the Torontos, is a fine player, an experienced director, a genial gentleman, and a good fellow."[68]

The Torontos made their 1885 Canadian League debut at Guelph on June 10. Toronto lost 3–2 in twelve innings. McKinley started at shortstop and later moved to third base. He was hitless in three at-bats.

The next day, Toronto notched their first Canadian League victory. Playing in Hamilton against the Primroses, Toronto was behind 6–2 after five innings. The Torontos rallied for three runs in the sixth inning and seven more in the eighth, and ultimately won by a score of 12–8. McKinley started the game at third base but came in to pitch late in the game. Box scores do not say in which inning he entered the game or whether he got credit for the win.

McKinley pitched regularly and played third base when he was not "in the box." There were no mounds at the time. Instead, the pitchers worked from a box that was chalked onto the infield.

On June 24, with McKinley manning the "hot corner," Bill Stemmyer pitched for Toronto at home against the Hamilton Clippers. Stemmyer

Bill Stemmyer.

was a twenty-year-old righty from Cleveland. On this day, the Clippers could not touch the 6'2", 190-pound hurler. The baseball scribe of the *Globe* wrote, "They tried banging, then pounding, then bunting, but Stemmyer's balls were never where they expected them to be, and the poor Clippers retired every time with a variety of emotions depicted on their crest-fallen countenances."[69]

Stemmyer walked four and the Torontos made eleven errors (one by McKinley), but the Clippers made nary a hit. Stemmyer pitched a "no-no" and the Torontos won 6–4. It would be another twenty-three years before another no-hitter was thrown by a pitcher in a Toronto uniform.

James McKinley emerged as Toronto's best pitcher. He put up some excellent numbers in 1885: a WHIP of less than 1.00, and just 1.6 walks per nine innings. He allowed seventy hits, walked sixteen, and whiffed seventy in ninety and a third innings. He topped the Torontos with nine victories and lost only three times. He allowed a total of forty-eight runs, but it is not known how many were unearned. His ERA would have been 4.78 if all of those runs had been earned. Considering the fact that errors were more commonplace in those days than they are now, his ERA was almost certainly much lower.

Stemmyer had a WHIP under 1.00 as well, but his win–loss record was only 6–10. He was Toronto's hard-luck hurler.

In 1886, Harry Spence left the Torontos and joined the Portland, Maine, club in the New England League. James McKinley went with Spence. There were six teams in the New England League, including the wonderfully named Newburyport Clamdiggers.

McKinley lost his Portland debut but pitched well. As Independence Day neared, McKinley had at least nine wins and three shutouts. Then, on July 4, the Boston *Globe* proclaimed that McKinley had requested his release. He wanted to quit baseball.

As it turned out, McKinley had gone AWOL after being fined $50 for "poor play" in an 11–9 loss to Boston. He claimed that he had received a telegram from home, saying that his wife was very ill. He responded by going home to Toronto. Just days later, he wrote to the Portland club, claiming that he wanted to return to Maine. He wanted to settle some unpaid bills and "show the people of Portland that he can pitch good ball."[70]

McKinley was back in the pitcher's box on July 14. He took his turn in the rotation for less than a month. Then, on August 13, he returned to Toronto for a second time. After a couple of weeks back home, he once again contacted the Portland club and asked to be reinstated.

This time, club officials said no. They also blacklisted McKinley so that he could not play for anyone else.

On September 4, the Boston *Globe* reported that the Torontos wanted McKinley. Several days later, the Portland club reinstated him from the blacklist and sold his contract to Torontos for $500.

McKinley's record with Portland could not be found, so it was cobbled together from box scores in newspapers. He had a win–loss record of 13–8. He appeared in twenty-one games, started them all, and completed twenty. McKinley threw three shutouts and struck out at least ninety-three batters in at least 180 innings.

James McKinley went home and rejoined the Torontos, who were now playing in the International League. He threw a pair of late summer shutouts for Toronto. On September 10, he threw a four-hitter as Toronto defeated Hamilton 9–0. There was only one Hamilton club in the International League, as opposed to two in the 1885 Canadian League. Hamilton was whitewashed by McKinley again on October 9. This time, Toronto won 5–0. McKinley held Hamilton to five hits.

A tumultuous 1886 season ended for McKinley with a pair of exhibition game defeats against a pair of major league clubs. The 1887 campaign started in much the same way. McKinley was hit hard by two major league opponents during spring training.

Baseball rules were in a state of flux in the 1880s and nowhere is that more apparent than in a game that James McKinley pitched for Toronto in Utica on May 10. Toronto eked out a 6–5 victory, scoring the game-winning run in the bottom of the ninth. In this game, the visiting team batted last.

The "walk-off" hit was rather controversial. Here's how it happened: Toronto had one out with first baseman Jay Faatz on first base. The score was 5–5. Centre fielder Pat Gilman stepped up to the plate. With three strikes on him, Gilman got a hit.

Stop the presses! Gilman got a hit after three strikes were called? Yes. In 1887 — and 1887 only — it took four strikes for a batter to strike out. Not three. Four.

Faatz flew around the bases and tried to score. He passed the catcher to avoid being tagged out, but then missed the plate and did not attempt to touch it thereafter. The catcher tagged the plate and never touched the runner. He then threw to second, and Gilman was tagged out. An argument ensued. Time was not called. Third base was left open. Gilman stole third. He was then picked off third.

The umpire ruled Faatz out and Gilman safe. The next batter, third baseman Jerry McCormick, singled home Gilman to end the game.

The umpire correctly called Faatz out. Faatz had missed the plate and never attempted to touch it after he missed it. Under such circumstances, the catcher need only touch the plate and appeal to the umpire.

On the other hand, the umpire should have called Gilman out when he was picked off second by the catcher. Gilman should also have been called out when he was picked off third.

Another unusual rule came into play on May 21. McKinley was on his game, throwing a four-hit shutout. Toronto gave visiting Buffalo a 13–0 pasting. On the face of it, there's nothing unusual about that. However, in 1887, walks counted as hits. Three of Buffalo's four "hits" were actually walks. But because of the "walks are hits" rule, McKinley is credited with a four-hitter. Had the rule not been in place at the time, his performance would have gone into the books as a one-hitter. The "walks are hits" rule was in place for the 1887 season only.

Box scores could be found for seven games in the 1887 season that McKinley appeared in. His record in those games was 4–3. In early August, *Sporting Life* reported that he was released.

James McKinley's last year in pro ball was 1888. He pitched a couple of games for Toronto, in June, and that was it.

That same year, Harry Spence managed the Indianapolis Hoosiers of the National League. That was the extent of his major league managerial career. In April of 1890, the Hamilton *Spectator* incorrectly reported that Spence had died of consumption in Savannah, Georgia. The newspaper described him as "an old base ball player who at one time belonged to the [Guelph] Maple Leafs."[71] In fact, Spence lived another eighteen years and died in 1908 at age fifty-five.

Bill Stemmyer went 22–18 for Boston of the National League in 1886. That year, he started forty-one games and finished them all. Stemmyer pitched almost 350 innings that season. He struck out 239 batters and walked 144. By 1889, Stemmyer was out of pro ball. He died in Cleveland, his hometown, at the age of seventy-nine.

James McKinley remains one of Toronto's longest serving homebrews, pitching for professional teams in Hogtown for parts of four years. If one adds his New England League record (13–8) and his 1887 Toronto record (4–3) to those on the Internet (14–5), his lifetime record becomes 31–16. McKinley passed away in Toronto, *his* hometown, in 1932, at seventy-three.

Bill O'Hara: Stole 'Em All

William Alexander O'Hara was born in Toronto and grew up on Sherbourne Street, just south of Dundas (then called Wilton Avenue). His dad, James, was a buyer for a wholesale dry goods company. It was only a half-hour's walk from the O'Hara residence to Sunlight Park, where Toronto's pro baseball teams played when Bill was growing up.

The Nonpareils, a team in the Toronto Junior League, used O'Hara at second base. He emerged as the league's best hitter in 1898. O'Hara played senior ball for a team called Park Nine, city champs in 1900. The following year, he joined a team in Gananoque, near Kingston.

The Gananoque fans loved their team. For example, O'Hara and his teammates were feted after a satisfying 5–0 win over the Kingston Ponies. The victors travelled by train that day and were met by a band at the station when they got back to Gananoque. "A torch light procession was formed and the 'conquering heroes' paraded through the streets," said the anonymous baseball correspondent of the Kingston *Daily News*. "The reception was on a par with that given to the heroes of the South African war."[72]

Pro baseball was being played at Diamond Park by the time O'Hara began his pro career in 1902. He spent part of that season as a member of the Montreal Royals in the Eastern League (EL). Toronto was one of the other cities in the eight-team loop. The EL was renamed the International League after the 1911 season.

When the Royals visited Toronto in July of '02, O'Hara was with the team. He played third base, hit a double, and scored Montreal's lone run in a 3–1 loss to the Maple Leafs in a late July contest. Montreal player-manager Charles Dooley was impressed. "He will be a dandy next year," Dooley said to the *Globe*.[73]

Dooley's prediction proved correct. O'Hara played over 200 games in the Pacific Coast League (PCL) in 1903 and accumulated at least 765 at-bats and 225 hits (records might be incomplete). The PCL had a very long schedule at the time, taking advantage of the fine weather. Four of the league's six teams were based in California.

Bill O'Hara participated in five no-hitters during his career and was on the wrong end of the score twice. The first of those was a PCL game that took place in early November of 1903. Doc Newton of Los Angeles completely neutralized the offence of the Oakland Recruits in a 3–0 win. O'Hara led off for the Recruits and played centre field. Only a pair of errors prevented Newton from throwing a perfect game.

After what turned out to be his only season out west, O'Hara moved closer to home. He spent some time as a member of the Toledo Mud Hens, who were then in the American Association. He returned to the EL with Baltimore in 1905. In September of 1906, Fred Burchell of the Orioles no-hit the Leafs 2–0 in the second game of a twin bill in Toronto. O'Hara led off and played left field for the O's.

O'Hara put on an uncharacteristic display of power one day in June of 1908. Playing at home, the Orioles defeated Buffalo 3–1 in the first game of a doubleheader. O'Hara hit two home runs for the O's, one with a runner on base. When he hung up his cleats for good, O'Hara had played in over 1,500 games and hit just seventeen homers.

The 1908 season saw O'Hara and the O's win an Eastern League title. By then, the fleet-footed Toronto native had established himself as an outstanding defensive outfielder. He could run, too — O'Hara led the EL in stolen bases in 1907 and 1908. These strengths attracted the attention of the New York Giants, who signed him in late September.

• • •

Some 16,000 fans were in the stands at Robison Field in St. Louis on Sunday, August 8, 1909. Their Cardinals were down 2–0 in the top of the ninth. Johnny Lush, normally a starter, came in from the bullpen.

Bill O'Hara, rookie left fielder for the visiting New York Giants, was due to bat third. O'Hara had appeared in all of New York's ninety-one games so far in the 1909 season. He was proving to be an "all-field, no hit" type of ballplayer. His batting average was .220 going into this game. O'Hara had stolen nineteen bases so far in his debut National League campaign. His speed and defence kept him in the lineup of New York manager John McGraw.

Third baseman Art Devlin led off the inning against St. Louis and was retired for the first out. Next up was Jack "Chief" Meyers, the New York catcher. Meyers and O'Hara had both made their big-league debuts on Opening Day.

Lush coaxed an out from Meyers. Two gone. Nobody on.

Up to the plate stepped Bill O'Hara. His objective: get on base. And that he did, via a walk.

Al Bridwell, the New York shortstop, batted next. O'Hara took his lead, then took off for second base. Safe! Man on second, two out. O'Hara had just stolen his twentieth base of the campaign. And his pilfering ways were not over yet. He stole third base, too.

Johnny Lush had walked almost 120 batters back in 1906, his first full season in the majors, but his control had improved dramatically since then. Nevertheless, he issued his second free pass of the frame. Bridwell trotted to first. There were now two out, with runners on the corners. Fred Merkle stepped up to the plate.

Merkle had made a memorable baserunning blunder in September of 1908. He was on first base with two out, another runner on third, and the score 1–1. The batter hit what should have been a "walk-off" single, but Merkle left the field without touching second base. He was ruled out and no run scored on the play. The game was called due to darkness. It was made up at the end of the season, out of necessity because the Giants and the Chicago Cubs were tied for first place. The Cubs won the replay and advanced to the World Series. If not for Merkle's blunder, the Giants would have been in the Series instead.

Stepping up to the plate against Johnny Lush, you can bet that Fred Merkle had learned his lesson. But the Giants had a plan with a task that preceded Merkle putting the ball into play. They successfully pulled a double steal. O'Hara's steal of home gave the Giants a 3–0 lead, and that proved to be the final score.

Bill O'Hara was only the twelfth big leaguer to steal second, third, and home during one trip around the bases. This rare feat put him into a select group that now includes the likes of Honus Wagner, Ty Cobb, Rod Carew, Paul Molitor, and Rogers Hornsby. O'Hara was the first rookie to do it. Kevin Pillar of the Blue Jays accomplished the feat in 2018.

Despite playing just 60 percent of New York's games at that position, O'Hara led all National League centre fielders with sixteen assists. He participated in four double plays, which was a league-best at that position.

Despite his accomplishments, Bill O'Hara was put on waivers in November of '09 and picked up by the St. Louis Cardinals. Late in the following month, back in Toronto, O'Hara and a business partner opened up a billiard hall. Located on Yonge Street, just north of King, the business lasted until the mid-1920s.

O'Hara's stay in Missouri was short, but it gave him an experience that proved to be one of a kind in his baseball career. On a Monday in early May of 1910, the Cardinals were scheduled to play a makeup game in Cincinnati. National League president Tom Lynch had forgotten to find an umpire to do the game. The two umps from the previous day's game had already left Cincinnati. The best available umpire was Jim Maginnis, a local amateur. He declined the offer at first, then agreed to officiate.

Cincinnati scored five runs in the bottom of the first to go ahead 5–1. Maginnis made a couple of marginal calls in favour of the home team, but nothing serious. Roger Bresnahan, the St. Louis player-manager, was unimpressed. He protested by moving some of his players to unfamiliar positions in the second frame. First baseman "Big Ed" Konetchy relieved starting pitcher Frank Corridon. Coming in to play first base was Bill O'Hara, who took Corridon's number nine spot in the batting order.

To his credit, Konetchy went four innings and gave up just two runs. Then, in the sixth, he swapped positions with Bill O'Hara. Like Konetchy, O'Hara had never pitched as a pro. Well, wouldn't you know it: O'Hara retired the Reds one-two-three in the sixth. All three outs were fly balls to St. Louis centre fielder Rebel Oakes.

Bill O'Hara never pitched again. By throwing a scoreless inning against the Reds, he joined a select group of non-pitchers who took the mound and kept their opponents off the scoreboard in a major league game. That group now includes the likes of César Tovar, John Cangelosi, and Rocky Colavito.

Bill O'Hara made his final big-league appearance less than a week after taking the mound in Cincinnati. That was the bad news. The good news, for Toronto baseball fans at least, was that he was coming home. O'Hara was joining the Leafs.

Patrolling centre field and batting third for Toronto, O'Hara played in two no-hitters in September of 1910. On September 5, at Rochester, righty George McConnell held the "Leaves" (as they were called in the local press) hitless in a 5–0 victory. McConnell had spent his first five pro seasons as a first baseman. He would go on to win thirty games for Rochester in 1911 and twenty-five more for the Chicago Whales of the rebel Federal League in 1915.

Dick Rudolph was Toronto's losing pitcher in McConnell's "no-no." On September 12, at home, Rudolph beat the Montreal Royals 1–0 in twelve innings at the island. Rudolph threw a no-hitter for ten frames, then allowed one hit in the eleventh and another in the twelfth.

In days of yore, that sort of performance "counted" as a no-hitter because one team was held hitless for nine innings. But the definition of "no-hitter" has changed. Now it means "no hits allowed — period." Unless the game in question is less than nine innings long, e.g., a regulation game that is called early due to bad weather (or, more likely in days of yore, due to darkness). No-hitter or not, Rudolph's feat is worth a mention. The fans certainly

Tim Jordan.

got their money's worth that day. Rudolph's gem was the first game of a doubleheader.

O'Hara batted sixth and was at his usual post in centre field when Fred Herbert of the Leafs held Baltimore hitless in a 15–0 thrashing in July of 1914. The game was a seven-inning affair, the first half of a twin bill.

Batting .304 and hitting thirteen triples, O'Hara led the Leafs to the 1912 International League (IL) pennant. The Leafs finished five games ahead of Rochester. Toronto first baseman Tim Jordan led the league in home runs with nineteen. That was an impressive total in the so-called dead ball era. The 1913 IL leader in dingers hit a measly eight.

Bill O'Hara and Tim Jordan were two of thirteen Leafs whose images were immortalized in a set of ninety International League cigarette cards in 1912.

O'Hara et al. comprised the 1912 Imperial Tobacco C46 set. The cards have an attractive format: an oval black-and-white photo surrounded by

Dick Rudolph.

what looks like a carved wooden frame. The player's surname is printed below the photo in uppercase letters. The back of each card contains a brief blurb about the player, and the number of the card is in the lower right-hand corner.

Dick Rudolph was another Leaf in the set. Rudolph topped the Toronto pitching staff with a 25–10 win–loss record; 1912 was his sixth and final season as a Maple Leaf. Indeed, it was his last year as a minor leaguer. During spring training in 1913, Rudolph walked out on the Leafs and threatened to quit baseball altogether unless he was sold to a major league team. His demands were not unreasonable. His career record as a Leaf was 120–70, and all that he had to show for it was a couple of "cups of coffee" with the New York Giants. Rudolph, a native New Yorker, was twenty-five years old. He had no more to prove at the top rung on the minor league ladder.

Rudolph got his wish and was dealt to the Boston Braves. The 1914 season, his second with Boston, proved to be a memorable one. Midway through the schedule, the Braves were languishing in last place. Then they caught fire, winning the NL pennant by ten and a half games. Rudolph went 26–10 as the Braves defeated the heavily favoured Philadelphia A's in the World Series. Rudolph had two complete game victories in the Fall Classic, allowing just one earned run in eighteen innings. He went on to win 121 games as a Brave.

In the end, Bill O'Hara spent five-plus seasons with his hometown team. He played in over 700 games as a Leaf. At his post in the Island Stadium outfield, he participated in many memorable contests. Some were wins, and some were not.

Of all the games that O'Hara played in a Leafs jersey, the best known by today's fans is one of the defeats. It transpired on a Saturday in early September of 1914. The Providence Grays furnished the opposition for Toronto starting pitcher Ellis Johnson. Providence was still in the thick of the IL pennant race. The Leafs were not.

Just twenty-one years old, Johnson had gotten into a few games with the Chicago White Sox two years earlier. He was in his second full season of pro ball as he bore down on the Providence leadoff hitter. Johnson walked him. Later in the first frame, he walked in a run.

For a while, Johnson settled down. In the meantime, his Providence counterpart was mowing down the Leafs with ease. The Grays clung to a 1–0 lead through five innings. Their bats then exploded for eight runs over the last four frames. The Leafs managed nothing in response. The final score was 9–0 for Providence. They teed off on Ellis Johnson's offerings, blasting him for fifteen hits. Johnson stayed on the mound until the bitter end.

Billy Kelly, Johnson's batterymate, got Toronto's only hit of the game. Kelly was twenty-eight years old and had been in the big leagues for two full seasons and parts of two others. Oddly, Kelly's stats with the Leafs in 1914 are missing from two of the largest historical baseball stats websites on the Internet. His numbers for the season, assembled from newspaper box scores, are as follows: 102 games played, with seventy-five hits in 328 at-bats, thirty-one runs scored, eleven doubles, a triple, six sacrifice bunts, and a .229 batting average.

Providence's biggest hit was a three-run homer by their pitcher, a blast that Bill O'Hara watched as it flew over the fence in right field. The Grays pitcher, still a teenager, was nearing the end of his first professional season. He threw and batted left-handed. He was a big kid, as strong as an ox, too, or so it seemed after the home run. Who, then, was this "Paul Bunyan–esque" southpaw?

His name was George Herman Ruth. Not yet a big-league slugger, but already known as "Babe." Which, of course, was the name of Paul Bunyan's ox.

Ruth struck out seven, walked one, and allowed just one hit. The homer turned out to be the only one that he ever hit in the minors. Ruth had started the 1914 season with Baltimore, his hometown. He won fourteen games for them and was then sold to the Boston Red Sox. Boston then sent him to Providence.

The Babe hit his homer on a three-and-two count. According to legend, the baseball landed in Lake Ontario. Some people believe that the ball is still there today. Could this be true? After all, that home run was hit over a century ago. That's over a hundred autumns, winters, springs, and summers. The poor ball would contract in the cold and expand in the heat. One should also keep in mind that the waters of Lake Ontario have occasionally been, well, filthy. Also, a dangling red stitch might have proven irresistible to a sea monster like the one seen near the Stanley Barracks in 1882. That's mighty close to the site of Island Stadium.

Theories involving cryptids notwithstanding, aerial period photos do show that the configuration of Island Stadium was conducive to hitting a home run over the right field fence and into Lake Ontario. It does not seem unreasonable that Ruth's homer went into the lake. As for whether or not it's still there …

• • •

The next season, 1915, proved to be Bill O'Hara's last. In May, he asked to be released. Bill Clymer, Toronto's manager, asked O'Hara to stay. Just over a month later, he was given his unconditional release. After hanging up his cap, O'Hara wore a lot of hats. Some were related to baseball jobs, and some were not.

First on his post-playing agenda was the First World War. O'Hara went to England and flew up and down the coast as a member of the Royal Flying Corps, patrolling the skies rather than the outfields of the International League. After crashing a plane, he was moved to the balloon corps. Not finding that to his liking, he was transferred to the 24th Battalion of the Canadian Expeditionary Force. He was wounded in battle and was mustered out of the army in the summer of 1918.

O'Hara then became a celebrity of sorts. He went on the lecture circuit, talking about his experiences. He appeared in vaudeville as well. His previous association with the Giants may or may not have helped him onto the stage.

During his first winter back home, O'Hara went fur trapping up north. A rather quirky sense of humour was plain to see in a letter that he wrote to the *Globe*:

> We learned a few things during the war. One of the chief difficulties is in getting the fur to market — when one has any fur. Airplanes will do the trick. We have also applied to the War Office for an observation balloon from which to scan the country roundabout, machine guns to mow down herds of moose and deer, hand grenades for bear dens, and searchlights to blind the denizens of the wild at night. Next week we are going to resort to gas. That ought to get 'em without spoiling the pelts.[74]

As the war continued, the U.S. government hired O'Hara to give lectures at steel and cotton mills. His objective was to coax increases in production for the sake of the war effort. His tour lasted about six months.

O'Hara was briefly a boxing promoter in the early 1920s. He rejoined the Leafs, too, as business manager, road secretary, scout, and first base coach. Occasionally, he stepped in as acting manager. For example, O'Hara took the reins when manager Dan Howley had to return home because of a death in the family.

Midway through the 1927 campaign, Leafs manager Lee Fohl resigned. O'Hara was named manager in his place. Toronto finished the season eleven games over .500, but that was only good enough for fourth place. Buffalo won the IL pennant with an excellent 112–56 win–loss record.

In March of 1931, long-time Leafs executive Lawrence "Lol" Solman passed away at the age of sixty-seven. The ball club was at spring training in Columbus, Georgia, at the time. At one time or another, in addition to his association with the Leafs, Solman had managed the Royal Alexandra Theatre. He also ran the Toronto Ferry Company, which took people to Island Stadium and back.

Bill O'Hara had nothing but praise for Solman when he was interviewed by the *Globe*:

> I have lost a close personal friend. It was a pleasure to work for such a man. In the 20 years that I have been associated with the Toronto Ball Club and other interests of Mr. Solman, his kindliness, his sage advice, his willingness to give the other fellow better than an even break, are virtues that have endeared him to me and won the respect of all who knew him. I could not feel more bereaved had he been a near relative.[75]

On June 15, quite suddenly, Bill O'Hara died. He had been travelling with the Leafs, who were playing in Jersey City. O'Hara had been ill for several days. He had been confined to his bed in the city's Plaza Hotel. O'Hara went into convulsions while a friend from nearby Newark was visiting him. The friend found a doctor, who called for an ambulance. By the time it arrived, O'Hara was dead. His body was sent home by train. The cause of death was a heart problem. He was only forty-nine years old.

Ed Holly, then the manager of the Montreal Royals, was a teammate of O'Hara in Toronto in 1912 and 1913. "I am shocked and grieved to hear of Bill O'Hara's death," Holly told the Montreal *Star*. "He was a great fellow, was popular all over the league and counted his friends by hundreds [*sic*]. He was a close personal friend of mine and he will be missed. They didn't come any better."[76]

Bill O'Hara is buried at Mount Pleasant Cemetery in Toronto.

Bob Prentice: Bitter Coffee

Bob Prentice lived the life of a journeyman minor leaguer. In a ten-year career, he played for ten different teams. He also played for multiple teams in a single season in four different years.

All that travelling must not have bothered Prentice much. When he hung up his cleats, he became a successful scout.

Prentice played football at Riverdale Collegiate and was good enough at that sport to attract attention from the CFL's Argonauts, but he stuck with baseball as his potential meal ticket.

While playing for a team called Turners in the Greenwood Park Junior Baseball League, Prentice once hit a ball over a barn beyond the left-field fence.

Prentice signed with the Cleveland Indians in late September of 1947. He had just turned eighteen the previous month.

After starting his career with Batavia in the Class D Pennsylvania-Ontario-New York (PONY) League in 1948, Prentice was promoted to the Class C Pittsfield Indians of the Canadian-American League.

Prentice hit a career best .314 in '49 for the Indians, who were based at Wahconah Park. Wahconah Park has a capacity of 3,500. The grandstand is

Bob Prentice as a Leaf.

made of wood, one of the few left in the country. The ballpark, built in 1919, is listed on the American National Register of Historic Places.

Daniel Okrent once wrote in *Sports Illustrated* that going to a game at Wahconah Park was "baseball heaven." It's just possible that Bob Prentice felt the same way.

The years rolled by, and Prentice continued to climb the minor league ladder. At Cedar Rapids of the Class B Illinois-Indiana-Iowa (Three-I) League, in 1950, he knocked in an even one hundred runs. Three years later, he smacked a career high twenty-four home runs with Tulsa of the AA Texas League. He reached AAA in '54.

The 1956 season was to be Prentice's ninth in pro ball. In the spring of that year, he went to spring training with the Toronto Maple Leafs at Fort Pierce, Florida. If he made the team, he would be going home. Though playing in the big leagues was his primary goal, suiting up for his hometown team was also important to him.

When the roster was set, Prentice's name was on it. On Opening Day, on April 18, the Leafs won 3–1 at Richmond. Prentice rode the pine.

Four days later, at Columbus, Prentice made his first regular season appearance for the Leafs. He pinch-hit for pitcher Tony Jacobs in the top of the ninth inning and grounded out. The game was tied 6–6 when it was called in the top of the eleventh due to bad weather.

On April 26, the Leafs were playing in Miami. In the seventh inning, Toronto pitcher Robert Lowe was due up. Once again, Bob Prentice was sent in to hit.

This was an uncommon matchup. Prentice, then twenty-six years old, was in his ninth season of pro ball. The pitcher, a lanky African American right-hander, was forty-nine, easily old enough to be Prentice's father. And that was his "official" age. Some speculated that he was older.

Bob Prentice was facing the great Satchel Paige.

Paige was in the middle of his third season with the Birmingham Black Barons of the Negro National League when Prentice was born.

The Satchel Paige of 1956 was a lot more than a seemingly ageless hurler with a rocking chair to sit on in the dugout. Used as a starter and a reliever, Paige appeared in thirty-seven games for Miami that season. His win–loss record was 11–4 and he sported a puny 1.86 ERA.

Paige had entered the game against the Leafs in the seventh inning.

Prentice ended up singling and later scored. He remained in the game and got a second, unsuccessful, crack at Paige later in the game. Miami won the contest 11–8. Paige threw the last three innings for Miami.

Bob Prentice never got another hit as a member of the Toronto Maple Leafs. In late May, he was demoted to the Mobile Bears of the AA Southern Association. As a Leaf, he had appeared in only a handful of games, all as a substitute, spread over a period of about five weeks.

Prentice was not happy with the demotion. "I'm thoroughly disgusted," he told the Toronto *Daily Star*. "I've been playing pro ball for eight years and I have to come home to Toronto to get the worst deal of my career."[77] But Leafs manager Bruno Betzel felt that the club had better options. Prentice's cup of coffee with his hometown team was over.

Prentice batted .301 for Mobile in 1956. The next year, he returned to Tulsa. His last year of pro ball was 1957.

Prentice then turned his attention to scouting, becoming Canadian scout for the Detroit Tigers. He signed his fair share of players. Some were busts. Others were successes. In a couple of cases, Prentice hit the jackpot.

Duncan Wood, a 6'4" right-handed pitcher, was one of Prentice's more unusual signings. Wood was born in Dundee, Scotland, and saw his first baseball game at the age of ten. He was pitching for People's in the Leaside Baseball Association junior league when he was signed in June of 1964. Wood pitched in the Tigers system for three years.

Infielder John Fallis, nineteen, was signed by Prentice shortly after Wood. Another Leaside junior, Fallis lasted only one season in the minors.

Prentice signed Gary Jeffries of Burlington in 1966. Jeffries was a second-generation minor leaguer. His uncle Walt played for three years in the late 1940s. In fact, Walt Jeffries and Prentice had played against one another in the PONY League. Gary Jeffries played in the minors for two years.

Malvern Collegiate student Bernie Beckman was still in grade 12 when he was signed by Bob Prentice. A 6'4" southpaw who was born in the Netherlands, Beckman played as high as AAA during a pro career that spanned parts of nine seasons and pitched a no-hitter in the Texas League in 1976.

George Korince, a right-handed pitcher, was one of Prentice's earlier signings. An Ottawa native, Korince earned call-ups to Detroit in 1966 and 1967.

Before he was summoned to Detroit in '67, Korince pitched for the Tigers' International League affiliate in Toledo. In June of that season, Korince got the starting assignment for a game at Maple Leafs Stadium. There, he hit the first homer of his pro career in an 8–2 loss. He pitched in the minors for six years.

Mike Kilkenny was another Canadian pitcher signed by Bob Prentice. A native of Bradford, Ontario, Kilkenny threw a no-hitter for Daytona Beach of the Florida State League in 1965. He played pro ball for a decade, including three full seasons with Detroit. The 6'3" southpaw also pitched for Oakland, Cleveland, and San Diego in the big leagues.

Bob Prentice hit paydirt when he signed Scarborough native John Hiller. More about Hiller in a later chapter.

The Detroit Tigers had no fewer than thirteen Canadian players in their system in the spring of 1970. The Expos had six. "The Red Sox have three or four, and that's about it," Prentice told Jack Dulmage of the Windsor *Star*. "I don't know of any other big-league clubs with any in the minors."[78]

It was no coincidence that most of the Canucks in the Tigers organization were pitchers. As Prentice explained during his Detroit scouting days, "If a pitcher has a strong arm, we can have patience with him, teach him things he must know. The Tiger system allows for this development. It is the only one that does."[79]

Canadian position players were at a competitive disadvantage at the time. "I was an infielder myself and I hate to admit it, but coaching in Canada is not good. The players are not taught the strategy of the game … the fine points, the proper way to make relays, backup plays, cutoffs, throwing to the correct base. American boys get these things."[80]

In 1970, the Detroit Tigers had no fewer than thirty scouts. Prentice was one of only three full-time Canadian scouts in major league baseball.

Prentice scouted for the Tigers until 1976. The next year, he became the first director of Canadian scouting for the expansion Toronto Blue Jays.

Frank Repchik: Blanked Braves

Toronto's Frank Repchik split the 1952 season between the junior and senior teams of Milwaukee Sports of the West Toronto League. The nineteen-year-old southpaw had a combined record of 11–3 with a pair of no-hitters.

That December, Repchik was signed to a pro contract by the Maple Leafs. The signing was reported in a wire story, which was picked up by newspapers as far away as Saskatchewan, Alberta, and British Columbia.

Repchik went to spring training with the Leafs in '53 and went north with the club when they broke camp. That was no small feat for a first-year pro. Repchik had won a place on the pitching staff over established hurlers with major league experience, like Phil Haugstad and Sam Zoldak.

The International League regular season was almost three weeks old, and Frank Repchik had not yet pitched for the Leafs. Finally, on May 11, he got his chance. Repchik was chosen to start in a midseason exhibition game against the Milwaukee Braves at Maple Leaf Stadium.

Repchik answered the call by allowing just one hit in three innings. The one hit was by Braves third baseman Eddie Mathews, a future Hall of Famer.

Frank Repchik as a Leaf.

The Leafs won the game 3–2. Yes, it was "only" an exhibition game. Yes, Milwaukee skipper Charlie Grimm replaced his starters midway through the contest. However, the starters remained in the lineup for as long as Repchik was on the mound.

Repchik's performance was deemed print-worthy by the sports editors of newspapers all over North America. His achievement was duly noted in the pages of the Baltimore *Sun*, the Chicago *Tribune*, and many other dailies.

Just three days after keeping the Braves at bay, Repchik was demoted to the Hamilton Cardinals of the Class D Pennsylvania-Ontario-New York (PONY) League. He struggled with the Cardinals, going 3–5 with a 5.61 ERA in sixty-nine innings.

In late July, Repchik was on the move again. The Leafs sent him to the Bluefield Blue-Grays of the Appalachian League, another Class D loop. He found his stride in Bluefield, reversing his Hamilton win–loss record, trimming his ERA from 5.61 to 3.71, and issuing far fewer free passes per nine innings.

In mid-August, Repchik threw what was probably the best game of his pro career. He twirled a three-hit, 2–0 shutout against the Welch Miners at Bluefield. The Miners were slugging it out for first place with the Johnson City Cardinals, while Bluefield was in last place in the six-team league.

Four days after the shutout, Bluefield crushed the Cardinals 16–8. Repchik went the distance for the Blue-Grays. What made this game stand out for Repchik was his performance at the plate rather than on the mound. He went four-for-five, scored a run, and drove in three.

In his next start, Repchik threw another shutout and held the Bristol Twins to five hits in a 3–0 win. This was his second whitewash in nine days.

As for the Appalachian League pennant race, Johnson City finished a game ahead of Welch. Bluefield ended the season a whopping forty games off the pace.

The Leafs rewarded Repchik for his Bluefield success with a late season call-up to Toronto. Repchik was given a start on September 13 in the first game of a Sunday doubleheader against the Ottawa A's at Maple Leaf Stadium.

This was not a meaningless game — Toronto was in the thick of a hunt for a playoff spot and needed to win both games in order to stay in the race for a postseason berth.

Though they weren't exactly the Milwaukee Braves, the A's could not be taken lightly. Six of the players in the Ottawa starting lineup had either played or would go on to play major league ball.

The Leafs opened the scoring in the second inning. Third baseman Kal Segrist walked and scored on a double by catcher Hal Keller.

Inning by inning, the score remained 1–0. Repchik was cruising, while Ottawa hurler Dick Rozek could not find the plate. Rozek walked seven Leafs that afternoon, but only the free pass of Segrist proved to be costly.

Like Repchik, Rozek was a lefty. Wildness plagued Rozek throughout his pro career. Back in '48, with Wilkes-Barre of the Eastern League, he had walked 180 batters in 198 innings. In parts of five major league seasons, he walked more than twice as many batters as he struck out.

Going into the top of the ninth inning, the score was still 1–0. Then, with a runner aboard, centre fielder Joe Taylor homered to put Ottawa ahead 2–1. Taylor was a twenty-seven-year-old African American from Alabama who was no stranger to Canada. His first three years as a pro were spent with Winnipeg of the independent Mandak League and Farnham and Saint-Hyacinthe of the Quebec Provincial League. Taylor played for Toronto in 1955 and had two stints with Vancouver of the Pacific Coast League. He hit .249 in 119 big league games.

The Leafs were unable to score against Rozek in the bottom of the ninth. Ottawa prevailed, 2–1, and Frank Repchik was charged with the loss. He scattered seven hits, walked just one Ottawa batter, and struck out none.

The Leafs lost the second game of the doubleheader as well. They were finished for the season.

Repchik rode in a local parade, billed as Toronto's up-and-coming baseball prospect. He sat in a car with a banner on the door that read, "And now Toronto's own Frank Repchik."

Frank Repchik was promoted to the Burlington Bees of the Class B Illinois-Indians-Iowa League in 1954. After going 0–5, 5.50, in fifty-four innings, he was demoted to Grand Forks of the Class C Northern League. That North Dakota town proved to be the end of the line as far as his pro career was concerned. He went 2–9 with a hefty 8.42 ERA in seventy-eight innings.

Repchik returned to senior ball in Toronto in 1955 and played for teams like Concords and Honest Ed's. All the while, he kept the banner that he rode with in the parade. He also kept his Association of Professional Ball Players of America membership card.

Goody Rosen, Fan Favourite

Goodwin "Goody" Rosen was a baseball hero in Toronto and in Brooklyn, an all-star who nearly won a National League batting title. Not bad for a scrawny kid from Parkdale Collegiate who trekked all the way to Florida so that he could try out as a professional ballplayer, only to be told that he needed to gain some weight.

Rosen played sandlot ball in Toronto for the likes of St. Andrew's bantams, St. Francis bantams, and the Elizabeths (better known as the "Lizzies"). He won titles with all three teams.

Playing — and winning — in the amateur ranks was great, but Rosen wanted something more out of baseball. He wanted to play pro. So, with a buddy, he took a bus to New York, bought a used car, and drove to Tampa. The pair got work pruning orange trees. Then they got a break. One of Rosen's brothers got word of a tryout in Little Rock, Arkansas.

The distance from Tampa to Little Rock is almost a thousand miles (1,600 kilometres). Undeterred, the pair hitched rides and hopped freight cars. The Little Rock gig did not pan out. The pair eventually participated in a set of tryouts in Memphis. There, they learned that they were too small. Rosen weighed just 135 pounds at the time.

It took a couple more years, but Goody Rosen finally made it to the pros, signing up with the Stroudsburg Poconos of the Class D Interstate League in 1932. Stroudsburg was sitting atop the standings when the league folded in late June.

Somehow, the Stroudsburg team stayed together and played exhibition games after the league went bust. In early September, the Poconos played one such game against the Philadelphia Athletics. Stroudsburg won the game, too, 8–7 in ten innings. Rosen batted in the leadoff spot and played centre field for Stroudsburg. He had recently celebrated his twentieth birthday.

The Louisville Colonels of the AA American Association were Rosen's next stop. Rosen played for Louisville for five years. He hit .300 or better in four of those five seasons, amassing 905 hits in the process. But they were lean times for the Colonels, who finished above .500 just once while Rosen played for them.

On the last day of the 1936 campaign, Rosen made what turned out to be the only pitching appearance of his pro career. The game was played at Indianapolis. It wasn't pretty. Rosen took the mound in the home half of the eighth inning with Louisville behind 9–3. Goody was tagged for four hits, a walk, and three runs. The final score was 12–4.

Just before Louisville's final game of the 1937 season, the Colonels' radio station announced that Goody Rosen had won a trophy as the team's most popular player. Rosen was so pleased with the award that he homered in his first at-bat.

Goody made his first big-league start in the second game of a doubleheader at Crosley Field in Cincinnati on September 14, 1937. Rosen led off for Brooklyn, played centre field, and went two-for-five with a run scored, an RBI, and a stolen base. The Dodgers cruised to an emphatic 11–2 win.

"I can't see how he can miss for a regular spot next year," Brooklyn manager Burleigh Grimes told *Star Weekly*.[81] And that's exactly how the 1938 season played out for Rosen. He hit .281 and played all three outfield positions.

On June 15 of that year, Rosen played a minor role in a game that was doubly significant in the annals of baseball history. The Dodgers were hosting the Cincinnati Reds at Ebbets Field. Johnny Vander Meer, the starting pitcher for the Reds, had pitched a no-hitter in his previous game.

Vander Meer was wild against the Dodgers. Through eight frames, he had walked five Dodgers. But he was also untouchable. Going into the bottom of the ninth, Vander Meer had a no-hitter going.

Buddy Hassett, the Brooklyn left fielder, grounded out to Vander Meer to lead off the ninth. Catcher Babe Phelps and third baseman Cookie Lavagetto both walked. Rosen was sent in to pinch-run for Phelps. First baseman Dolph Camilli walked. The bases were loaded with one away. Goody Rosen was on third for the Dodgers. Centre fielder Ernie Koy then hit a grounder to the Reds' third baseman, Lew Riggs, who forced Rosen at the plate. Shortstop Leo Durocher then flew out to centre fielder Harry Craft for the final out.

Johnny Vander Meer had thrown back-to-back no-hitters. This was a major league first, and it has not happened since. It was also the first-ever night game at Ebbets Field.

The Brooklyn Dodgers employed Babe Ruth as their first-base coach in 1938. The Babe and Goody Rosen were keen cigar smokers. "Babe accused me once of stealing cigars, but I pointed out that my brand was different," Goody once told Jim Proudfoot of the Toronto *Star*. "So we set a trap for the thief. We changed the top row in his box to exploding cigars."[82]

The Dodgers were on a train bound for Boston. "After dinner, I see the trainer preparing to light up a cigar." Goody grabbed Ruth's attention just in time for the indoor pyrotechnics. "Babe had vowed to murder the guy, but he looked so funny, with his face all covered with soot, we couldn't do anything for laughing."

Rosen split the 1939 season between Brooklyn and the Montreal Royals, their International League affiliate. This was his first stint in the IL, which meant that he would be playing in Toronto for the first time in his pro career.

Goody's first game at Maple Leaf Stadium on July 20, 1939, was heralded as "Goody Rosen Night." Prior to the game, Rosen was presented with a radio, a suit, a watch, shirts, a floor lamp, a hat, and a sports jacket. Goody's wife was given a suit and a bouquet.

Playing first base for the Royals, Rosen had a pair of hits and stole a base. The Leafs won the contest 3–2, scoring the winning run on a bases-loaded wild pitch in the eleventh inning.

Rosen was a full-time minor leaguer from 1940 to 1943 inclusive, spending most of those seasons playing for the Syracuse Chiefs of the IL. As a result, he was a regular visitor to Maple Leaf Stadium during that time.

Goody finally returned to Brooklyn in 1944, spending the season with the big club and Syracuse. He was determined to spend all of '45 in the majors. "Because it was wartime and there were travel restrictions, we had spring training at Bear Mountain, N.Y., near West Point," Goody recounted to Al Sokol of the Toronto *Star* in 1974.[83] "One day I paid some rookies to pitch to me. I must have hit for three straight hours because my hands were blistered raw and I could barely swing. Because I was so tired, I squared my stance and just tried meeting the ball. Suddenly I was hitting nothing but line drives."

The 1945 season turned out to be a "breakout year" for Rosen. He batted .325 for the Dodgers, third best in the National League and better than anyone in the American League. He was selected to the NL All-Star Team. Alas, due to the Second World War, there was no All-Star Game that year.

The Flatbush faithful loved Rosen, and the feeling was mutual. "The fans in Brooklyn were the best in baseball: a wonderful place to play in. If those fans took a liking to you, then you could do no wrong. Mind you, if they didn't like you, they'd run you out of town."[84]

Early in the 1946 season, Rosen was traded. "We were playing the Giants at the Polo Grounds, and I hopped on the subway. When I opened the [New York] *Daily Mirror*, I read that I had been traded to the Giants."[85]

Right after the trade, the Dodgers played a doubleheader at the Polo Grounds. Goody wanted the Dodgers to pay for letting him go. He wanted the twin bill to be a memorable one. He was a man on a mission. Sure enough, he went five-for-seven with a home run, four runs scored, and three runs batted in. The Giants won both games.

Rosen was back in the International League when the curtain rose on the 1947 season. This time, Goody was a Maple Leaf. Hitting in the cleanup spot and playing centre field, he went hitless. The Leafs beat Baltimore 4–1 in front of over 14,000 fans.

Goody turned thirty-five a couple of weeks before the end of the IL season. His last day at the office was a doubleheader in Montreal on the final day of the season. The Leafs, dead last in the league, won both games. In doing so, they knocked the Royals out of first place. Montreal was beaten at the wire by Jersey City.

No missive about Goody Rosen would be complete without mentioning his love of horses. The cigar-chomping ex-ballplayer actually had a horse named after him. The equine Goody was a standardbred partly owned by his human namesake. Goody the horse ran at the Meadowlands, not far from the site of Roosevelt Stadium in Jersey City, where Goody the outfielder ran down flies for Toronto, Montreal, and Syracuse.

Rolf Scheel: Baseball Über Alles

It was only a preseason game, but it briefly featured one of the most unlikely batteries in baseball history.

It was late March of 1959. The Baltimore Orioles were hosting the Kansas City Athletics. The game was tied 3–3 after nine innings. Catching for Baltimore was Joe Ginsberg, a secular Jewish native of New York City. Ginsberg had entered the game as a replacement for starting receiver Gus Triandos.

Coming into the game to pitch the top of the tenth for the O's was Rolf Scheel, an ethnic German who was born in Yokohama, Japan, in 1932.

Scheel and his parents spent the Second World War in Germany. During the war, he had learned Nazi songs and was allegedly a member of an organization that was similar to Hitler Youth. He knew how to shoot a rifle. He knew how to throw a hand grenade.

As it turned out, Scheel also knew how to throw a baseball.

After the war, the U.S. military had an installation in Bad Homburg, where Scheel lived. Some MPs were playing baseball on the grounds. A home run went over the fence and into a tennis court, where Scheel was playing tennis. He picked up the baseball and hurled it some 345 feet to home plate. This feat did not go unnoticed by the MPs, and before long the teenage German was practising with them.

Scheel was not allowed to play in games with the MPs, but he later joined a German team called the Stuttgart Phillies. "I played my first game of baseball when I was seventeen," he told the Miami *Herald* in 1959.[86] As a member of the Stuttgart squad, Scheel met pitcher Curt Simmons of Philadelphia's Phillies in early 1952; Simmons was in the military at the time.

Later that year, Rolf Scheel and his mom immigrated to Canada and settled in Toronto. Scheel attended tryouts at Maple Leaf Stadium. The tryouts had been organized by the St. Louis Browns (forerunners of the Baltimore Orioles), then the parent club of the Leafs. Scheel impressed the organizers and was signed to a pro contract.

Scheel was twenty years old when he made his pro debut with Valdosta of the Class D Georgia-Florida League in 1953. It quickly became apparent that he had problems with his control. Scheel walked 119 batters in 130 innings with Valdosta.

Despite his wildness, in 1954 Scheel was promoted to Aberdeen of the Class C Northern League. He spent two years at Aberdeen, walking more than 110 batters in each season.

Scheel was demoted back to Class D in 1956. Pitching for Paris of the Sooner State League, he had a breakout season. Scheel cut his average walks per nine innings by more than 50 percent. His 2.10 ERA was less than half of his previous best.

Until this point in his pro career, pitching was a means to an end that was not related to baseball. "I didn't take baseball serious [*sic*] until after my fourth year in the minors. I wanted to be a geologist and I started playing professional baseball in hopes of making enough money to further my studies."[87]

Back in C ball in 1957, Scheel won a career best eighteen games for the Phoenix Stars of the Arizona-Mexico League. The six-team loop had two teams south of the border, in Mexicali and Cananea. Phoenix won the league pennant with a .650 winning percentage, 10.5 games ahead of second place Cananea. The Stars' player-manager was Bob Hooper, a native of Leamington, Ontario.

Scheel climbed a couple of rungs to the top of the minor league ladder in 1958, when he was assigned to the Louisville Colonels of the AA American Association. He was Louisville's hard-luck hurler, sporting a 3–17 win–loss record despite a 3.69 ERA. He lost his first nine starts, finally putting up a "W" in mid-June by shutting out Omaha. He went 2–8 thereafter. "Over the last six weeks of the 1958 season I didn't allow more than two runs in any game. But I was the winning pitcher only once," he lamented to the *Herald*. "We were shut out five or six times when I was pitching."[88] One of those goose eggs was a 3–0 loss in which Scheel's Omaha counterpart threw a no-hitter.

Not discouraged by Scheel's record, the Orioles invited him to spring training with the parent club in 1959. It was there that he teamed up with catcher Joe Ginsberg. Scheel pitched a scoreless tenth frame, allowing one hit by the A's. Baltimore won it with a run in the bottom of the inning. Scheel was the winning pitcher.

That same spring, after a game against Boston, Scheel and a Baltimore teammate approached Ted Williams and asked his advice for pitching to American League players. Over two hours later, Williams had gone through every hitter in the league.

Rolf Scheel pitched in the minors for a few more years. Perhaps inspired by his season in the Arizona-Mexico League, he spent the better part of two seasons in the Mexican League.

Scheel signed with the Leafs in early September of 1962 but did not make any appearances for the club. He was invited to spring training in 1963 and signed a contract in late April. Scheel made his Leafs regular season debut on May 4 in Rochester. Scheel pitched two shutout innings, but the Leafs lost 7–3.

Scheel made his Maple Leaf Stadium debut on May 9 against Richmond. He pitched seven innings of relief, struck out five, walked none, and gave up just two runs in a 7–4 defeat. After that, he was much less effective. Scheel was released in late May.

Scheel had one last kick at the can in 1966, when he went to Baltimore's minor league spring training camp in search of a job. "They didn't promise me anything," Scheel told the Brantford *Expositor*. "But I'm familiar with their organization. [They] were in dire need of long relief pitching last year."[89] Scheel caught on with Stockton, Baltimore's Class A affiliate in the California League. Scheel then went into coaching, first in the California League and then at UC Santa Barbara.

Rolf Scheel was one of the first professional baseball players who learned the game in Europe.

PART VII

OTHER TORONTONIANS

Jimmy Archer, Early Squatter

Jimmy Archer was born in Dublin, Ireland, and grew up in Toronto. He learned about baseball as a new Canadian on the sandlots of his adopted hometown. Archer went on to enjoy a successful big-league career that was spread over parts of twelve seasons. Mostly a catcher, he participated in pretty much every type of baseball competition that a professional could in the early part of the twentieth century.

Not bad for a fellow who was badly injured in a horrific industrial accident just before he turned pro.

Archer described the incident to *Baseball Magazine* many years later. "It was in the slack winter season of 1902 and work around Toronto was scarce. I had just got a temporary job helping out in a cooperage shop. Part of my employment consisted in placing the heads of barrels in a vat so that the sap could be boiled out of them."[90] It was near quitting time, and Archer slipped while removing a barrel from the vat.

His right arm and right leg went into the bubbling sap: "The flesh on my arm was seared to the elbow and my right leg was also scalded to the knee." A well-meaning coworker tried to help by tearing off a protective jersey that

Jimmy Archer.

Archer was wearing. "In doing so he tore all the skin off my arm to the elbow and a good bit of the flesh with it."

The road to recovery was long. "The next two months I spent in the hospital, the better part of the time trying to persuade the doctors to cut the arm off." Archer added, "That was before the days of skin grafting and as a result my arm is pretty well scarred and ridged. It is also bent and stiffened at the elbow."

As a result of the accident, Archer's right arm was an inch shorter than his left arm. "I went to a tailor's, and while being fitted for a suit the clothes maker called my attention to the shortage in the right arm," Archer once told the St. Louis *Dispatch*. "Since then it has alarmed more than one tailor."[91]

Remarkably, Archer could still throw. In fact, he could throw hard and accurately from a crouching position. Throwing from a squat became his specialty. This was not a common practice at the time.

Archer cut his teeth as a professional baseball player in 1903 as a member of the Fargo club of the Class D Northern League. The four-team loop included the Crookston Crooks and the Grand Forks Forkers.

The 1904 season saw Archer join the Boone Coal Miners of the Iowa League of Professional Baseball Clubs, another Class D organization. Boone's opponents included the Fort Dodge Gypsum Eaters, the Waterloo Microbes, and the Ottumwa Standpatters.

Archer's worst on-field injuries were sustained while he was playing for Boone. "I ran at top speed to catch a foul ball that was alighting near the edge of the field. First thing I knew I didn't know anything, for I had crashed into a hitching rack used by farmers to tie their horses during the game."[92] Archer had separated a shoulder and broken a collarbone.

After recovering from the crash, Archer batted .299 for the Coal Miners and earned a trial with the Pittsburgh Pirates. His big-league debut took place on the day after Labour Day in the second game of a doubleheader against Cincinnati. Playing shortstop and batting cleanup for the Pirates was Honus Wagner. Archer caught and batted eighth. In his first at-bat, he hit a run-scoring single. He hit another single in the ninth. Pittsburgh lost 7–3.

Charles Louis "Deacon" Phillippe, Archer's batterymate that day, was near the end of a mediocre 1904 regular season. Phillippe had been a twenty-game winner in each of the previous four years. He had another twenty-win season in 1905, but by then Jimmy Archer was no longer a Pirate. Instead, he was back in the minors, catching for Atlanta of the Southern Association.

According to the Wilkes-Barre *Times Leader*, Archer set a pair of pickoff records while playing for Atlanta. Both occurred in games against Memphis. The first was catching three men off base in one inning on four pitches, while the other was catching seven men off first in one game.

After toiling in Atlanta for two years, Archer had another memorable campaign in 1907, spending the entire season as a backup catcher for the American League champion Detroit Tigers.

Archer did not play much for Detroit. In fact, he had fewer at-bats as a Tiger (forty-two) than he did as a member of the Wellingtons (forty-four) in Toronto's brief 1902 City Amateur League season. The Wellingtons played fourteen games. The Tigers played 153.

The 1907 Detroit Tigers featured future Hall of Famers Ty Cobb, Sam Crawford, and Hughie Jennings. Cobb was only twenty years old and in his second full season. He won his first batting title that year.

Late in his career, Ty Cobb had a six-hit game in St. Louis against the Browns. That is one more hit than Jimmy Archer had for Detroit in the entire 1907 season.

The association of Archer with the Detroit Tigers was brief and bittersweet. On the one hand, he was with the Tigers for the whole season. On the other hand, he hardly played. His Detroit curtain call came in the last game of the 1907 World Series. Archer caught that game, a 2–0 defeat at the hands of the Chicago Cubs. The winners stole four bases with George Mullin on the mound and Archer behind the plate. Batting seventh in the Detroit order, Archer was hitless in three at-bats. He was removed in favour of a pinch-hitter in the bottom of the ninth.

Archer was back in the minors in 1908. His new employers were Buffalo of the Eastern League. Of course, one of Buffalo's rivals was the Toronto Maple Leafs. This meant that Jimmy Archer had the opportunity to play in the city where he grew up.

The Bisons played ten games at Island Stadium that year; Archer caught in six of those games. In twenty-one at-bats at the island, he had just two singles. The 1908 season turned out to be Archer's worst at the plate. He hit .208, and it looked like his stock was falling.

Enter the Chicago Cubs, who were looking for a catcher. They signed Archer and put him on the bench. He did not get into a game until Chicago's sixteenth game of the season, on May 3. In that game, the Cubs were behind 7–1 in the second inning. Archer replaced Pat Moran behind the plate.

Archer sat for two weeks after his Chicago debut and then came in as a substitute for Moran again on May 17. He then rode the pines for over a month before replacing Moran in midgame yet again on June 23. Finally, on June 25, Archer was in the starting lineup. It was the fifty-fifth game of the season for the Cubs. The next day, Archer was behind the plate again as righty Ed Reulbach threw a one-hitter against the Reds.

Quite quickly, Archer became the number-one catcher for the Cubs. There was a good reason for that: he was a great defensive backstop. Snap throws from a squatting position were his forte. Such throws were an innovative anomaly in Archer's time. "The squat throw is a freak delivery, pure and simple," Archer said to *Baseball Magazine*.[93] "It is an accident, the result of an accident," he added, referring to the unfortunate event at the cooperage. "I tried it simply because I had to. I could not throw successfully any other way. My arm is so bent at the elbow that when I stand on my feet I have a tendency to throw down. I cannot control the ball well from that angle."

Baseball Magazine was happy to sing Jimmy's praises. "Archer was undoubtedly the greatest of modern catchers. Mechanically, he was perhaps the greatest catcher who ever lived. Certainly, it will be a long time before his like appears again."[94]

With the Cubs, Archer quickly emerged as a top defensive catcher. The fact that the Pirates and the Tigers let him slip through their fingers was not lost on the Wilkes-Barre *Times Leader*, which noted that Hugh Jennings of Detroit and Fred Clarke of Pittsburgh were great managers, but they made a mistake by not retaining Jimmy Archer.

The Cubs finished the 1909 season with 104 wins, which was only good enough for second place. The Pittsburgh Pirates claimed the National League pennant, six and a half games in front of the Cubs. Pittsburgh beat Detroit in the World Series, four games to three.

While the Pirates and the Tigers were battling it out for baseball supremacy, another interleague best-of-seven series was played in Chicago, an annual competition between the Cubs and the White Sox called the City Series. Up for grabs were bragging rights as Windy City champions. Oh, and prize money. Players were paid a share of the gate receipts, and the winners received more than the losers.

The City Series was a big deal; the games received the same level of local coverage as the World Series. Early editions of newspapers included midgame line scores and play-by-plays on the front page. Attendance at some games was higher than it is at certain major league games today.

The 1909 edition of the City Series started on October 8, just two days after the end of the regular season. The Cubs won the series in five games. Archer played in the first four games and had three hits in twelve at-bats. Total attendance for the series was 74,512. The White Sox received $455.44 per player. Archer and his teammates got $727.32 each. That's the equivalent of more than $21,000 in 2023.

The dust had barely settled on the City Series when the Cubs played a three-game series against the Chicago Leland Giants, an African American club led by player-manager Rube Foster, now acknowledged as the man most responsible for the formation of the Negro National League in 1920. Foster was voted into the Baseball Hall of Fame in 1981.

The Cubs defeated the Giants 4–1 in the series opener. Jimmy Archer started behind the plate. He suffered a minor injury to one of his hands and played centre field in the second game. Foster pitched for the Giants, who scored five runs in the top of the third inning and led 5–2 going into the bottom of the ninth. The Cubs rallied for four tallies and won 6–5. Foster threw a complete game for the Giants. Archer had a pair of singles for the Cubs.

Cubs pitcher Mordecai "Three Finger" Brown stole the show in the third and final game. Brown threw a four-hit shutout and knocked in the game's only run with a sacrifice fly in the third frame. Once again, Jimmy Archer played centre field.

The 1909 season was still not over for Archer. He joined a group of players who travelled to Cuba in early winter to play six games each against Almendares and Havana, the two best teams in Cuba's modest three-team winter league. The tourists were simply called the "All-Stars."

Archer had one of the All-Stars' two hits in a 3–1 loss against Almendares. The opposing pitcher was José Méndez, a righty who went on to play for the Negro National League's Kansas City Monarchs for seven seasons. Méndez was inducted into the Baseball Hall of Fame in 2006.

There were two future Hall of Famers on the pitching staff of the All-Stars. One was Three Finger Brown; the other was Addie Joss of the American League's Cleveland Naps. Joss was only thirty-one years old when he died from tubercular meningitis in the spring of 1911.

The All-Stars were less than halfway through their twelve-game tour when they cut their visit short and returned to the USA. Jimmy Archer told the Buffalo *Courier* why the team came home early: "You know, when a fellow is playing his regular schedule of games in a league it's mighty fascinating, meeting new friends among the players every few days, playing in different parks and always with something to play for."[95] The tour was lacking in variety. "But when we went to Cuba playing the same teams and before the same people with nothing to play for even when the box office receipts were big, it was listless, tiresome work."

Homesickness was a factor, too: "When we saw that we were to put in a Christmas away from home the most of us began to think of snowflakes and Christmas trees and sleigh parties and so on and made up our minds to beat it for home and let Cuba to pot. That's what we did and I am mighty glad of it."[96] Ultimately, the All-Stars played five games in Cuba. They won twice.

Jimmy Archer's first two seasons in Chicago coincided with the last two of one of the most famous double-play combinations in major league baseball history. As a catcher, Archer had one of the best vantage points for watching the trio do their thing. The trio, of course, was Joe Tinker, Johnny Evers, and Frank Chance.

Over the years, baseball broke Jimmy Archer's bones on many occasions. "The thumb has been dislocated and the joint is swelled to double its natural size," Archer said to *Baseball Magazine*. "The index finger has been broken no less than four times, and every joint is gnarled and bent. The bones of the second finger have been shattered on three occasions, the third once, the little finger has been dislocated several times and its joints creak like a rusty hinge."[97] These quotes were from an interview that Archer gave while recuperating from a broken elbow, which was in a plaster cast at the time.

As a hitter, Archer was no superstar. Nevertheless, at least one Hall of Fame hurler preferred not to pitch against him. "I used to find more trouble in beating the Cubs than any other team," said Grover Alexander. "They were a wise old bunch. And although he never led any league in batting averages, I think Jimmy Archer was the worst man at-bat I ever faced."[98] That's "worst" as in "most difficult."

The Cubs made it to the World Series in 1910. Archer looked on from the bench as the American League champion Philadelphia A's won Game One and Game Two. He played first base in a losing effort in Game Three. Archer was back behind the plate in Game Four. The Cubs narrowly avoided a sweep. Chicago was behind 3–2 going into the bottom of the ninth. The Cubs tied it up and sent the game into extra innings. Then, with one out and nobody on in the tenth, Archer doubled. The next batter was retired. Up to the plate stepped Jimmy Sheckard, the Cubs' left fielder. Sheckard slashed the first pitch of the at-bat for a single. Archer scampered home. The Cubs had lived to fight another day. But that was it. The A's won Game Five and were crowned World Series champs. Archer caught Game Five and had a hit in four at-bats. He never played in the World Series again.

The City Series was cancelled in years when the Cubs or the White Sox played in the World Series. Thus there was no City Series in 1910. The competition returned in 1911 and was played every October until 1917, when the White Sox played in (and won) the Fall Classic.

Jimmy Archer played in seven City Series, thirty-three games overall. He had twenty-seven hits in 102 at-bats, a .265 batting average. He hit eleven doubles and scored six runs.

Archer had an extraordinary knack for throwing out wannabe base stealers and picking off baserunners who had wandered too far from safety. According to the Brooklyn *Daily Eagle*, he nabbed 100 runners in 1912 and 105 in 1913. A quarter-century after Archer's retirement, Harry Grayson of the Kingston *Whig-Standard* wrote, "In '12 he threw out 81 would-be base thieves. He tossed out 19 New York Giants in 22 games, and the Polo Grounders ran lickety-split that season."[99]

Jimmy Archer played his last big-league baseball game in 1918. He died in Milwaukee, age seventy-five, of "tuberculosis of the spine." His fellow Cubs catching great, Gabby Hartnett, was one of the pallbearers at his funeral. Archer was inducted into the Canadian Baseball Hall of Fame in 1990.

Vince Barton, Outlaw

Vince "Firpo" Barton was born in Edmonton, and the Barton family moved to Toronto when he was ten years old. He played sandlot baseball in Toronto, and his adopted hometown was where he hung his hat for most of his life. In the 1936 Toronto city directory, Barton's occupation is listed as "professional baseball player."

Seems rather sedentary for an outlaw.

For a while, it seemed that Barton might chase pucks instead of fly balls; he played hockey in flooded playgrounds with the likes of Charlie Conacher, Red Horner, and other members of the hockey Leafs.

Ultimately, he pursued a baseball career. He felt he could go further in baseball than in the rink. He was also concerned about the potential for injury, which was greater in hockey than in baseball.

Ironically, famed hockey executive Frank Selke was largely responsible for Barton becoming a professional baseball player. In addition to his hockey activities, Selke ran a baseball team that Barton played for. Selke sent him to Baltimore when he thought Barton was ready to play professionally. The Orioles were an International League team at the time.

Barton was signed to a pro contract by Jack Dunn in time for the beginning of the 1928 season. That was Dunn's twenty-fourth and last campaign as a minor league skipper. Six of the squads that Dunn managed made a top-100 all-time minor league teams list in 2001. The list was made to celebrate the centennial of the National Association of Professional Baseball Leagues.

Barton went two-for-two for the Orioles in his pro debut. But there was a problem: Dunn could not give his twenty-year-old Canadian prospect enough playing time. As a result, Barton was sent down to the Class D Eastern Shore League (ESL). There, as a member of the Crisfield Crabbers, Barton hit up a storm against the likes of the Cambridge Canners, Easton Farmers, and Parksley Spuds.

Season stats could not be found for the 1928 ESL. However, Crisfield box scores were found for sixteen games in which Barton played. In those games, he batted .393 (twenty-two–for–fifty-six) with seven home runs. Soon after, Dunn shuffled the Orioles deck and Barton was back in Baltimore. The ESL folded in July.

An awful tragedy struck the Barton family in Toronto on April 19, 1930. Alice Barton, eighteen, was killed in the family home by her brother Frank. Alice had been murdered with an axe. Her body was discovered by another brother, Jack.

Alice, Frank, and Jack Barton were Vince's siblings.

Frank Barton was found not guilty of murder by reason of insanity. He had recently been in a traffic accident that left him with a fractured skull; the injury had altered his personality.

Vince Barton, then with the Orioles, was called home to be with his family in the aftermath of Alice's death. Barely a week after the murder, on April 27, he smacked a three-run, pinch-hit home run in Buffalo against the Bisons. He went on to have the best season of his career. Barton had 201 hits, a .341 batting average, thirty-two homers, and eight-three extra-base hits for Baltimore. On July 27, in the first game of a doubleheader against Jersey City, Barton hit three home runs.

In the autumn of 1930, Barton was sold to the Chicago Cubs for a reported $25,000 (the equivalent of about $750,000 as of this writing). He went to Chicago's spring training complex on Catalina Island, about an hour by ferry from the California mainland.

Barton made a big impression right away. In his very first batting practice at-bat, he smashed a baseball some fifty feet beyond the right field fence. It landed on the roof of a house. Chicago *News* correspondent James Crusinberry wrote that the other players were shocked into silence. Ultimately, Barton started the 1931 season with Los Angeles of the Pacific Coast League. He was called up by the Chicago Cubs in July.

Barton made his Chicago debut at Wrigley Field against the New York Giants on July 17. He pinch-hit for pitcher Guy Bush in the bottom of the eighth with the Cubs behind 7–6. Barton was retired by New York hurler Bill Morrell and there was no further scoring. Two days after his debut, Barton got his first big-league hit in a 10–6 loss against Brooklyn.

Barton then slumped badly and was hitting .140 when the Cincinnati Reds rolled into the Windy City on August 3. Facing Reds righty Si Johnson, Barton clubbed his first big league home run and knocked in four runs in an 8–0 route at Wrigley. The next day, in the second game of a doubleheader, Barton hit a pair of round-trippers and had four RBIs in a 7–3 win.

On August 9, in St. Louis, Barton hit a solo homer that proved to be the only run of the game. The home run was his fifth in a week. The gopher ball had been served up by Cardinal righty Paul Derringer. Like Barton, Derringer was a rookie in 1931. He went on to win 223 games in a fifteen-year major league career.

Barton had four hits, including a double and his eleventh dinger, in an 8–7 win over Boston in the second game of a twin bill on September 16. The next day, he was a home run away from hitting for the cycle. He went three-for-four as the Cubs nipped Brooklyn 4–3.

The Cubs hosted the Pittsburgh Pirates for a season-ending double dip on September 27. Pittsburgh was leading the second game 4–2 in the middle of the seventh frame. Chicago rallied for six runs, highlighted by Barton's grand slam, and went on to win 8–4.

Vince Barton finished the 1931 season with thirteen homers and fifty runs batted in as a Cub. He put up those numbers despite playing only sixty-six games for Chicago — less than half the season.

The next year, Barton struggled in Chicago, and his offensive numbers declined. He ended up spending most of the 1932 campaign back in the International League. As it turned out, Barton would never play in the majors again. He was only twenty-four years old.

After a subpar 1933 season, Barton made a comeback of sorts in 1934 as a member of the Newark Bears. He hit thirty-two home runs, good enough for a tie for the lead in the IL. The Bears won the pennant and faced third-place Toronto in the best-of-seven semifinals.

The Leafs won the first two games of the series in Newark and went on to win the series in seven games. Barton was almost invisible at the plate, with a measly three hits in twenty-eight at-bats. He was hitless in twelve at-bats at Maple Leaf Stadium.

Barton returned to Baltimore in 1935 and hit .286 with twenty-seven homers in just 381 at-bats.

Then the bottom dropped out. In 1936, Barton hit neither for power nor for average. He spent part of the season in the Southern Association, one rung below the International League.

By the second week of July, Vince Barton had played his last game of so-called organized pro ball. That is, he would no longer play in a loop that was part of the National Association of Professional Baseball Leagues (NAPBL). Instead, Barton joined the Carolina League (CL), an independent pro league. An "outlaw" league, as far as the NAPBL was concerned.

The modest, six-team league was in its first season in 1936. The teams were located in mill towns. Barton signed with the Kannapolis Towelers. The CL town farthest from Kannapolis was less than 100 miles (160 kilometres) away. Road trips were much longer in many NAPBL leagues.

Full statistical records for the 1936 CL season could not be found. What is known about Vince Barton's stint with Kannapolis that year is that he played at least eighteen regular season games, batting .391 (twenty-five–for–sixty-four) in those games with four homers and twenty runs batted in. He then hit .389 (seven-for-eighteen) in the playoffs. Kannapolis lost their best-of-five semifinal series in five games. Barton re-signed with Kannapolis during the off-season and rejoined them in the spring of 1937.

On the field, Barton was nothing but trouble for opposing pitchers. Off the field, apparently, he was just plain trouble. According to one source, this was something that was known at least as far back as his time as a Chicago Cub.

Barton allegedly exhibited "rambunctious behaviour" that was a thorn in the side of CL club owners. He was chucked out of the Wayside Grill, a well-known establishment in Concord (another CL town). The Kannapolis team's president, Henry Whitley, owned a furniture store. Whitley once locked Barton — and others — in the store to prevent them from getting into trouble.

There was more. Barton missed a substantial portion of the 1937 season because he was recovering from a gunshot wound to his side. He had been shot at a poker house in Kannapolis.

Between the lines, Barton had a great year. He hit .320 and led the CL with twenty-seven home runs. Kannapolis won the CL pennant but was defeated in the postseason finals.

Because of his reputation for off-the-field shenanigans, Kannapolis did not want Barton back in 1938. He signed with the Hickory Rebels.

On August 26 of that year, Vince Barton accomplished a feat that has never been accomplished in major league baseball, before or since. This feat has been achieved only a handful of times in professional baseball. That day, Barton hit five home runs in a single game.

Hickory was playing at home against Kannapolis. Amazingly, Barton grounded out in his first at-bat. He then proceeded to hit one over the fence in each of the third, fifth, sixth, seventh, and eighth innings. One of his homers travelled an estimated 500 feet.

The first three of Barton's dingers came against Mike Roscoe, the right-handed Kannapolis starting pitcher. The last two were served up by Tracy Hart, a southpaw. Barton's blasts knocked in a total of nine runs. Hickory won the game by a 17–8 score.

Barton finished the 1938 season with a .324 batting average and twenty-six homers, just one behind the league leader. He topped the CL with ninety-seven runs scored. The Rebels lost in the playoff finals.

In 1939, Barton joined the Granby Red Sox of the Quebec Provincial League (QPL), another "outlaw" loop. In seventy-three regular season games, he batted .286 with seven homers and fifty-five runs batted in. That July, he played in the QPL All-Star Game.

And so ended the professional baseball career of Vince Barton. He managed Hollinger, a club based in Timmins, Ontario, to a pair of Northern Baseball Association senior championships. He moved to Porcupine, just east of Timmins. Eventually, Barton returned to southern Ontario and died of a heart attack in Port Credit at age sixty-five.

The site www.baseball-reference.com is a fantastic source of baseball stats, but it is not always complete. In Vince Barton's case, at least seventy-one minor league home runs are missing:

7 with Crisfield in 1928
4 with Kannapolis in 1936
27 with Kannapolis in 1937
26 with Hickory in 1938
7 with Granby in 1939

Likewise, 333 hits are not on the site:

22 with Crisfield in 1928
25 with Kannapolis in 1936
96 with Kannapolis in 1937
117 with Hickory in 1938
73 with Granby in 1939

According to the website, Barton hit 132 minor league homers. Add the seventy-one missing dingers and the total becomes a much more impressive 203. Throw in his sixteen big-league bombs and the grand total is 219.

The 333 missing hits increase Barton's minor league total from 764 to 1,097. He had eighty-seven more as a Cub for a grand total of 1,184 as a pro.

It could be argued that numbers like those merit consideration of Vince Barton as a candidate for induction into the Canadian Baseball Hall of Fame.

Doug Beckett: From BP to AAA

Doug Beckett had an uncommon clause in his contract when he signed with the Boston Red Sox. The Red Sox agreed that Beckett would not have to report for duty until after the school year was completed; he was a second-year math student at the University of Toronto when he signed.

"It was the summer of 1966. I was playing junior baseball in Toronto for the Columbus Boys Club," Beckett recalled. "I was nineteen then and I had finally grown into my body."[100]

Suddenly, he was attracting attention from professional baseball people. "A few local scouts were looking at me. Bob Prentice was with the Detroit Tigers at the time. Detroit seemed to have a leg up on everyone else when it came to Canadian talent."

Ron Roncetti was another local scout. "He was affiliated with the Red Sox. As it happened, so were the Toronto Maple Leafs. Ron arranged for me to come down and throw some batting practice, expose me to some of their personnel and to see what professional baseball was all about."

Beckett's routine soon included working out at Maple Leaf Stadium. "Any time that the Leafs were in town and I was available, I would pitch batting practice unless I was pitching for Columbus the day after or the day before. I would shag fly balls in the outfield with the other pitchers."

Beckett was accompanied by Bucky Reed, the Columbus junior team's catcher. "They invited him to come down, too. He generally caught when I pitched batting practice."

Pitching to the Leafs was a memorable experience. "I was a bit awestruck. These guys were the pros. This was the team that my dad used to take me to see. We took advantage of those Sunday doubleheaders. That was a frequent outing for us when I was a little guy."

Beckett remembers one potentially disastrous incident on the field. "Reggie Smith was the most outstanding prospect on the Leafs team. I would pitch at-batting practice speed, and they'd ask me to spin a curveball now and then."

Reggie Smith won the International League batting title that season and went on to swat 314 homers in seventeen major league seasons. "At one point Reggie says, 'Okay, kid, let's see what you've got. Give me your best fastball.' So of course, I reached back and tried to give him a little bit extra, which is never a good thing. The ball went right at his head."

Reggie was okay. "He got out of the way, but he went flying. His helmet went one way. His bat went another way. He got up, dusted himself off, and said, 'Okay, that's enough BP for me.'"

Toronto pitcher Gary Waslewski stands out as someone who treated Beckett particularly well. "He had a very good season that year for Toronto. He had a major league career. In fact, he started a game in the World Series the next season."

Waslewski started for Boston in Game Six of the '67 World Series. He had gone 18–11 as a Leaf in 1966, sharing some pitching tips with Beckett along the way. "I was a fastball-curveball guy, and he showed me a few grips. He showed me how to throw a slider, though I didn't start throwing one for a couple of years."

Beckett signed a contract with the Red Sox in early August of '66. "I remember sitting around the dining-room table with Ron and my mom and dad. My dad grew up in Windsor, so he was a big Tiger fan. He might have been a bit disappointed that I went with the Red Sox rather than the Tigers."

Toronto manager Dick Williams was full of praise when he assessed Beckett for the Toronto *Star*. "He's got a good fastball that moves naturally. He can be taught to throw breaking pitches, but nobody can teach you to throw the fastball."[101]

The Sox were okay with Beckett missing spring training and reporting late for a couple of years. "Reporting late probably put me behind the eight ball a little bit, but at least I was able to work out in a gym before I reported. No game experience, but it was better than nothing."

Beckett signed for $3,000. "There certainly wasn't a lot of money available for a Canadian kid in those days."

Waterloo, Iowa, was the first stop of Doug Beckett's professional baseball career. There, he pitched for the Hawks of the Class A Midwest League.

His season got off to a rocky start. In his debut, a starting assignment against the Quad City Angels, he was yanked in the second inning after walking four batters and giving up three hits and a pair of runs.

Beckett's second start was even worse; he was relieved with just one out in the first inning after surrendering two walks, two hits, and three runs.

At the end of June, Beckett had a 0–4 record. He rebounded thereafter, going 6–3 the rest of the season. A four-hit, 1–0 shutout of Cedar Rapids in late August was his best performance of the campaign. The game was a seven-inning affair, the first half of a doubleheader. Two of the Cedar Rapids hits came off the bat of future Hall of Famer Ted Simmons, who had recently celebrated his eighteenth birthday.

Beckett returned to the Hawks in 1968. That season, his new teammates included pitcher Bill "Spaceman" Lee and catcher Carlton Fisk.

Lee was just out of college, but he was already ruffling the feathers of baseball's establishment. "Bill Lee once called Rac Slider, our manager, 'Coach.' Rac said to Lee, 'You can call me "Rac." You can call me "Skip." But don't you ever call me "Coach." It's a U.S. college thing. You didn't call the manager 'Coach' in pro ball. At least not then. Bill's reply was, 'Okay, Coach!'"

Bill Lee's time in Waterloo coincided with one harsh punishment that Slider gave to his hurlers. "We had a night game after a seven-hour bus ride that got us in at something like three o'clock in the morning. We'd probably lost a few games on that trip, so Rac had all the pitchers report to the ballpark at eight o'clock a.m. to run sprints. Bill Lee was the starting pitcher that night. He threw a two-hit shutout. He was soon on his way up." Lee ended up pitching for Boston for ten years, then another four for Montreal.

Unlike Lee, Carlton Fisk spent the whole season in Waterloo. "I knew that he was highly respected as a prospect in the organization. I wouldn't say that he was fast-tracked, but he was on the move. Nothing was given to him."

Fisk understood the significance of fraternizing with his pitching staff. "He hung out with the pitchers, and that makes a big difference when you are pitching to a catcher who does that."

Beckett briefly pitched at AAA Louisville in 1969 and again in 1970. This team was the former Toronto Maple Leafs. Beckett's batterymate in this one particular game was Bob Montgomery, who had caught for the Leafs in '66 and '67.

"I was pitching to Steve Demeter," recalled Beckett. Demeter was nearing the end of a nineteen-year pro career in which he hit 272 home runs, including sixty-eight as a Leaf between 1960 and 1963.

Beckett continued, "I was working on a slider at the time, but I didn't have confidence in it. Anyway, Bob Montgomery put down three fingers for a slider. I shook him off, and I guess I wasn't supposed to do that. He was a veteran, and I was just a rookie up from A ball."

The pitcher versus batter battle quickly became a pitcher versus catcher battle. "So he puts a three down again. I shook him off again. I really didn't want to throw that pitch. So he puts a three down a third time. This time, I thought, okay, so I threw Demeter a slider. Demeter ripped it for a double."

Doug Beckett pitched in the minors for four years. He never made it to the big leagues, but he did pitch for the Toronto Maple Leafs for two years. Those were not the International League Leafs. Rather, they were the Ontario Senior Intercounty Baseball League semipro team. He was with the Intercounty Leafs when they won their first league title in 1972.

Gladys Davis: The Scarlet Pimpernelle

Toronto's Gladys "Terrie" Davis (née Anthony) won the 1943 All-American Girls Professional Baseball League batting title. That was the league's first year. Davis hit .332 and was the regular shortstop for the Rockford Peaches, who finished the season at the bottom of the four-team loop.

Davis was just twenty-three years old when she first suited up for Rockford, but she had played senior softball since she was a teenager. Actually, she did more than simply play. She excelled. In 1937, in her mid-teens, she was awarded a silver tea service for winning the batting crown in the Olympic Ladies Senior Softball League. Davis hit a hefty .470 for Langley's that season. Langley's swept the best-of-seven playoff final series at Sunnyside.

In 1938, Davis left Langley's and joined a team called Sunday Morning Class. That season, "SMC" won the Ontario provincial championship and participated in the Amateur Softball Association of America Nationals Tournament in Chicago.

Davis and her SMC teammates played in the nationals again in 1941 and finished fourth in a field of thirty-six teams. The competition took place in Detroit that year and in the following year as well. Only nine teams participated in the '42 Nationals. SMC finished last, winning one of three games.

Sunday Morning Class returned to Detroit in 1943. Gladys Davis was not a member of the team that year. Instead, she was playing professional baseball.

Davis was one of some 200 players who descended on Chicago for tryouts. She won one of the sixty available roster spots. The All-American Girls Professional Softball League ("Baseball" later replaced "Softball"), her new employer, was supported by Philip Wrigley, the chewing gum mogul. Each team was to have a roster of fifteen players. Each player was contractually committed to her team for the duration of the season. Moonlighting of any sort was not allowed.

Players were assigned to teams with a view toward making the level of parity in the league as high as possible. Davis and the rest of the Peaches did not arrive in Rockford until just a few days before the beginning of the regular season.

Opening Day for the Peaches was May 30, a Sunday doubleheader in South Bend, Indiana. Davis started at shortstop and batted in the cleanup spot. Rockford manager Ed Stumpf, a former minor league catcher, was confident that Davis would be one of the better hitters in the new loop. If the first game of this Opening Day twin bill was any indication, he was right. Davis had a pair of hits and a sacrifice fly, but Rockford lost the game 4–3 in thirteen innings. Davis had a busy game in the field: five putouts, five assists, and an error.

Davis had a good game at the plate in the nightcap as well. She had a single and a triple, knocked in a pair of runs, and stole a base. Rockford scored four runs in the top of the eighth inning to go ahead 9–8. South Bend responded with a four-run outburst of their own in the bottom of the frame and held on to win 12–9.

The first no-hitter in the fledgling league's history took place at Rockford on June 10, thrown by Olive Little, a Manitoban. Little struck out eight and walked five as the Peaches defeated Kenosha 7–2. Rockford made five errors in the game. Davis had three hits.

On June 12, at South Bend, Davis clubbed two triples and four hits in all. Rockford lost 9–4.

The league's first All-Star Game took place at Wrigley Field on July 1. It was played in the evening under a temporary set of lights. It was the first ever night game at the stadium. Since there were only four teams in the AAGPBL, each All-Star squad consisted of players from two league teams. Wisconsin was made up of players from Kenosha and Racine, while Illinois-Indiana was comprised of Rockford and South Bend players. Gladys Davis played shortstop for Illinois-Indiana and went hitless in four at-bats.

On August 15, Olive Little threw her second no-hitter of the season. Unlike her first, this one was a shutout. The Peaches won 2–0 at South Bend. It was a rare 1943 outing for Gladys Davis. She went hitless.

The Peaches and their opponents were contractually bound to various "no-no's" that had nothing to do with baseball. For example, no liquor, no obscene language, no driving one's own car beyond city limits, no social engagements unless approved by the team chaperone, no trousers, and no haircuts that could be classified as "boyish bobs." Transgressions meant a $5 fine for a first offence, $10 for a second offence, and a suspension for a third.

It was not a no-no to sport a pair of very long braids that might have been the inspiration for "Pippi Longstocking." That's just as well, or Davis would have been fined for sure.

There were team groupies, apparently. These were referred to as "Clubhouse Clydes" and "Locker Room Leonards." There was no shortage of admirers. "Wherever we were, guys used to hang outside our hotel, hollering up to us," one AAGPBL alum admitted in 1992. "We'd throw our bras down to them."[102] This specific activity was not, apparently, a no-no.

Olive Little narrowly missed a third no-hitter on the last day of August. It was the first game of a doubleheader against Kenosha, scheduled to be a seven-inning contest. Kenosha's lone hit came with two out in the sixth frame. Little settled for a 5–0, one-hit win.

Gladys Davis cooled off as the season wore down, but she still won the batting title by a wide margin. Coming up empty at the plate rankled Davis.

Eddie Stumpf told the Milwaukee *Journal* that getting walks instead of base hits made her angry, and she would chew out pitchers on her way to first base.

The AAGPBL expanded to six teams in 1944. Davis returned to Rockford but moved on to the Milwaukee Chicks, one of the two new clubs, in midseason. She was in the right place at the right time. The '44 schedule was cut into two halves. The winners of each half played a best-of-seven playoff series to determine the league championship. Milwaukee won more than two-thirds of their games to win the second half. The Kenosha Comets, first-half winners, had a dreadful second half. Going into the finals, momentum favoured Milwaukee.

Kenosha won the first two games of the series. Milwaukee gained an emphatic 7–0 victory in Game Three. Davis had three hits and three stolen bases in the one-sided contest. The Chicks then levelled the series with a 7–1 Game Four win. Coming back from two heavy defeats, the Comets crushed the Chicks 9–0 in Game Five. Milwaukee had their backs to the wall.

An estimated 2,130 fans were on hand for Game Six. The game was scoreless through ten innings. Kenosha scored once in the eleventh, only for Milwaukee to score twice in the bottom half of the frame and even the series. Gladys Davis scored the winning run on an overthrow at third base. Connie Wisniewski, the Milwaukee hurler, gave up just three hits.

The Chicks clinched the series with a 3–0 win in Game Seven. All three runs were unearned. Wisniewski threw another three-hitter, despite not logging so much as a single strikeout. The box score for the game indicates that Wisniewski induced a heap of ground-ball outs. The Milwaukee first baseman had twenty putouts. The attendance was 3,166.

Wisniewski pitched a complete game in all four of Milwaukee's victories. Davis had at least one hit in all but one game of the finals. In all, she had nine hits in twenty-eight at-bats. That's a .321 batting average, not exceedingly high for a series of seven games. However, it is worth noting that Milwaukee hit just .178 as a team. In that context, .321 is outstanding. For Davis, it was a pleasing way to finish a disappointing summer. She batted only .246 in the regular season.

Gladys Davis lived three lives. In addition to her baseball and family-related responsibilities, she had her own interior design business. She was married and had a young son who was of primary school age. She took the 1945 season off and changed clubs again when she became a member of the Muskegon Lassies. She did not join the '46 Lassies until midseason. According to a story in the Muskegon *Chronicle*, this was because she had to find someone to manage the business while she was away playing ball.

The Lassies finished the 1946 season twenty games under .500 and twenty-eight games behind the first place Racine Belles. Davis batted just .202 and appeared in just over half of Muskegon's games. She was mostly a shortstop, but she spent time at second base, third base, and right field as well.

As far as the AAGPBL was concerned, Davis was finished. She returned to Toronto, where she jumped through a mess of administrative hoops in order to be reclassified as an amateur softball player. Her AAGPBL experience had rendered her a professional.

When Davis finally got her amateur status back, she rejoined Sunday Morning Class. SMC played in front of crowds that were as big as, or bigger than, those at AAGPBL games. For example, some 3,500 fans saw SMC lose an eleven-inning, 2–1 contest against a team from Phoenix, Arizona, played in late June of 1948 at Oakwood Stadium, near the corner of Oakwood Avenue and St. Clair Avenue West. In addition to softball, the stadium was used for football and stock car racing.

Gladys Davis remarried, became Gladys Smith, and had another child. She played for and managed several softball teams, at least until the mid-1950s. Then, at least as far as softball is concerned, her trail goes cold. A gathering of Canadian former AAGPBL players took place when they were inducted into the Canadian Baseball Hall of Fame as a group, at St. Marys, in 1998. Gladys Davis Smith (née Anthony) was not among them. Her fate was unknown.

The AAGPBL played its final season in 1954. The league has its own website. Each former player has a dedicated page. Included on each page is a link to an obituary, if applicable. Until recently, there was no obit for Gladys "Terrie" Davis. Her fate was unkown.

What happened to her? For now, the answer to that question could be described by a parody of the famous poem "The Scarlet Pimpernel":

They seek her here, they seek her there;
Clubhouse Clydes seek her everywhere.
Be she in Hogtown, or Racine with the Belles?
That elusive shortstop, Pimpernelle.

In fact, Davis passed away in Fort Erie, Ontario, in 1991. She was 72.

Doug Gostlin: "Goose"

Doug Gostlin was nicknamed "Goose," like former major league great Goose Goslin. But unlike Goslin, Gostlin was a pitcher. A pitcher who threw his share of goose eggs.

Gostlin made the news at the age of sixteen when he threw a seven-inning no-hitter for Bonitas, a Toronto sandlot team, in 1946. He faced the minimum twenty-one batters, striking out eleven and walking just one. The lone baserunner was subsequently caught stealing.

Two years later, Gostlin was chosen to be a member of the North Toronto Baseball Association All-Stars. The All-Stars faced a visiting team from Brooklyn at Maple Leaf Stadium. The game was to be followed by a banquet at the swank King Edward Hotel, if you please.

Goose started on the mound but ultimately failed to live up to his name. He was tagged with the loss as the Torontonians lost 4–2. Gostlin could be forgiven for his subpar outing against the American tourists: The previous day, he had pitched a four-hit shutout for Earlscourt in a West Toronto Senior Baseball League (WTSBL) game.

Gostlin threw a three-hit shutout in the WTSBL playoffs. A week later, he allowed four hits in a 0–0 tie that was called for reasons unknown, presumably a curfew, bad weather, or darkness.

In 1950, the year that he turned twenty, Goose was recruited to play for the Delisle Gems of the semipro Northern Saskatchewan Senior Baseball League. The NSSBL consisted of two teams in Saskatoon and one each in Delisle, North Battleford, Prince Albert, and Colonsay. Delisle is about twenty-eight miles (roughly forty-five kilometres) southwest of Saskatoon.

Gostlin came to the attention of the Gems via a hockey connection. Sid Smith, star forward for the hockey Leafs, knew about Gostlin and recommended him to Max Bentley; Smith and Max Bentley were hockey teammates in Toronto.

Max was one of the Bentley brothers, the best-known hockey siblings of their time. Max, Doug, and Reg all played in the NHL. The brothers were from Delisle and played baseball for the Gems during hockey's off-season.

The *Leader-Post*, Regina's daily newspaper, predicted that the 1950 Delisle Gems would have four Bentleys in the lineup on a regular basis, on the corners of the infield and in two of the outfield positions. A fifth Bentley was to share the catching chores.

Goose faced one particularly well-known hockey player in a mid-June game against the Saskatoon Legion nine. Batting fifth and playing first base for Saskatoon was none other than Gordie Howe. "Mr. Hockey" hit a two-run single against Gostlin that was pivotal in the Legion's 5–4 victory.

Howe also stole a base in the game. It's not known if he slid in with his elbows up.

The NSSBL final pitted the Gems against the Saskatoon Cubs in a best-of-five series. Delisle swept the series in three games. Gostlin whiffed eighteen and allowed one hit in the clincher, an emphatic 7–1 Delisle victory.

Goose Gostlin was not scouted. In the spring of 1951, he went to Vero Beach, Florida, and asked the Dodgers to give him a tryout. The Dodgers granted his request, liked what they saw, and signed him to a contract.

Gostlin made his pro debut for Newport News of the Class B Piedmont League. Gostlin started on the mound on Opening Day and allowed just six hits, going the distance in a 4–3 win at Richmond. Goose was wild, though; he issued seven free passes.

Newport News manager Clay Bryant, a former pitcher who won nineteen games for the Chicago Cubs in 1938, had employed some psychological strategy prior to Goose's debut. Bryant did not tell Goose that he was starting until twenty minutes before game time. "I didn't want him to get nervous," Bryant told Shelley Rolfe of the Richmond *Times-Dispatch*. "I know how it is. When I was starting out I used to get real nervous before a game I was supposed to pitch."[103]

Gostlin thoroughly earned the win. With two runners on base and two out in the bottom of the ninth, Richmond manager Billy Herman put himself into the game as a pinch-hitter.

Herman, forty, had been a major league second baseman for fifteen years. He owned a .304 career big-league batting average. Sure, he was past his prime, but he was still a batter to be feared; he had hit .307 for Oakland of the Pacific Coast League in 1950.

Clay Bryant, who had played for the Cubs with Herman, rushed to the mound for a chat with his green hurler. "I said, 'Kid, he's got two arms and two legs and two hands just like you. Don't be afraid.' He wasn't."[104] Herman was retired. Game over.

Goose's opening day performance turned out to be his best with Newport News. In his next start, he walked nine batters in seven innings at Lynchburg. That game marked the beginning of a twelve-day stretch in which he pitched in five games.

In mid-May, Gostlin was optioned to Hornell of the Class D PONY League. Barely a month after joining Hornell, Goose had a 7–1 record and had pitched a three-hit shutout at Jamestown. He and two other hurlers led the PONY League with seventeen wins each in 1951.

Goose's performance at Hornell earned him a promotion to the Lancaster Red Roses of the Interstate League, a Class B organization, in 1952. He had climbed two rungs up the ladder in one fell swoop.

It was with the Red Roses that Gostlin pitched what would end up as the best game of his pro career. On August 5, the Red Roses were hosting a doubleheader against the Sunbury Giants. The twin bill was to consist of a seven-inning contest, followed by a nine-inning game.

Lancaster's manager was Jim Bivin, a retired journeyman pitcher who had thrown a pair of no-hitters in a professional playing career that spanned seventeen years.

Bivin might have endured an acute case of déjà vu as the first game unfolded. Goose was unhittable. The Giants could not touch him. The seventh inning came, and Gostlin was three outs from a no-hitter. Lancaster's Toronto twirler later admitted that he was "pretty tense" when he walked to the mound in the seventh.

Three outs later, Doug "Goose" Gostlin, of Toronto, had thrown a no-hitter.

A hat materialized and was passed amongst members of the crowd, all proceeds to Goose. A total of $81 was collected. That is the equivalent of over $900 as of this writing.

Gostlin's day was not over yet. In the top of the eighth inning, in the second game, Sunbury was ahead 5–4. Goose was summoned from the bullpen. There were two outs and two runners on base.

George Franko, the Giants second baseman, hit a two-run single to increase the Sunbury lead to 7–4. Goose then whiffed third-sacker Don Bailey for the final out. Hornell responded with a five-run rally in the bottom of the inning and hung on to win 9–7. Goose faced only two batters but got credit for the win.

Two victories, including a no-hitter, were not a bad day's work.

For the second year in a row, Goose Gostlin finished the season in a three-way tie for the lead in victories. The Interstate League trio logged eighteen wins each.

Gostlin was promoted again, spending 1953 with Elmira of the Class A Eastern League. He pitched at the A and AA levels in both 1954 and 1955. Over the years, he morphed from a starter into a reliever.

In 1956, Gostlin returned to Saskatchewan. This time, he joined the Saskatoon Gems of the Western Canada Baseball League (WCBL), an "outlaw" independent professional circuit. The Gems finished the season in second place, just a game behind the Edmonton Eskimos.

Goose finished second in the WCBL with eleven wins and a 2.33 ERA. He led the loop with thirteen complete games. Max Bentley played occasionally for the Gems in '56.

Gostlin split the 1957 season between the WCBL, the Western League, and the Northwest League. He fared poorly wherever he went. In Saskatchewan, he went 2–2 with a 6.92 ERA in ten games. The 1957 campaign proved to be Goose's last as a pro.

The list of Canadians who have thrown a no-hitter in the minor leagues is small. Oscar Judd, from Rebecca, Ontario (near London), threw one for the Maple Leafs in 1948. Oscar Tuero, Havana-born but raised and taught baseball in Toronto, threw four. Mike Kilkenny and Bernie Beckman each threw one. Goose threw one.

Likewise, few Canuck hurlers have ever topped a league in wins in any given season. Tuero did it twice, as did Gostlin. Goose did it in back-to-back years.

John Hiller, Comeback Kid

The ink was barely dry on his contract when John Hiller threw a no-hitter for Ruscos in the Scarboro [*sic*] Junior Baseball League. Hiller was signed by Detroit Tigers scout Bob Prentice in June of 1962. The nineteen-year-old southpaw was to report to Jamestown of the NY-Penn League in a year's time.

Hiller advanced quickly through the Detroit farm system. He was called up to the Tigers late in the 1965 campaign and made his Detroit debut on Labour Day at home against the Red Sox. Hiller threw a scoreless ninth inning in a 4–1 Boston win.

The following year, Hiller was pitching for the Syracuse Chiefs, Detroit's AAA affiliate. In late May, the Chiefs rolled through Toronto for their first series of the season against the Maple Leafs. The teams played a twin bill at Maple Leaf Stadium on Victoria Day. This was the first opportunity for Hiller's family and friends to watch him play pro ball in his hometown.

The nightcap was a thriller. Toronto led the seven-inning affair 1–0 after six innings. The Chiefs scored twice to take a 2–1 lead. Syracuse skipper

Frank Carswell then handed the ball to John Hiller. This game was Hiller's to win or lose.

Hiller coaxed a fly ball from the first Toronto batter. One away. Al Lehrer, hitting .149 at the time, singled. Bob Sadowski followed with a two-run, walk-off homer. The Leafs had eked out a dramatic 3–2 comeback win. Not the Maple Leaf Stadium debut that John Hiller was hoping for.

Just over a year later, Hiller was back at Maple Leaf Stadium. This time, he was a member of the Toledo Mud Hens, Detroit's new International League farm team. That affiliation survives to this day, as of this writing.

Hiller was summoned to the mound in the home half of the eighth inning. Toledo was behind 7–5. Hiller surrendered a couple of hits and a run, and the Leafs emerged with an 8–5 win.

No save for John Hiller in this game, either, but save opportunities would arise in abundance soon enough. In the meantime, Hiller had a World Series to pitch in and a heart attack to endure.

Hiller was called up to Detroit again not long after pitching for Toledo at Maple Leafs Stadium. He got his first major league win on July 23, 1967. The Tigers were hosting the New York Yankees in the second game of a doubleheader. Hiller came in as a reliever in the fourth inning and got credit for Detroit's 7–3 win. He also had a bases loaded, two-run single in the game. "I don't think I've got any future as a pinch hitter," Hiller joked after the game. "I don't get to bat much. I was only up about eight times last year."[105]

Coincidentally, Hiller's victory was nailed down by Mike Marshall, who rose to prominence as a closer for the Montreal Expos and LA Dodgers in the 1970s. "Iron Mike" logged over 200 innings in a jaw-dropping 106 appearances for Los Angeles in 1974.

Two days after Hiller's first major league win, the Tigers were forced to reschedule a home game against Baltimore. The cause was a sign of the times: rioting.

The 1968 World Series pitted John Hiller's Detroit Tigers against the defending champion St. Louis Cardinals. This was the year in which Cards pitcher Bob Gibson had a microscopic 1.12 ERA. Detroit's Denny McLain won thirty-one games. Carl Yastrzemski led the American League with a .301 batting average.

Hiller made his World Series debut in Game Three at Tiger Stadium. Mayo Smith, the Detroit skipper, inserted Hiller into the game in the top of the eighth. He allowed four hits and a walk in two innings but kept the Cards off the scoresheet. St. Louis won 7–3 and took a two-to-one lead in the series.

The very next day, Hiller was back on the mound. This time, however, he couldn't get anybody out. He was tagged for four runs, three earned, and St. Louis coasted to a 10–1 victory. The Cards were now one win from taking the series.

The Tigers roared back, winning three times in a row to take the Fall Classic in the maximum number of games. John Hiller made no more appearances in the series.

By this stage of his big-league career, John Hiller had settled into the roles of spot starter and long reliever. Between 1968 and 1970 inclusive, he averaged about forty-two appearances, eight starts, and 110 innings pitched. Hiller had no reason to think that things would be different in 1971.

Then, in January of '71, Hiller had a heart attack. He did not think too much of it at first and he neglected to tell his employers right away. Hiller convalesced for over a year. He changed his diet. He lost weight. He changed his smoking and drinking habits.

It took a while, but Hiller finally reached the point where he was ready to pitch again. On July 8, 1972, he made his first pitching appearance since October 1, 1970, pitching three innings of relief, giving up four hits and two runs in a 5–2 loss at Comiskey Park in Chicago. "I was more relaxed than I thought I'd be," Hiller told Jim Hawkins of the Detroit *Free Press* after the game. "I've been more nervous than this on the first day of Spring Training."[106]

One might wonder why it took eighteen months for Hiller to be declared fit for duty. At least part of the reason boiled down to concern for Hiller. He had suffered a heart attack. There was a risk he could suffer another one. This was on everyone's mind because Gil Hodges, Mets manager and former Dodgers great, was killed by a heart attack in April of 1972. The attack was not his first. Baseball people, partly in shock over Hodges' death, hardly wanted a similar fate for Hiller.

Billy Martin had taken over as Detroit's manager while Hiller recovered from his heart attack. Martin had entertained the notion of putting Hiller in his starting rotation. Seeing Hiller throw, Martin was impressed, but the idea of putting Hiller into the rotation quickly fell by the wayside.

Hiller finished the 1972 season with the Tigers. Near the end of that season, Clay Carroll of the Cincinnati Reds set the single-season major league record for saves. Carroll logged thirty-seven of them.

John Hiller had thirteen career saves going into Opening Day of the 1973 season. As the season unfolded, it became clear that Hiller might break Carroll's new record. And that's exactly what he did.

On September 21, 1973, Detroit was hosting the Boston Red Sox at Tiger Stadium. With one out in the top of the sixth and Detroit leading 3–1, Hiller was called in from the bullpen to relieve starter Jim Perry. Hiller was a bit wild, walking four, but he allowed just one hit the rest of the way. Detroit won 5–1. It was his thirty-eighth save, a new single-season record. For his efforts, Hiller won the *Sporting News* American League Comeback Player of the Year Award for 1973.

Hiller's record stood for a decade. Kansas City's Dan Quisenberry smashed it when he amassed forty-five saves in 1983.

Hiller was not finished with getting his name into the record book. In 1974, he set the single-season American League record for wins by a reliever with seventeen. That record was tied by Bill Campbell of the Minnesota Twins in 1976. Also in 1974, Hiller tied the AL single-season record for losses by a reliever with fourteen. This record had first been set by Darold Knowles of the Washington Senators in 1970.

It should therefore come as no surprise that John Hiller also holds the AL record for most *decisions* by a reliever in a season.

Over four decades have passed since John Hiller's last major league appearance. In a slightly different guise, he has pitched as recently as 2022, for the Fort Mackinac Never Sweats, an amateur side that plays nineteenth-century baseball. No gloves. No mound.

Yip Owens: The All-Ugly Club

Imagine that you are a newcomer in the big leagues, standing at the plate. The catcher starts talking to you, and he says something like, "I've got my eye on you." During your next at-bat, the catcher says, "I call you a real good prospect."

Congratulations! You have just been scouted as a potential member of the All-Ugly Club (AUC) managed by Toronto native Frank Walter "Yip" Owens.

Veterans knew about the AUC. When they went to the plate, Owens might say something like, "You know, I'm thinking about making you my captain. You are rising higher in my estimation every time I look at you."

For some players, this sort of one-sided banter went on for years. "You've got what it takes all right, but it happens I've got a lot of class on my club just now," Owens might say to a homely soul at the plate. "You bear down hard and get uglier than [so and so] and I'll put you on. But that's not easy."

When he wasn't managing the AUC, Yip Owens was a workhorse behind the plate. He routinely caught both ends of doubleheaders. On one occasion, when Owens was with the Minneapolis Millers of the American Association, he did this on two straight days.

Yip Owens in 1920.

Having caught four games in two days, Owens assumed that Joe "Pongo Joe" Cantillon, the Minneapolis manager, would give him the day off. With that in mind, Owens and teammate Earl Yingling stayed out past curfew that night.

The next day, before the game, the umpire asked Cantillon who would be forming the Millers' battery that day. Pointing to Owens and Yingling, Cantillon replied, "Those two nighthawks are working again."[107] The Millers won the game. Yip had caught five games in three days.

Owens started his pro career in 1905 with Lyons of the Empire State League. In mid-August of that year, while still a teenager, he was summoned by the Boston Americans, forerunners of today's Red Sox. The Boston pitching staff included the legendary Cy Young. At the age of thirty-eight, Young was old enough to be Yip's father. It is not known if Owens caught Young in the Boston bullpen during his brief stay in Boston. Cy Young had a losing record in 1905. By his standards, that season was … ugly.

After riding the pines for several weeks, Yip finally made his big-league debut. Boston was playing the second game of a doubleheader against Washington at the Huntington Avenue Grounds in Boston. Washington scored four runs in the first, sending Boston starter Ed Hughes to the showers in the process. Hughes was relieved by Norwood Gibson, who promptly surrendered six more runs in the second frame. The game was getting … ugly.

Boston player-manager Eddie Collins gave catcher Lou Criger a rest in the fourth inning and put Yip into the game. Owens threw out a wannabe base stealer and was hitless in two at-bats. Washington scored at least once in every inning except the sixth and cruised to a 14–0 win. Boston mustered just one hit against Washington pitcher Cy Falkenberg.

Yip caught three no-hitters as a pro. The first was in September of 1906, when Owens was with Memphis of the Southern Association. George Suggs was on the hill for Memphis, facing Nashville in the second game of a doubleheader. Owens was behind the plate. Memphis won the game 9–0.

Owens logged his second no-no in August of 1912. Bill Lelivelt held Toledo hitless in a 4–0 Minneapolis victory.

Minneapolis became Yip's adopted home; he played there for ten of the seventeen seasons that he played pro ball.

After four seasons as a Miller, Owens left Minneapolis for a couple of years and played in the Federal League (FL). This "rebel" major league competed for revenue with teams in the National League and American League. The FL did this aggressively by courting some big-name players and putting teams in cities that already had big-league clubs.

Owens joined the Brooklyn Tip-Tops of the FL in 1914 when the loop opened up for business as a third major league. Yip's skipper was Bill Bradley, who had just played three seasons with the Leafs in Toronto. One of Brooklyn's outfielders, Al Shaw, had also spent three summers playing in Toronto.

Yip caught his last no-hitter as a member of the Tip-Tops. Brooklyn hurler Ed Lafitte defeated the Kansas City Packs 6–2. The game was played in mid-September. It was the only no-hitter in the FL that season.

Bill Bradley.

Owens returned to the FL in 1915 as a member of the Baltimore Terrapins. There, he was reunited with George Suggs, whose no-hitter he had caught nine seasons before.

Long after Yip hung up his cleats, a former opponent named Jack Onslow paid him homage. Onslow was another retired catcher and a member of the AUC. "I was the no. 1 catcher on Yip's 'Ugly' club," Onslow told the Minneapolis *Star* in January of 1958. "You had to be ugly to make that team because Yip really scouted 'em. Of course, I sort of sneaked in because Yip would have been the catcher if he hadn't made himself manager."[108]

Owens was a member of the Chicago White Sox in 1909. For part of that season, one of his teammates was a pitcher from Ypsilanti, Michigan, named Frank Owen. His nickname was — you guessed it — Yip. On a couple of occasions, Yip Owen the pitcher and Yip Owens the catcher formed the Chicago battery. As a team, the White Sox had the yips.

Sorry. That joke was … ugly.

William Summers: Billy the Kid

Nowadays, William (a.k.a. Billy, a.k.a. "Kid") Summers would be hard-pressed to recognize much of the Toronto neighbourhood where he grew up. Mind you, that was about 150 years ago. The house on Denison Avenue where he lived with his parents and siblings is long gone. Many of the street names have changed. In fact, Denison is one of the few streets in his old stomping grounds that hasn't been renamed.

Even baseball, the sport that Kid excelled at, was different when he headed east to join the Kingston team in the new, professional Eastern International League (EIL). That was back in 1888. In those days, a walk was awarded after five balls. The pitcher was only fifty feet from the batter. Spitballs were legal. Foul bunts were not counted as strikes. The plate was square-shaped.

Kid was a catcher. When he first cut his teeth as a pro, there were no padded, pillow-like mitts for catchers. Mind you, that would change soon thanks to Harry Decker, a big leaguer who had caught for the International Association's Toronto nine "over the Don" that same year. More about him later.

The EIL at least partly lived up to its name. Two of its four clubs, Kingston and Belleville, were based in Canada. The other two, Watertown and Oswego, were American.

Robert Eilbeck, the Kingston manager, had summoned Kid from Toronto a couple of games into the regular season. Eilbeck was about as grizzled as a baseball veteran could be in eastern Ontario in 1888. Way back in 1873, he led off and played first base for St. Lawrence, Kingston's top amateur side, against the touring Boston Red Stockings. The result of that game was pretty much what you might expect when a top pro team plays an amateur squad that has only been together for a short time. Boston won 55–10.

Kingston was away at Watertown when Kid joined them. Getting from Toronto to Watertown was no small feat in 1888. The journey was partly by rail, partly by boat. Kid was plenty weary when he finally made it to the Watertown diamond. He had gotten only one hour of sleep the night before. Since this could be his first professional game, his adrenalin level was high.

Sure enough, Eilbeck inserted Kid into the starting lineup that day. Kid caught and batted fifth. He got a couple of base hits, but Watertown spoiled his debut by winning the game 7–5.

The season had barely started when there were problems. Watertown and Oswego had used pitchers who were under contract to other clubs, which was a direct violation of EIL rules. The pitchers in question were from stronger leagues as well. The American EIL clubs responded to Eilbeck's complaint by explaining that they had not been given the chance to sign eligible pitchers. After all, opening day was only a fortnight after the league was formed.

Four days after his debut, Kid had a four-hit game in a 17–15 loss to Oswego. Then, in a mid-June 15–4 win over Oswego, he collected five hits. Included was a double, his first extra-base knock of the season.

By now, only Oswego was out of the Eastern International League pennant race. They were also out of luck financially. A week after Kid's five-hit performance, the Oswego club folded. The league was down to three teams.

In early July, Kingston's new uniforms arrived. The shirts had red and white vertical stripes. The trousers were blue. The socks were red.

Alas, no amount of sartorial elegance was going to save the league. Watertown also dropped out of the league. The Belleville team moved to Brockville. Soon afterward, they folded as well.

Spalding had crafted and donated a large pennant for the league. It was twenty-five feet long and had blue and white bunting and the word "Champions" in the middle. Kingston held the pennant with a view toward presenting it to the champs at the end of the season. Now, as the last men standing, they could cheaply claim and fly the pennant while crickets chirped and tumbleweeds tumbled at the league's former grounds.

There was plenty of "chirping" of another kind as the clubs went under one by one. Club officials kicked up a fuss. Local newspapers lapped it up. For example, the Kingston *Whig-Standard* published a letter from the Belleville *Intelligencer*. The letter claimed that, among other things, the Oswego club had stolen over $100 from their Belleville rivals. The same letter blamed Brockville for the league's ultimate collapse.

If all else failed, one could always blame the umpires. The abilities of the lone ump at a Kingston-Watertown game were described as follows in the *Whig-Standard*: "The ump knew as much about ball as a ten-year-old baby, but his decisions were about as rank one side as the other."[109]

In a mid-June game between Watertown and Oswego, the Watertown manager was allowed to umpire. The alternative, according to a quote of the Oswego *Times* in the *Whig-Standard*, was a fellow who had officiated at a recent game between the two clubs. He was "a man with no brains and less conscience, who disgusted the Watertown people with his efforts to steal the game from Oswego."[110]

Kid acquitted himself well in his first season as a pro. In twenty-one games that he played for which box scores were found, Kid hit .364 in ninety-nine at-bats with twenty-two runs scored and twenty-four stolen bases. He batted cleanup in most of the games. In addition to his catching duties, he spent some time in the outfield and at third base.

Before Kid and his teammates parted company, they played three exhibition games against the barnstorming African American team, the Cuban Giants. Kingston won two of the games. Then it was time for Kid to go home. The Eastern International league was deader than a late-nineteenth-century baseball that had been in use for a full nine innings. He would have to find another league, another town.

Bob Eilbeck did not pursue a career in baseball management. Eventually, he heeded the call of the Klondike gold rush. He did not get rich panning for gold, but he did become the first sheriff of the Yukon. His jurisdiction was the entire territory — not just a town.

• • •

There was a brief note in an early March 1889 edition of the Buffalo *Courier*. "Kid Somers," a Toronto player, had signed with Springfield. Was this Kid Summers of Denison Avenue?

Following Kid's pro baseball odyssey becomes a bit tricky here. For starters, "Springfield" is a common city name in the United States. Multiple cities named Springfield had a pro baseball team in 1889. Which Springfield did Kid Summers play for during that season, if any?

Three variations of Kid's surname appear in box scores in the years that Kid played: "Summers," "Sommers," and "Somers." There were other professional baseball players in 1889 with those surnames. Newspapers of the time often referred to ballplayers by their last name only.

Thankfully — and mercifully — the Altoona *Times* published a team roster in February of 1890. Included on that city's team was William Somers, age twenty-one, from Toronto. The roster included each player's 1889 club. The entry for William Somers was "Springfield, O." Jackpot. Kid Summers and William Somers were one and the same. He played in the Tri-State League (TSL) during the 1889 season. That league included a team in Springfield, Ohio.

There were six teams in the TSL. The other five were Canton, Dayton, Mansfield, Hamilton, and Wheeling. Only Wheeling is not in Ohio. In 1889, "Tri-State League" was a misnomer.

Kid usually patrolled centre field in the TSL. The "Somers" variation of his surname was used regularly in the newspapers. Springfield finished in second place with a 60–48 win–loss record, nine games behind Canton.

The TSL had proved to be much more reliable and stable than the Eastern International League. All six teams played a full season.

Player stats for the 1889 TSL are hard to come by. The *Sporting Life*, baseball's primary information source in the late nineteenth century, did not publish box scores for the TSL that season. Local newspapers sometimes printed box scores that were missing the "at-bats" column. That is a rather key omission.

• • •

Kid's next stop was Altoona, Pennsylvania, of the Eastern Interstate League (EISL). This was another oddly named organization. All six EISL teams were based in Pennsylvania. Altoona opened the season at home with a three-game series against Harrisburg. Then, on May 5, Kid and his teammates went to Harrisburg for the first-ever game in that city's new stadium. The new ballpark was on an island in the Susquehanna River and was accessible by bridge. The stadium has since been rebuilt, but the current Harrisburg pro team plays on the same site to this day.

Crossing the bridge over the river, Kid Summers might have compared the experience with going "over the Don" to see a game at Sunlight Park in Toronto.

In a world where Jim Crow was in the process of slamming the door in the faces of Black professional baseball players, the EISL was partly integrated. The Harrisburg nine included Frank Grant, a twenty-four-year-old native of Pittsfield, in western Massachusetts. Grant had played in the top minor leagues for Buffalo, first in the International League and then in the International Association, from 1886 to 1888. Buffalo's opponents included Toronto. Grant was an excellent hitter and a versatile fielder who could play any position.

The EISL also included an entirely African American team. The York Monarchs were the strongest club in the league. They went on to win over 70 percent of their games in 1890. The Monarchs were led by their second baseman, Sol White. Just twenty-one, White led the Monarchs in batting average, hits, and runs scored. Later in life, he managed several African

American clubs for many years and wrote a well-known book titled *History of Colored Base Ball.* He was inducted into the Baseball Hall of Fame in 2006. Frank Grant was voted into the hallowed halls of Cooperstown the same year.

It was against the Monarchs that Kid hit his first and only home run of the season, on May 24. That is how, remotely, this Canadian celebrated Queen Victoria's birthday. Alas, the homer was in a losing cause. York won the game by a 9–7 score.

Kid was a regular in the Altoona lineup. He caught a bit but mostly played centre field. He batted second for the first two-thirds of the season, then moved to the cleanup spot. Though they were no match for the York Monarchs, Altoona was having a good season. Kid and his team were winning almost 60 percent of their games and occupied third place, close behind second-place Harrisburg.

Then, in late July, it happened. Lock, stock, and barrel, the Harrisburg club jumped to the Atlantic Association. Rather than continue with a five-team league, the EISL folded. The York Monarchs took to barnstorming for the rest of the season.

Without a team for the second time in three years, Kid managed to join Harrisburg. There, his new teammates included Frank Grant and a young catcher named Hugh Jennings. In Jennings's Harrisburg debut, he caught while Grant played shortstop and Kid manned centre field. All three could have been involved in a play in which the ball was hit to centre and relayed to the plate.

Hugh Jennings went on to play in the big leagues for many years, primarily as a shortstop. He batted .401 for Baltimore, then a National League team, in 1896. Jennings drove in 121 runs that year without hitting a single home run. He managed the Detroit Tigers for fourteen seasons and the New York Giants for parts of two more.

Back in those days, major league managers coached third base. Jennings made a reputation as an animated third-base coach. He danced. He whooped. He whistled. His best-known cry was "ee-yah," which was mimicked by Detroit fans when he stepped onto the field. In the off-season, Jennings went to law school. He passed the bar in 1905 and practised law during the off-season. He was posthumously enshrined at Cooperstown in 1945.

For as long as it lasted, Kid must have had fun playing baseball with Hugh Jennings. But when the 1890 Atlantic Association season ended, Grant, Jennings, and Kid went their separate ways. Frank Grant joined Ansonia, an African American team in the Connecticut State League. There, he teamed up with Sol White. Hugh Jennings played for Louisville of the major league American Association.

As for Kid, he joined Dayton of the Northwestern League. Dayton was dropped from that league in early August. For the third time in his four-year pro career (so far), his Opening Day employers failed to make it through the season. A few days before Dayton folded, Kid found work as a member of the Cedar Rapids Canaries of the Illinois-Iowa League. When their season ended, he joined Oconto of the Wisconsin State League.

While at Cedar Rapids, Kid's teammates included a feisty teenage shortstop named John McGraw. Known as "Little Napoleon," McGraw became manager of the Baltimore Orioles (then a National League team) in 1899. Three years later, in midseason, he became skipper of the New York Giants. He remained at that post for three decades, winning three World Series and ten National League titles along the way. McGraw was voted into the Hall of Fame in 1937.

The 1892 season saw Kid splitting his time between Quincy of the Illinois-Iowa League and Chattanooga of the Southern Association. Chattanooga played a higher calibre of baseball than what Kid was used to. The "Chatts," as they were called, had a second Torontonian on the team for part of the season. Larry Murphy, thirty-five, had spent most of the previous year in the major leagues with Washington of the American Association. Murphy was one of the many Chatts who had big-league experience.

• • •

Kid Summers had the proverbial major league "cup of coffee" in 1893. He had returned to the Southern Association and was playing for that league's team in Nashville. The National League's St. Louis Browns summoned Kid, and he arrived on July 31. Kid was filling a roster spot that was vacated when the Browns released Joe Gunson, a catcher. Gunson had made his big-league debut back in 1884 with Washington of the short-lived Union Association.

On August 2, Kid caught for the Browns in an exhibition game in Vincennes, Indiana. Three days later, he made his major league debut at Eclipse Park in Louisville. Kid played left field, made a catch and an error, and the hometown Colonels emerged with a narrow 7–6 victory. The next afternoon, in Cincinnati, Kid went behind the plate. He threw out a runner who was attempting to steal on him, and he made an error. The Browns won 12–8.

That was the end of Kid's cup of coffee. He played a total of eight innings. He was hitless in one official at-bat, was hit by a pitch in his only other plate appearance, and scored a run. He never played in the big leagues again.

• • •

Kid went back to Chattanooga and the Southern Association in 1895. Once again, he had latched on with a team that proved to be unstable off the field. The club abandoned Chattanooga for Mobile, Alabama, in midseason. Two teams, Memphis and Little Rock, dropped out of the league entirely.

Eight years into his baseball career, Kid Summers returned to Denison Avenue for the winter. It was time to rest up and prepare himself for the 1896 season. He was only twenty-seven years old. There was plenty of baseball left in him. If he decided to hang up his spikes, he could be a full-time upholsterer. That was his off-season job. Maybe, just maybe, he'd get another kick at the can. Another trip to the big leagues. Something more substantial than a cup of coffee.

Then, tragically and long before his time, Kid died. The cause of his death was a cerebral hemorrhage, which had followed bouts of typhus and malaria that lasted eleven days.

Ron Taylor: Doctor, Engineer

Okay, trivia fans, name a former major league pitcher from Toronto with a medical degree and an engineering degree. "Ron Taylor," you say? Well done! Now, name another one …

A Torontonian through and through, Ron Taylor played sandlot ball at Talbot Park in Leaside. There, he was scouted by Chester Dies of the Cleveland Indians.

Taylor threw batting practice for the Leafs at Maple Leaf Stadium. The Leafs offered him a contract, but he refused, feeling that he would have a better chance with a major league organization.

After a tryout at Municipal Stadium in Cleveland, the Indians made Taylor an offer that suited him perfectly. The offer included a $3,999 signing bonus. A larger bonus would have forced the Indians to keep him on their roster for a full season, so he would probably languish on the bench. Instead, he would be on a minor league team and get more opportunities to play.

The contract also included a clause stating that Taylor would not have to report to his minor league club until the end of the school year; Taylor was an engineering student at the University of Toronto and did not want baseball to interfere with his studies.

Over the course of six years in the Cleveland farm system, Taylor climbed the minor league ladder from Class D to AAA. Finally, in 1962, Taylor was called up by the Indians and was part of Cleveland's Opening Day roster.

Taylor made his major league debut on April 11, a start against the Boston Red Sox at Fenway Park. The game was a classic pitcher's duel. After nine innings, there was no score. At that point in the game, Boston starter Bill Monbouquette had allowed only one Cleveland hit: a single by Taylor.

Neither team scored in the tenth. Or the eleventh. The Indians were retired in the top of the twelfth. Then, in the bottom of the inning, Carl Yastrzemski tripled over the centre fielder's head. The next two batters were intentionally walked. Right fielder Carroll Hardy then smacked a grand slam to give the Red Sox a 4–0 victory.

Taylor was two-for-four at the plate. He and Monbouquette both went the distance in the game. It was the first twelve-inning complete game shutout in the majors since 1958.

On May 22, Taylor was sent down to the AAA Jacksonville Suns. Jacksonville was in the International League at the time, so their opponents included the Leafs.

On July 2, Taylor started on the mound for the Suns at Maple Leaf Stadium. It was the first game of a doubleheader. Jacksonville opened the scoring with a single run in the sixth. The Leafs tied it in the eighth. The Suns then staged a three-run rally in the ninth. Taylor, still on the mound for Jacksonville, retired the Leafs in the home half of the inning.

The final score was 4–1 in favour of the Suns. Taylor allowed six hits, all singles. He struck out five and walked two. The performance earned him a kiss from his mom and a handshake from his dad.

Taylor started against the Leafs again on July 26. This game was played in Jacksonville. Taylor threw a two-hit shutout and the Suns prevailed 2–0. Both runs scored on a homer by Mike de la Hoz in the bottom of the seventh.

A former Leaf, de la Hoz went on to play parts of nine years in the majors. He and Taylor had been teammates, on and off, since 1958. That year, they were members of the Minot Mallards of the Class C Northern League.

On July 31, back in Toronto, Taylor faced the Leafs again. For the third time in less than a month, he defeated the team from his hometown. The Suns won 6–3. Taylor went the distance; the win improved his record to 8–2.

"He's got a good fastball that sinks naturally, and a good slider, and he can put the ball where he wants," Suns skipper Ben Geraghty said to Neil MacCarl of the Toronto *Star* after the game. "Just give him an idea of how to pitch to the hitters, and he can do the job."[111]

The Indians had told Taylor to work on his overhand curve and changing speeds when they sent him down to Jacksonville. As he explained to MacCarl, "Out in Salt Lake last year, I relied mostly on a slider for a breaking ball because the curve didn't break much in the thin air."

Taylor was 12–4 with a 2.62 ERA when the Indians called him back up at the end of August. After the '62 season, he was traded to the St. Louis Cardinals. In 1964, his second season with the Cards, they played the New York Yankees in the World Series.

The Yankees led the series two games to one going into Game Four at Yankee Stadium. St. Louis starter Ray Sadecki was knocked out of the game in the first inning after allowing four hits and three runs. Roger Craig then pitched four and two-thirds innings of shutout ball. The score was still 3–0 after five complete innings.

In the top of the sixth, Cards third baseman Ken Boyer hit a grand slam off Al Downing (who would go on to give up Hank Aaron's record-breaking 715th career homer in 1974) to give St Louis a narrow 4–3 lead. Cards manager Johnny Keane then gave Ron Taylor the ball. Taylor proceeded to pitch four hitless innings and save the day. He allowed only one base runner, a walk to Mickey Mantle.

Neal Russo of the St. Louis *Post-Dispatch* had some unusual praise for Taylor in the wake of Game Four. "Ron Taylor this day was the greatest stretch runner to come out of Canada since Northern Dancer."[112]

The Cardinals won Game Five to take a 3–2 series lead. Game Six was played at Busch Stadium in St. Louis. New York led 3–1 in the bottom of the seventh. With one out with a runner on second, Taylor was brought in to relieve starter Curt Simmons.

Yankees pitcher Jim Bouton batted next and hit a line drive. Second baseman Dal Maxvill caught it and threw to shortstop Dick Groat, who stepped on the bag before the runner could get back to it. Double play. Taylor was pinch-hit for in the bottom of the seventh.

Taylor's Game Six heroics were all for naught in the end. The Yankees scored five runs in the eighth and went on to win 8–3. The series was now tied at three games apiece.

The St. Louis bullpen didn't see any action in Game Seven. Bob Gibson, the ace of the Cardinals staff, beat the Yankees 7–5. Ron Taylor had himself a World Series ring.

Fast-forward to 1969, and Taylor was back in the World Series, this time as a member of the New York Mets. In the previous seven years, the Mets had finished dead last five times and second-to-last twice.

Game One took place in Baltimore. Taylor pitched two shutout innings, but the Mets lost 4–1.

In Game Two, also in Baltimore, the Mets were clinging to a 2–1 lead going into the home half of the ninth. Mets starter Jerry Koosman retired the first two batters of the inning. He then walked Frank Robinson. Merv Rettenmund ran for Robinson. Koosman then walked Boog Powell.

Enter Ron Taylor. Up to the plate stepped the great Brooks Robinson. Taylor coaxed a ground ball to Ed Charles, the New York third baseman. Charles threw across the diamond to nab Robinson at first. Game saved. Series tied, 1–1. The Mets won the following three games to win the Fall Classic. A second ring for Ron Taylor.

That '69 championship team is nicknamed "The Miracle Mets." Ron Taylor said that the moniker is a misnomer, since they had had one of the best pitching staffs in the major leagues that season and were also very good defensively.

In four career World Series appearances, Taylor threw seven no-hit innings, allowed no runs, and had two saves.

After retiring from pro ball in 1972, Taylor pursued a medical career. He had thought about going into medicine once he finished his engineering degree but was almost in the majors at that time. He decided to give baseball a try for a couple of years and ended up in the big leagues for ten years.

Taylor was accepted into med school at the University of Toronto and got his degree in 1977. He became the team doctor for the Toronto Blue Jays two years later. He fulfilled that role well into the twenty-first century. Dr. Ron Taylor passed away on June 16, 2025, at the age of 87.

Oscar Tuero, Havana Heaver

Oscar Tuero was born in Havana. In June of 1904, he and his family sailed to New York. The passenger list of their ship shows Toronto as their destination. According to the list, Oscar was twelve years old at the time.

In Toronto, Tuero played baseball for teams like the Broadview Boys' Union Club and the Carltons. He suited up in the Don Valley League and the City Amateur League and played at Dufferin Park.

In 1912, Tuero went to Montreal and pitched for a team called the Athletics in a city sandlot league. He returned to the Athletics in 1913. Late that season, he was signed by Jersey City of the International League. Over the course of more than a quarter-century, he would pitch for over twenty professional teams from Class D to the major leagues, racking up over 270 victories and four no-hitters.

Tuero made his pro debut on the last day of August 1913 in Montreal. In the first game of a doubleheader, he pitched five innings of relief, giving up three runs on three hits and a walk. No strikeouts. Jersey City lost by an 8–5 score. Tuero was charged with the loss.

On September 2, in Providence, Jersey City starter Chick Brandom allowed six runs in the first frame and failed to make it through the second. Tuero came in from the bullpen and pitched the rest of the game. He struck out seven, walked three, and hit a pair of batters in a 13–3 defeat.

Tuero got his first start on September 7, a no-decision against Baltimore in Jersey City. Eleven days later, Tuero made his final appearance of the International League season. It was the second game of a doubleheader, scheduled as a seven-inning affair. Tuero went the distance as Jersey City scored a pair in the home half of the last inning to win 3–2.

His brief experience with Jersey City whetted Tuero's appetite for pro ball. In 1914, he joined the Class B New England League (NEL). The eight-team league had some wonderfully named clubs, including the Portland Duffs, Lawrence Barristers, Worcester Busters, Manchester Textiles, and Lewiston Cupids. Tuero pitched for the Duffs in '14 and the Cupids in '15.

Tuero threw two no-hitters for Lewiston in 1915. The first took place on August 7 at home against the more blandly named Lowell Grays. Three Grays reached base in the game, two on errors and one on a walk. Tuero struck out four. Lewiston won 5–0 in the first game of a doubleheader.

The teams agreed in advance that the second game would be only five innings. The abbreviated contest ended in a 1–1 tie. Lowell went hitless again. The Grays scored their run against Lewiston hurler Otto Rettig via a hit batter, an error, a fielder's choice, and a sacrifice fly. Lowell avoided a sweep despite going hitless in a doubleheader.

Lewiston's manager was Arthur Irwin, a Toronto native who had moved to Boston as a child and forged a playing and managerial career that lasted over forty years. Prior to managing Lewiston, Irwin had most recently skippered a pro baseball team in 1908. More about him in another chapter.

Tuero's second no-hitter, on August 31, has acquired a dreaded asterisk over the course of time. This is because Tuero did not allow any hits through nine innings, only to give up a couple in the tenth. First place Portland defeated Lewiston 3–2 in ten innings.

This game was a real heartbreaker for Lewiston fans — and for the Cupids. Portland scored single runs in the third and ninth innings. Both tallies were unearned. Tuero retired the first two Portland batters in the tenth, then gave up a double and a run-scoring single. Lewiston was held scoreless in the home half of the tenth.

• • •

From 1914 to 1917, Oscar Tuero amassed seventy-nine wins and suffered just thirty-six defeats while playing for three minor leagues in the American Northeast. He led the Eastern League with twenty-two wins in 1916. Tuero furnished an impressive 24–7 win–loss record with Wilkes-Barre of the New York State League in 1917. His 156 strikeouts were tops in the league.

Tuero started the 1918 season with Little Rock of the Class A Southern Association and was the starting pitcher in the season opener at Memphis on April 19. After seven innings, the game was scoreless. Tuero had a no-hitter going. In the top of the eighth, Little Rock pushed across a run. There were no hits, no runs for Memphis in the bottom of the inning. Little Rock failed to score in the ninth.

Closing in on a no-hitter, Tuero went to work against Press Cruthers, the Memphis second baseman. Cruthers reached first safely on an error by shortstop Norman "Kid" Elberfeld, the Little Rock player-manager. A forty-three-year-old veteran of almost 1,300 big-league games who was nearing the end of a long-playing career, Elberfeld didn't exactly live up to his nickname any more.

Next up was Dixie Carroll, the Memphis centre fielder. Nearing the halfway mark of his own twenty-year pro career, Carroll bunted Cruthers to second. Fred Bratschi, playing left field for Memphis, then hit an infield single to put runners on the corners. Cruthers then scored on a wild pitch. There was no further damage. In fact, the final score was 1–1. The game was called due to darkness after the eleventh inning. Tuero went the distance for Little Rock and gave up a solitary hit.

Less than six weeks later, on May 30, 1918, Oscar Tuero made his major league debut, summoned from the minors by the St. Louis Cardinals. The Cards were playing at Forbes Field in Pittsburgh. Southpaw Gene Packard started on the hill for St. Louis that afternoon. A few years earlier, Packard had put together a pair of twenty-win seasons for the Kansas City Packers of the outlaw Federal League.

Yes, the St. Louis hurler had previously been Packard of the Packers.

Early on, Packard held Pittsburgh at bay. The Pirates had a slender 1–0 lead midway through the fifth. Then, in the bottom of the fifth, it would not be inaccurate to say that Packard's wheels fell off. Tuero came in to pitch with one out. When the smoke finally cleared, Pittsburgh had scored five times and led 6–0. Tuero finished the game for St. Louis, giving up four hits, two earned runs, and three runs over all in three and two-thirds innings. He walked one batter and struck out none. The final score was 8–0.

The Pittsburgh cleanup hitter that afternoon was a right fielder who went one-for-three with a run scored and a run batted in. He was no slouch as a player, as his .284 career batting average shows. Nevertheless, he shone most brightly as a manager. His name was Casey Stengel.

Batting fourth for St. Louis was twenty-two-year-old Rogers Hornsby. Then mostly a shortstop, Hornsby made a staggering forty-six errors at that position in 1918. That was down from the fifty-two fielding blunders he had made the previous season. Hornsby batted just .281 that year. That's seventy-seven points lower than his career batting average.

Tuero's catcher against the Pirates was Miguel "Mike" González. Like Tuero, González was a Havana native. The Tuero-González tandem was a rare early example of an all-Cuban big-league baseball battery.

One of the umpires that day was Bob Emslie, a native of Guelph. Emslie umpired in the National League for over thirty years. A former pitcher, he won thirty-two games for Baltimore of the (then big-league) American Association in 1884. That remains the record for most victories by a Canadian in one season. Emslie also pitched for Toronto's International League club in 1886. He started twenty-seven games that year and completed all of them.

Tuero was half of an all-Cuban pitching matchup in Cincinnati on September 2. In the second game of a doubleheader that afternoon, the Reds put Adolfo Luque on the mound. Luque, also a Havana native, had pitched for the Leafs in 1915. He and Tuero had shutouts going until the bottom of the seventh. Tuero's control then let him down. Cincinnati scored on a wild pitch, and that turned out to be the only run of the game. Tuero gave up just two hits.

• • •

The 1919 edition of the St. Louis Cardinals included Oscar Tuero from start to finish. The Cards had a new manager that season, Branch Rickey. The new skipper used Tuero as a starter and reliever. Tuero appeared in forty-five games for the Cards and finished the season with a 3.20 ERA in just under 155 innings. His stock seemed to be rising, but it wasn't.

Tuero's pitching repertoire included the spitball. This might have been a problem, since the spitball was banned from the major leagues after the end of the 1919 season. From 1920 onward, only pitchers who were previously acknowledged as spitball throwers would be allowed to throw a wet one.

Why was this a problem for Tuero? After all, he had spent the entire 1919 campaign with St. Louis. Why would he not simply be "grandfathered in" as a spitball user? Tuero answered that very question in a 1930 interview with the *Times* newspaper of Shreveport, Louisiana. According to Tuero, spitball throwers were capped at two per club. Bill Doak and Marv Goodwin, the two leading winners on the St. Louis 1919 staff, threw the pitch. They continued to do so in 1920, while Tuero was consigned to the minors to learn to throw the curveball. "I lost my chance in the big leagues because of the spitball," lamented Tuero. "I believe if I had been given a fair chance with St. Louis, I would be in the major leagues yet. Everyone got to believing I was only a spitball pitcher and it hurt my chances."[113]

After spending most of the 1920 season in the minors, Tuero played for Habana in the Cuban Winter League. Mike González was the club's player-manager. Habana was one of only three teams in the modest league, joined by Almendares (a Havana suburb) and the Atlantic City Bacharach Giants, an independent, African American pro club whose lineup included future Hall of Famers Louis Santop and Oscar Charleston.

The Habana pitching staff included Walter "Lefty" Stewart, a teenager who later pitched for the Leafs for three seasons. Stewart won sixty-three games as a Leaf and lost just thirty-two times. He went on to win over a hundred games in the majors, mostly with the St. Louis Browns.

• • •

The 1921 season turned out to be Tuero's best as a pro. Pitching for the Memphis Chickasaws, he had a fantastic 27–8 win–loss record and led the Southern Association in victories. Memphis won the league pennant to earn a berth in the Dixie Series against Fort Worth, the winners of the Texas League. Fort Worth won the best-of-seven affair four games to two. Tuero lost the sixth and final game by a score of 3–0. He allowed just six hits and chipped in with a pair of singles.

The Reading Keystones of the International League were Tuero's employers in 1924. This was his third and final stint in the IL. He began his pro career in the IL with Jersey City, back in '13. More recently, Tuero had spent part of the 1918 season with the Binghamton IL club. But those tours of duty did not include any games in Toronto. Now, finally, he got a chance to work in his adopted hometown.

His first game at Island Stadium was played on May 13. The next day, the game's box score was published in the *Globe* under a boxed title that read, simply, "Too Much Tuero." That title said it all. The Leafs managed only four singles against the former Toronto sandlot star and were defeated 4–0. The losing pitcher was none other than Lefty Stewart.

On July 11, Tuero played at the island again. He pitched five and two-thirds innings of relief, giving up three runs on five hits in a 6–0 loss to the Leafs. Starting pitcher Jim Clary took the loss. Three days later, Tuero made his last appearance in Toronto in a seven-inning second-game of a double-header. Tuero threw a complete game for Reading but lost 2–1.

• • •

For most of the next four years, Tuero pitched for the Waco Cubs in the Texas League. His third career no-hitter was against the Shreveport Sports in Waco, on June 24, 1925. Tuero whiffed eight batters in the game and walked four. He also hit a double. The game took all of ninety-five minutes to play.

Though he would not have been allowed to throw the spitter in the majors anymore, Tuero was not restricted from using the pitch in the minors. "When I joined the Texas League, I was not really a spitball pitcher but [player-manager] Derrill Pratt wanted me to use it," Tuero explained to the Shreveport *Times*. "He was the boss and I listened. The day I pitched a no-hit-no-run against the [Shreveport] Sports, while serving with Waco, I never threw one spitball. My curve ball was breaking good."[114]

The very presence of Oscar Tuero seemed to be a good luck charm of sorts for Del Pratt, who was back in the minors in 1925 after spending thirteen seasons in the big leagues. He hit forty-three homers in those baker's dozen years. During the four campaigns that Tuero spent in Waco, Pratt hit ninety-nine home runs. Tuero left Waco after the 1928 season, and Pratt's power disappeared as quickly as it had appeared.

Tuero remained in the Texas League and pitched for Shreveport. There, his arm was showing signs of wear. "During the last two months of the 1929 season my arm was very sore," Tuero admitted to the *Times* in July of 1930. "No one really knew what was the matter with me. The only thing the catchers knew when I was on the mound last year was to signal for a spitball or a curve. It wore my arm down. This year I am mixing up the delivery. My arm feels as fine as it did in the spring, and I believe there will be no letdown."[115]

After three full seasons in Shreveport, Tuero embarked on a descent to the low minors that included stops in the West Dixie League, the East Texas League, and the North Carolina State League. He got his final no-hitter in the latter loop, as a member of the Newton-Conover Twins, on August 5, 1937. Tuero was forty-three years old. His victims, the Cooleemee Weavers, lost 2–1.

Oscar Tuero played his last minor league game in 1941 at the age of forty-seven. He pitched in over 700 games spread over twenty-six seasons. Toronto's spitballing adopted son passed away in 1960, a couple of months before his sixty-seventh birthday.

Jimmy Williams, Traveller

Playing winter ball in Cuba was a working holiday for Toronto native Jimmy Williams. The long-time minor leaguer was an outfielder for Cienfuegos during the 1958–59 season.

Students of history might raise an eyebrow at that time period. They would be correct. Jimmy Williams was playing baseball in Cuba when the revolution took place. He arrived in the country when Fulgencio Batista was in power. A few months later, when Williams left, Fidel Castro had seized power.

Jimmy Williams should not be confused with Jimy (with one "m") Williams, the former manager of the Blue Jays.

A multisport athlete at Toronto's De La Salle College, Jimmy Williams was signed to a professional baseball contract by the Brooklyn Dodgers after attending tryouts in Maryland. He had played sandlot ball in Toronto for the likes of the Kiwanis and Columbus boys' clubs.

Williams batted .367 in his first professional season, had fifty-four extra-base hits, knocked in 121 runs, and stole twenty-four bases. Though he never again hit for such a high average in his eighteen-year career, he did bat .300

or better multiple times. Most notably, he hit .330 for the Montreal Royals of the International League in 1955. That was his first year at AAA, and his ninth as a pro.

Like many AAA players and major leaguers during the 1950s, Williams had a winter job: playing baseball. Over the course of his career, he suited up for teams in Panama, the Dominican Republic, Venezuela, and Cuba.

In the winter of 1956–57, Williams manned centre field for the Leones del Caracas. Los Leones won the Venezuelan league championship, which gave them a berth in the Caribbean Series. At the time, that competition pitted the winter league champions of Cuba, Panama, Puerto Rico, and Venezuela against one another. The format of the tournament was a double round robin, followed by a final between the top two teams.

The 1957 Caribbean Series was played in Havana. It was the ninth edition of the competition. Games were played at the Estadio Latinoamericano, where Williams would play for Cienfuegos two years later.

The massive ballpark first opened in 1946 and was home to the International League's Havana Sugar Kings in the summer, from 1954 to 1960, and to the Cuban winter league. Visitors included the Toronto Maple Leafs. Jimmy Williams frequently played against the Sugar Kings at the stadium as a member of the Montreal Royals between 1955 and 1957.

The Estadio Latinoamericano is nestled in an area of Havana called Cerro. In fact, the ballpark used to be called Estadio del Cerro. It is a tremendous structure with one of the largest capacities of any baseball stadium in the world. It is still in use today.

Caracas opened their Caribbean Series account with an emphatic 10–3 victory over Mayagüez, the representatives of the Puerto Rican winter league. Williams went one-for-four at the plate and stole a pair of bases for Caracas.

Marianao, the Cuban league champs, gave Caracas a 7–1 pasting the next day. The day after that, Caracas lost a narrow 2–1 decision to Balboa, from Panama.

On day four of the tournament, Caracas beat Mayagüez 7–3. Jimmy Williams hit a two-run triple in the fifth and scored on a double by Johnny Roseboro, his Montreal teammate. Roseboro went on to enjoy a long big-league career, mostly with the Dodgers.

After splitting their first four games, Caracas had a good shot at a place in the finals. Their next opponents were Marianao. Caracas opened the scoring in the top of the second on consecutive hits by Williams, Roseboro, and shortstop Chico Carrasquel. A member of the Venezuelan Baseball Hall of Fame, Carrasquel played in the majors for a decade. Los Leones scored again in the third inning to go ahead 2–0. Marianao promptly scored a pair of runs in the home half of the frame to tie the game.

There was no more scoring until the top of the seventh, when Caracas pushed across two runs to take a 4–2 lead. But the proverbial wheels fell off for Caracas in the bottom of the ninth. Marianao scored three times for a 5–4 comeback victory.

On the last day of the group round, Caracas would qualify for the finals if they beat Balboa, and Mayagüez lost to Marianao. The latter game turned out to be irrelevant for Caracas as they were defeated 4–0 by Balboa.

Two winters later, Jimmy Williams was in Havana, playing for Cienfuegos. The Cuban winter league was a modest loop containing just four teams: Almendares, Marianao, Cienfuegos, and Havana.

Williams began his commitment to Cienfuegos with an epic car journey. After spending the summer season with the Spokane Indians of the Pacific Coast League, he drove to Key West, Florida, and took a ferry to Havana. The distance from Spokane to Key West is over 3,000 miles (4,800 kilometres).

Once Williams arrived in Havana, he did not have to cope with road trips. All games were played at the Estadio Latinoamericano.

"Cuban baseball was as close to major league quality as you could get," Williams told the Baltimore *Sun* in 1999.[116] Rosters were filled with AAA and major league players. Williams was paid about $1,500 a month in Cuba, comparable to his AAA salary.

The Cienfuegos outfield also included Román Mejías. A Cuban, Mejías hit twenty-four homers for the expansion Houston Astros in 1962. He played for the Toronto Maple Leafs in 1965. The Cienfuegos pitching staff was led by Camilo Pascual, a righty from Havana who won 174 major league games over the course of eighteen seasons.

Williams attended a New Year's Eve party on the last day of 1958. That very date marked the end of Fulgencio Batista's dictatorship. When party guests heard an airplane fly by, someone remarked that it was Batista fleeing the country.

The revolution was fairly quiet for Williams. "Every now and then, you might have heard a little gunfire, but we never felt we were in jeopardy." He added, "I remember on New Year's Day seeing a young man waving a Castro flag and I didn't know what to make of it."[117]

The winter league games planned for New Year's Day were postponed. The schedule resumed after several days. Languishing in last place on New Year's Day, Cienfuegos rebounded slightly and finished in third place.

The schedule was long, seventy-two games. Jimmy Williams suited up for Cienfuegos not long after playing 142 games for Spokane. The Cuban winter season finished in early February, giving players a short breather before spring training. The break was shorter, of course, for the team that won the winter league title and moved on to the Caribbean Series.

Jimmy Williams played pro ball until 1964, then hung up his cleats. He proceeded to manage in the minors for seventeen years, then coached in the majors for eight more. He was first-base coach for the Baltimore Orioles when they won the 1983 World Series. Williams was inducted into the Canadian Baseball Hall of Fame in 1991.

Flatbush Farmhands Aplenty

From the late 1940s until the mid-1950s, a disproportionately large number of Toronto sandlot ballplayers were signed by the Brooklyn Dodgers. Some of the signees played in Brooklyn minor league towns that were a world away from Toronto. All of the players mentioned in this section were Torontonians.

Many of the aspiring Dodgers were signed by a Toronto-based scout named Bill Harris. Harris should not be confused with the former big-league hurler of the same name who was a native of New Brunswick, or the Buffalo Bison who threw a perfect game against the Leafs in 1936. Harris helped to run baseball clinics in Brantford and Welland and was officially hired as Brooklyn's full-time Ontario scout in early 1951, but he was already working in a similar capacity part-time.

As of October 1947, there were seven Torontonians in the Dodgers farm system. An additional seven were from elsewhere in Ontario.

None of the Torontonians signed by the Dodgers made it to Brooklyn. However, some of the players were prominent members of their teams. Their names adorn the minor league record books. Two such players were

Doug "Goose" Gostlin and Jimmy Williams, who are covered in chapters of their own.

• • •

Gordon Roach, a 6'4" righty, pitched a no-hitter for the Eau Claire Bears of the Class C Northern League, on August 28, 1952. Roach was nearing the end of his fourth and final season of pro ball.

The no-hitter came in the second game of a doubleheader, a seven-inning contest in which the Bears defeated the Aberdeen Pheasants by a score of 10–1.

Roach walked eight batters and had as many strikeouts. The Aberdeen run was scored in the third inning, the result of a walk, a stolen base, a throwing error, and a wild pitch.

Wildness plagued Roach throughout his pro career; he walked a hundred or more batters in three of his four seasons, despite never throwing more than 169 innings in a single season. As a rookie, in 1949, he issued a jaw-dropping 147 free passes in just 122 innings.

Roach spent part of 1949 and all of 1950 pitching for the Cairo Dodgers of the Kentucky-Illinois-Tennessee League. Widely known as the "KITTY League," this Class D loop was not yet integrated at the time. All of Roach's teammates and opponents were white.

Cairo (pronounced "CARE-oh") is located at the southern tip of the state of Illinois, where the Ohio River empties into the Mississippi. The Gem Theater, Cairo's downtown movie house, was also segregated — Black customers had to sit in the balcony.

• • •

Mike Witwicki, a right-hand hitting outfielder, played pro ball from 1949 to 1955. In 1953, as a member of the Great Falls Electrics, he led the Class C Pioneer League in runs scored (132) and stolen bases (forty-four).

Before he joined Great Falls, Witwicki played the better part of two seasons for Brooklyn's Cotton States League affiliate in Greenwood, Mississippi.

Witwicki's speed might have proved useful on May 18, 1951. That was Farm Night at Legion Field in Greenwood. Events included a chicken-catching contest, in which a dozen chickens were let loose and captured by the players. In another contest, the players had to capture and hold down a greased pig. Witwicki was spared the egg-throwing contest; that was for pitchers only.

Whether he caught the greased pig or not, Witwicki hit a key double and scored the first of Greenwood's four runs in the seventh frame en route to a 5–2 win over Hot Springs.

Like the KITTY League, the Cotton States League was segregated.

• • •

Haig Lavery was familiar with Greenwood, too, but not the town in Mississippi. The Greenwood that Lavery knew was Greenwood Park in Toronto's east end. He played sandlot ball there.

Lavery played for thirteen teams in a six-year pro career. He made it as high as AAA, briefly, early in the 1954 season. He had tried out for Richmond, a new team in the International League. Richmond hosted a series against the Toronto Maple Leafs about a week into the regular season. Lavery got into five games against his hometown team. He had four hits in nineteen at-bats in those games.

Fast-forward several years, and one could excuse Haig Lavery if he was getting a sense of déjà vu while watching *The Andy Griffith Show* on TV. One of the many towns where Lavery played pro ball was Mount Airy, in North Carolina near the Virginia border. Mayberry, the fictional setting of *The Andy Griffith Show*, was modelled on Mount Airy; Griffith was from the town. As a student, he patronized a local luncheonette called Snappy Lunch, which is mentioned in an episode of the program. It's still in business today.

• • •

Moe Galand had a short but successful pro baseball career, playing in the Brooklyn farm system from 1951 to 1953. He batted .307 overall. As a rookie, playing for the Sheboygan Indians, he led the Class D Wisconsin League with fifteen triples.

In June of 1953, Galand was playing for Hornell of the PONY League. In a 16–5 drubbing of Bradford, Galand went six-for-six. All of his hits were singles.

Galand was also an accomplished hockey player and played at the "senior A" level for several seasons. He also played for the Clinton Comets of the Eastern Hockey League, a defunct minor pro league.

• • •

Murray Richardson played junior ball in Toronto for a team called Pete Woods. In their 1947 Ontario Baseball Association (OBA) quarterfinal, Richardson was summoned from the bullpen after his opponents scored four runs in the second inning. Richardson threw no-hit ball for the rest of the game.

A southpaw, Richardson pitched Pete Woods to the provincial finals against a team called the Kitchener Rangers. Richardson threw eighteen innings in three days, striking out twenty-five and giving up just twelve hits. But it wasn't enough. Kitchener won the OBA junior championship, taking the best-of-three final series in two games.

In 1948, his first season as a pro, Richardson was sent to Greenwood, Mississippi. He had an excellent year: a 13–6 win–loss record, a 3.70 ERA, and a solid 3.4 walks allowed per nine innings.

Richardson's control deserted him in 1949. That year, he averaged 6.2 walks per nine innings. That figure rose to an alarming 7.3 in 1950. That was his final year as a pro.

• • •

Ted Seddon, a righty hurler, also had problems with his control. Seddon played just one season in the minors, in 1947, as a member of the Kingston Dodgers of the Class D North Atlantic League. That's Kingston, New York, which is about an hour's drive south of Albany.

Seddon had a fine 13–4 win–loss record for Kingston, but he walked an average of 6.2 batters per nine innings. He threw two consecutive shutouts. The Dodgers won the North Atlantic League pennant, finishing four games ahead of second-place Carbondale. Kingston was then upset in their best-of-seven playoff semifinal series against Peekskill, four games to one.

• • •

Billy Weir was a left-handed, power-hitting first baseman who played sandlot ball in Toronto for Staffords of the Viaduct Major Baseball League. He should not be confused with the Billy Weir who pitched a no-hitter for Toronto in 1939.

Weir was signed by Bill Harris in July of 1951, shortly after a set of tryouts in Brantford. He began his pro career in 1952 with the Hazard Bombers of the Class D Mountain States League. Hazard is in Kentucky, about a two-hour drive southeast of Lexington.

The Bombers ran away with the pennant, winning over 70 percent of their regular season games. They were defeated by the Morristown Red Sox in a best-of-five semifinal, three games to one. Weir led his team with twenty-seven doubles and ten triples. He missed just one of Hazard's 119 games.

In 1953, Weir clubbed twenty-one homers for Hornell of the PONY League and was voted to the Second All-Star Team. Hornell finished the season in second place but was swept in the best-of-five semis by third-place Hamilton.

Weir was promoted to the Bakersfield Indians, Brooklyn's farm team in the Class C California League, in 1954. There, he played less than half the season. Weir then came home to southern Ontario, where he briefly played in the Intercounty League before returning to sandlot ball in Toronto. He passed away in 2017 at the age of eighty-five.

• • •

Lidio "Red" Tallevi joined the Zanesville Dodgers of the Class D Ohio-Indiana League in 1948. In mid-August of that year, he pitched a twelve-inning, three-hit shutout against the Muncie Reds. A week later, he went the distance in a 16–3 thrashing of Lima. Tallevi helped his own cause with a home run, a single, and four runs batted in.

Zanesville finished the regular season in first place, a meagre half-game ahead of the second-place Portsmouth A's. The Dodgers swept Springfield in their best-of-seven semifinal and then defeated Muncie in six games in the finals.

Tallevi spent the 1949 season as a member of the Sheboygan Indians. This is the same club that Moe Galand would play for a couple of years later. The Indians were managed by Joe Hauser from 1946 to 1953. During that eight-year period, the club won four pennants and finished in the bottom half of the standings just once.

• • •

Right-handed pitcher Alf Williams also played for Joe Hauser at Sheboygan. That was in 1948, which was one of the seasons in which the Indians won the pennant.

Williams became an unlikely hero in Sheboygan's sixth game of the season, at home against Oshkosh. He pitched a scoreless top of the ninth with the score tied 2–2. Then, with a runner on and two out in the bottom of the frame, Williams stepped up to the plate. He put all of his 200 pounds into a pitch that sailed down the right field line for an opposite field, game-winning triple. It was the only triple of his brief minor league career.

Alf Williams played just one year of pro ball and finished the season with a 10–7 record. His WHIP was 1.79, and he had a 5.79 ERA.

Sheboygan finished the season atop the standings with an 85–40 record, 10.5 games ahead of the second-place Wisconsin Rapids.

• • •

Bill Harris, who had a hand in the signing of many of the players mentioned in this chapter, died of a stroke in February of 1954. He was only forty-eight years old.

PART VIII

TALES OF WOE

Arthur Irwin: Bigamist

Arthur Irwin was born in Toronto on Valentine's Day, 1858. The city of his birth was in Upper Canada back then, rather than Ontario. The Irwin family moved to Boston when he was a kid.

Irwin grew up playing baseball. He was a shortstop who made his professional debut in 1879 and went on to play big-league ball for teams in Worcester, Massachusetts, and Providence, Rhode Island, among other cities.

Wedding bells rang out in Boston for Irwin and his bride in 1883. But something was amiss. The new Mrs. Irwin later admitted that early in their relationship members of her family had warned her that something was not quite right with Irwin and that there were probably other women. Mrs. Irwin decided to ignore the warnings.

The Providence Grays, with Irwin as their regular shortstop, won the first interleague major league championship (a prototype World Series, essentially) in 1884. The Grays, representing the National League, defeated the New York Metropolitans of the rival American Association in three straight games.

In 1889, Irwin tried his hand at managing. Two years later, he skippered the Boston Reds of the (then major league) American Association to a pennant. The Reds won almost 70 percent of their games against the likes of the Louisville Colonels, Columbus Solons, and Cincinnati Kelly's Killers (so named because their player-manager was future Hall of Famer Mike "King" Kelly).

Irwin managed in the National League from 1894 to 1896. He was at the helm of the Philadelphia Phillies for two years and then spent a single term with the New York Giants. That year in Gotham may have been of some significance to Irwin in relation to his life outside of baseball.

Next up for Arthur Irwin was a return to his hometown. He was the manager and general manager of the Eastern League's Toronto Maple Leafs in 1897. "Toronto will have the best team procurable in the Eastern League next season," Irwin told the Ottawa *Daily Citizen* in January of '97. "And it will not be any fault of mine if baseball does not boom in this city this year."[118]

The Maple Leafs finished the regular season in second place, three and a half games behind the Syracuse Stars. Irwin's crew was led by outfielder Buck Freeman, one of the most prolific power hitters of the time. Freeman blasted a league-leading twenty homers for the Leafs in 1897.

After the 1897 regular season, Toronto and Syracuse played for the Steinert Cup, the Eastern League's playoff championship trophy. The series was to be a best-of-seven affair.

The Leafs won the first three games by scores of 9–2, 6–2, and 14–12. The teams combined for thirty-five hits and eleven errors in the third game. Syracuse won the fourth game, and the fifth contest was a tie that could not be completed.

The series then ground to a halt because the teams could not agree on where to play the next game. Ultimately, the Steinert Cup was awarded to Toronto.

Having assembled a championship team and steered it to a league title, there seemed little doubt that Arthur Irwin was a competent multitasker. Almost a quarter of a century later, this would become apparent in a different manner.

Irwin scouted and managed in the minor leagues, on and off, into the early 1920s. He was based in New York when he scouted. Now in his early

Arthur Irwin.

sixties, he tipped the scales at about 190 pounds. This was thirty pounds more than his playing weight.

When the curtain went up on the 1921 Eastern League season, Irwin was the manager of the Hartford Senators.

In mid-June, Irwin saw a doctor; he had been experiencing pain in his side. He was diagnosed as having appendicitis. X-rays were taken. The diagnosis was changed to neuritis. Irwin was told to rest. His woes were generally referred to as "abdominal trouble," and he was admitted to hospital. According to the Hartford *Courant,* he lost forty pounds.

On Thursday, July 14, Irwin left the hospital. However, he was clearly in distress. He told friends that he was "waiting for the undertaker." Irwin went to Springfield, Massachusetts. There he saw Jack Flynn, the manager of that city's Eastern League club. When they parted, Flynn said that they would see each other again. Irwin replied that he had seen the last of Arthur Irwin.

The next day, Irwin boarded the *Calvin Austin*, a steamship sailing from New York to Boston. Some time on the night of July 15, he disappeared. When the ship arrived in Boston the next day, Irwin was missing.

It was generally agreed that Arthur Irwin had thrown himself overboard. There's no proof of this. Nobody saw Irwin jump. Theoretically, he might have fallen. He might have been pushed. His body was never found.

Irwin was last seen on board by some friends and a ship steward. He had allegedly told friends that he was going to Boston to die. Irwin told the steward not to be surprised if he found him dead in his stateroom in the morning.

Several days after Irwin's disappearance, the true nature of his malady was disclosed. The St. Louis *Post-Dispatch* revealed that he had terminal cancer.

In the wake of Irwin's demise, it was also revealed that he was a bigamist. He had a wife in New York and another in Boston. They will henceforth be referred to as "Ms. Boston" and "Ms. New York."

Irwin fathered children with both women. The ladies only learned of Irwin's duplicity when it was revealed by his brother, John.

Somehow, Irwin lived his double life undiscovered for more than a quarter of a century. While already married to Ms. Boston, he wed Ms. New York in Philadelphia in 1894.

Arthur Irwin did not provide for Ms. Boston. This had been the situation for a period of several years. She was supported financially by her children.

John Irwin (also a former major leaguer) claimed that his brother's valuables were missing from his stateroom: diamond rings, diamond stickpins, and a watch. Other items were missing, too, like a $1,000 cheque from the Hartford ball club for the balance of his pay as the team's manager. It was learned later that Irwin had given the cheque for his back pay to Ms. New York. His Boston son, angry that his father had seemingly favoured his New York family, vowed to investigate the matter with the help of a lawyer.

In one "theory" relating to Irwin's demise, he boarded the steamer with $5,000. Then, during the voyage, he was robbed and thrown overboard. This hypothesis made it into print but was quickly discounted.

The three children of Ms. Boston feared how she might react to the news of their father's long-term infidelity. When she did find out, she was outwardly philosophical, feeling confident that despite having another woman, he had been on his way back to her to die in her arms.

Ms. Boston passed away in late August of 1922. "Mrs. Arthur A. Irwin Dies of Broken Heart," cried the Hartford *Courant.* According to the story under that sad title, Ms. Boston was already in poor health when she learned that Arthur had another wife.

Neither Ms. Boston nor Ms. New York were referred to by their actual names in news articles relating to Arthur Irwin. Instead, they were referred to as "Mrs. Arthur Irwin." This can make the stories difficult to understand because there were two of them.

Harry Decker: Inventor, Crook

The 1887 Toronto Canucks loved to run. International Association pennant winners that year, the Canucks pilfered no fewer than 414 bases in 104 games. Leading the way was right fielder Mike Slattery with 112.

Harry Decker, who played left field, third base, and catcher, stole thirty-one bases for Toronto. He returned to the Canucks and swiped thirty-seven bases in 1888.

It soon became apparent that habitual thieving came naturally to Harry Decker off the field as well. In particular, the thefts of other people's identities. Decker was a forger.

Harry Decker was born in Lockport, Illinois. He was just twenty-two when he joined the Toronto club. Decker had already bounced around in the majors and had appeared for big-league clubs based in Kansas City, Indianapolis, Detroit, and Washington, D.C.

Decker signed with three different clubs prior to the beginning of the 1887 campaign: Washington, Rochester, and Toronto. He received advances in the form of cheques from the three teams and promptly tried to cash them all. Decker went so far as to try to cash two of the cheques with the

Harry Decker.

same banker. What's more, the banker in question was a director for the Washington club!

After his caper failed, Decker impersonated two other catchers and convinced clubs to send him advance cheques made out to them. The addresses that he gave the clubs were empty lots. Decker was found pacing a nearby street, waiting for the postman.

One of the catchers who Decker claimed to be was David Oldfield. Decker and Oldfield were teammates with the Canucks, and both had played for Washington the previous season.

Despite his criminal antics, Decker was signed by the Toronto club. The *Globe* sang his praises during spring training: "Decker is a first-class catcher, a hard, reliable hitter, a fast baserunner, and a good fielder."[119]

The 1887 Canucks were Toronto's first pennant winners. The club won sixty-five games, lost just thirty-six, tied three, and finished three games ahead of second-place Buffalo. Decker was one of the stars of the team. He batted .335 and cranked out 151 hits in just ninety-nine games.

Decker ultimately played professional baseball for eight years, from 1884 to 1891 inclusive. His criminal proclivities ramped up as his playing career wound down.

Sometime in 1890, Decker was charged with infidelity. He rented a room at a hotel with a young lady who he claimed was his wife but was not. Decker's actual wife ultimately dropped the charges.

Decker lamented that he was irresistible. "I think I am a most unfortunate man," he told the Pittsburgh *Press*. "It seems to me that if I merely look at a girl she fancies me so much that a breach of promise suit is the result."[120]

In March of 1891, Decker was arrested for forgery and grand larceny in New Haven, Connecticut, where he was a member of the New Haven Nutmegs of the minor league Eastern Association. One of Decker's victims was Alfred Reach, a former player who was then president of the Philadelphia Phillies. Decker was a member of the Phillies for part of the 1890 season. Reach later became a sporting goods manufacturer and publisher of annual baseball guidebooks.

Decker could not make bail and was sent to jail. He made restitution and was released. Less than two months later, he was again arrested for forgery. This time, his New Haven teammates took up a collection and bailed him out of trouble. But Decker was through as a Nutmeg. The New Haven club wanted nothing more to do with him. In fact, his professional baseball career was over.

Decker's woes later took on a whole new dimension. In 1893, he was again charged with forgery. This time, he was declared insane. After spending a month at the Elgin Insane Asylum, west of Chicago, he was declared cured and released.

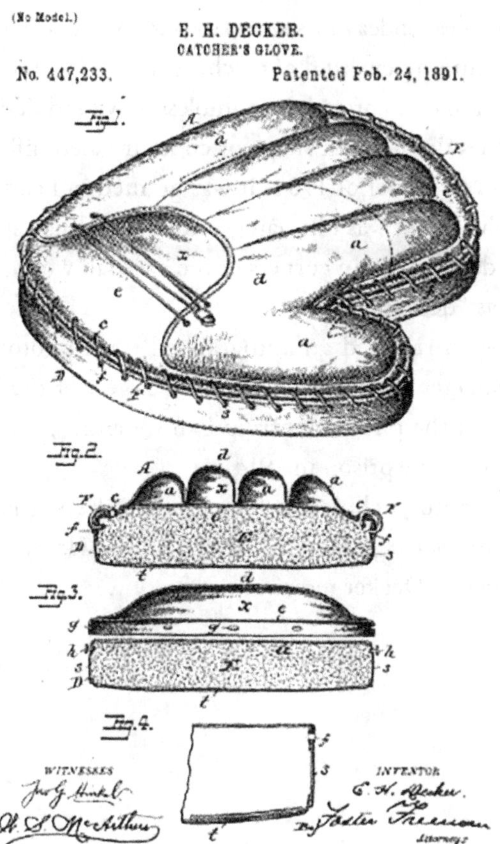

Catcher's mitt patented by Harry Decker.

Whether he was mentally ill or not, Decker exhibited odd behaviour. The *Globe* quoted the Chicago *Tribune* as follows: "Decker's hallucination is that he owns the city of Chicago. He was in the habit of entering saloons and ordering wine for everybody present and then walking out with the belief that the place belonged to him and he could give away his own wares if he saw fit."[121]

Decker stole a horse and forged the signature of a post office inspector on multiple cheques in 1894. He was arrested for forgery multiple times that year. One of his victims was none other than Albert Goodwill Spalding, the former pitcher turned sporting goods mogul. Decker was charged with bigamy as well.

Not all of Decker's business endeavours were crooked. Most famously, he invented what was at the time a new kind of catcher's mitt. He wrote in his patent application that he aimed to provide a thumbless glove and design the cushion so that it would retain its given shape or contour when inflated. A patent was applied for in November of 1904. It was granted in February of 1906, number 812921. The patent was ultimately sold to Spalding's sporting goods company. To this day, in certain corners of the baseball world, catcher's mitts are referred to as "deckers."

In 1915, Wallace Hogan received an autographed team photo in the mail. Hogan was the manager of the Venice/Vernon Tigers of the Pacific Coast League. The team in the photo was from San Quentin prison. The Tigers had given uniforms to the prison in 1914.

The players in the photo included a fellow with the surname of "Davenport." According to *Sporting Life*, Mr. Davenport was Harry Decker.

The ultimate fate of Harry Decker remains a mystery …

Vallie Eaves: Sozzled

It is somehow appropriate that a knuckleballer would be a drunk. The flight of a knuckler is erratic and unpredictable, just like the wobbly gait of someone who has had a few too many. Enter Vallie Eaves. Knuckleball pitcher. Boozehound.

Leafs manager Tony Lazzeri could not claim that he wasn't warned when Eaves was plucked from the Chicago White Sox in mid-May of 1940. Lazzeri had called Jimmy Dykes, manager of the White Sox, to see if he had any surplus pitching. Dykes replied that he did, and his price was reasonable.

But there was a catch. The Montreal *Gazette* quoted Dykes as saying that Eaves was unreliable and had gotten into a fight with a policeman — taking a beating in the process — just before the club left home, so he was not brought along.

Lazzeri decided to take a chance on Eaves. Toronto's newest hurler showed up a few days later wearing sunglasses that did not quite cover the remnants of a black eye. Lazzeri asked Eaves about it. Eaves claimed that he had been hit in the eye with a ball during batting practice.

The Toronto skipper then told Eaves that he knew the truth. Eaves promised to behave himself. Eaves was apparently great at making promises but not so good at keeping them.

Less than a month before Eaves joined the Leafs, he had a particularly wild outing for the White Sox. Pitching against the Detroit Tigers at Comiskey Park, he walked no fewer than twelve batters. Amazingly, he left the game in the eighth inning with a lead. Eaves ended up with a no-decision after the Tigers scored twice in the eighth and held on for a 6–5 win.

As a Maple Leaf, Vallie Eaves struggled. In parts of two seasons, 1940 and 1941, he had a combined 7–26 win–loss record and a 5.09 ERA. Not that the team was much better. Toronto had 104 victories and 208 defeats in those two years combined.

Eaves was suspended for "infraction of training rules" by new Toronto manager Lena Blackburne in late May of 1941.

The Leafs sold Eaves to the Milwaukee Brewers, then a minor league club in the American Association, midway through the 1941 season. The Brewers were owned by Bill Veeck, the imaginative owner who once sent in three-foot-seven-inch Eddie Gaedel to pinch-hit in a big-league game.

The day that he was dealt to Milwaukee, Eaves had to rush to Toledo. The Brewers were playing in that city, and Eaves was selected as the starting pitcher. Toronto's general manager put Eaves on a train. Game time came, and Eaves was AWOL. Veeck finally found him at a local bar, passed out.

Once resuscitated, Eaves was bundled onto a train to Columbus, the next stop on Milwaukee's itinerary. The next day, he was forced to pitch both ends of a doubleheader.

According to Veeck, Vallie Eaves was a harmless drunk. Nevertheless, Eaves was not beyond pulling a knife on a bartender after being told that he had had enough to drink for the evening. Veeck made it his mission to educate Milwaukee barmen, explaining that Eaves could easily be disarmed if shown a little sympathy.

After pitching well in Milwaukee, Eaves was picked up by their parent club, the Chicago Cubs. Eaves was thrilled by this, so much so that he offered to pitch for the Brewers and the Cubs on the same day. He could play in Chicago in the afternoon, then rush to Milwaukee to play in the evening. This was a nice gesture from Eaves, but it was not allowed.

Alcohol abuse continued to plague Eaves. In May of 1942, he was back with the Cubs, who were scheduled to play a doubleheader against the Brooklyn Dodgers. Eaves was sent home to Chicago and suspended when he allegedly turned up drunk at Ebbets Field.

A few years later, Eaves was pitching for the San Diego Padres, then a Pacific Coast League club. The Padres were managed by Pepper Martin, who had been the third baseman for "The Gashouse Gang," the rowdy St. Louis Cardinals of the late 1920s to mid-1930s. Martin was no shrinking violet.

The Padres were in Oakland to play the Oaks. Martin admitted that he slapped Eaves at the team's hotel, but witnesses claimed that the "slap" was actually a solid right-handed punch that hit Eaves in the chin. "Pepper had punched his big right-handed pitcher into the middle of next week for acting up in public," Emmett Watson of the Seattle *Star* later wrote.[122]

Whether it was a slap or a punch, Martin must have been a believer in the old adage "The bigger they are, the harder they fall." Martin was 5'8" tall. Eaves was 6'2".

A syndicated AP story quoted Martin as follows: "He had it coming to him. He let me down during the game yesterday, besides upsetting the discipline of the club and setting a bad example for the rest of the players."[123]

The previous day, Eaves had pitched three scoreless innings in relief of the San Diego starter. It is not clear how that constituted Pepper Martin being "let down." In any case, Martin and Eaves seemed to have let bygones be bygones. Eaves went on to finish the 1945 season with a 21–15 record in a career high 312 innings pitched.

Eaves gained some notoriety in San Diego for missing trains. Pepper Martin did his best to cope with the situation, trying various ways of getting Eaves to reform, including taking him to church. That didn't work.

In early July of 1948, as a member of the Gladewater Bears of the Class C Lone Star League, Eaves was suspended for "disciplinary reasons" yet again. By this point in his career, he was sliding down the minor league ladder.

Ed Terrell of the Marshall *News Messenger* lamented, "Nobody in professional baseball ever had a more brilliant future before him than did Eaves, but one weakness proved to be his downfall."[124]

Frank McGowan of the Birmingham *News* had this to say about Eaves in March of 1949: "Eaves holds some kind of record for drawing suspensions and fines and could have been a major league star if he had controlled himself."[125]

Eaves went on to win over 200 games in the minor leagues, spread over a period of nineteen years. He had four seasons with twenty or more victories.

Len Koenecke: A Sad Fate

Baseballs were flying all over the place on a mid-September Saturday afternoon at Wrigley Field in 1935. The Cubs led 8–0 after three innings and 16–4 after six. When the dust finally settled, Chicago emerged with an 18–14 win over the Brooklyn Dodgers.

The two teams combined for thirty-three hits in that game. One of those hits, a single, was smacked by Brooklyn centre fielder Len Koenecke. That single wound up being the last hit of his career.

Koenecke made his big-league debut in 1932, when he got into forty-two games with the New York Giants. In 1933, with the Buffalo Bisons of the International League, Koenecke batted .334 and amassed 201 hits. In the sixth and final game of the best-of-seven finals, he hit three doubles and a single to lead the Bisons to a Little World Series berth against Columbus of the American Association. Koenecke joined the Dodgers in 1934 and had a breakout season: a .320 batting average, thirty-one doubles, and fourteen homers. He walked almost twice as often as he struck out.

His 1935 season had not been quite so successful. Fewer of his hits went for extra bases. His strikeouts outnumbered his walks. His batting average was hovering around the .280 mark. That was good, but it was nowhere near what it had been the previous season. Still, there were two weeks left in the season. Casey Stengel, then the Dodgers manager, might give Koenecke a chance to make up ground on what had turned into a lost summer.

Or maybe not. With nothing to play for but pride, Stengel decided to send three players back to Brooklyn and give some prospects a chance to shine. One of the three ousted Dodgers was Len Koenecke.

After the Chicago series, the Dodgers travelled southwest to St. Louis. There, Koenecke and two pitchers, Bob Barr and Les Munns, were told that their 1935 season was over. They received plane tickets back to New York via Chicago and Detroit. This was odd because major league teams usually took the train. Furthermore, there was no need to hurry.

The first leg of the journey was from St. Louis to Chicago. Koenecke boarded the plane with a bottle of whiskey in one hand. He was a bit tipsy. Then, on the way from Chicago to Detroit, Koenecke became unruly. Ultimately, he knocked down a flight attendant and had to be restrained for the duration of the flight. On arrival at Detroit, he was removed from the plane. Barr and Munns continued without him.

Koenecke then arranged to charter a pilot and plane to take him to Buffalo. The pilot was a fellow named William Mulqueeney. The small, single-engine plane took off with three people on board: Koenecke, Mulqueeney, and a friend of the pilot named Irwin Davis.

According to Mulqueeney, Koenecke wanted to experience a stunt flight. "After the takeoff at Detroit, Koenecke suggested I nose the plane down and do some stunting. I told him we couldn't do that, that we were over Canada and to stunt would be a violation of regulations. This was about an hour after we left. Soon Koenecke tried to grab the controls."[126]

Davis intervened. Koenecke responded by starting a fight with Davis. Mulqueeney grabbed the plane's fire extinguisher and hit Koenecke in the head with it several times.

"It all happened so quickly," Mulqueeney told the *Globe and Mail*. "I hardly knew what it was all about. My first thought was self-preservation. It was a question of three or one. We intended only to subdue Koenecke, who was in a violent state."[127] Koenecke was on the floor of the cabin, unconscious, as Mulqueeney regained control of the plane.

By now, the plane had been in Canadian airspace for quite some time. People on the ground near the shore of Lake Ontario had seen it flying erratically. At about one o'clock in the morning, after narrowly missing some high-tension wires, Mulqueeney was able to land the plane on the infield of Toronto's Long Branch Racetrack. The track, which operated from 1924 to 1955, was near the corner of Kipling Avenue and Horner Avenue. Incidentally, the track was located just across a train track from today's Connorvale Park, where Joey Votto played amateur baseball for the Etobicoke Rangers.

There would be no more baseball for Len Koenecke, professional or amateur. Koenecke was dead. His belongings were used to identify him. Among them was a cheque made out to him from the Dodgers.

Ironically, Koenecke had once worked as a stoker in a locomotive. He fed fires in trains. Now he was dead, beaten to death by a fire extinguisher.

Mulqueeney was grief-stricken. "My god," he said to the Toronto *Star*. "I wish I could take those blows back. It's all so terrible. I hardly know what happened. If I could only meet his wife, I would assure her it was most unfortunate and tell her how sorry I am." He added, "I walloped him over the head — it was his life or ours."[128]

The fire extinguisher was heavily dented and looked like it had been used to whack someone in the head multiple times. The small plane was damaged on landing. It had come to rest perched on its left wheel and the tip of its right wing. It looked like a broken mechanical dragonfly. It was guarded by members of the RCMP.

Mulqueeney and Davis were charged with manslaughter and held in remand without bail. At no time did they deny killing Koenecke or point the finger at one another. They planned to enter a plea of self-defence. There was talk of bringing in Casey Stengel to testify that Koenecke was insane, at least temporarily. Edward Murphy, KC, was the defence lawyer for Mulqueeney and Davis. Murphy stated that Koenecke was trying to commit suicide and that his attempt failed because of the actions of the co-defendants. That was a strange thing to say, since Koenecke's actions led directly to his death.

Back in Brooklyn, Les Munns did not believe that Koenecke had attacked Mulqueeney and Davis. He was also upset that Koenecke had been allowed on an airplane under the circumstances. "What we can't understand," he told the Brooklyn *Daily Eagle*, "is why a commercial airplane would take a man in that condition after he had been ejected from another plane." Munns added, "I can testify that he was in no condition to be taken on a plane."[129]

Magistrate William Keith dismissed the case outright. "I am inclined to believe this man's death was caused by these men defending themselves," he told the Toronto *Daily Star*. "There is no evidence of criminal intent or negligence. The men may have used a little more force than necessary, but the circumstances were unusual."[130]

Less than a week after the case was dismissed, Mulqueeney flew the plane back to Detroit. Accompanying him was George Bonning, the mechanic who had repaired the damage. Irwin Davis went home by car.

Len Koenecke was not known as a drunk or a hothead. He left his wife and his young daughter back home in Wisconsin. His seemingly out-of-character behaviour on that September night cost him his own life and very nearly the lives of two other people.

One can only imagine how Casey Stengel felt about Koenecke's death.

EPILOGUE

Bridging the Gap

It was Labour Day, 1967. The Leafs were hosting the Syracuse Chiefs. Toronto was going nowhere as far as the International League season was concerned. The best that any of the Leafs could hope for was a summons to Boston, where the Red Sox were embroiled in a battle for the American League pennant.

Maple Leaf Stadium was mostly empty, as it had been all season. The Leafs drew just 67,216 fans in 1967, seventh in the eight-team International League.

Nobody knew it yet, but the Leafs were playing their final game in Toronto.

That very day, a half-dozen players and one manager were involved in other professional games in other cities. They had something in common, but they wouldn't know it for another decade.

• • •

Phil Roof of the Kansas City Athletics had a tiring Labour Day in 1967. Roof caught both ends of a doubleheader in Detroit that day. Phil Roof played briefly for the Leafs back in '63.

The Tigers won the first game 8–4. Roof went zero-for-two. The A's and their twenty-six-year-old receiver fared much better in the nightcap. Kansas City won 4–2. Roof had a single and a double in four at-bats. Incidentally, the double was hit against Toronto native John Hiller.

• • •

Chuck Hartenstein also had a busy Labour Day in 1967. His Chicago Cubs hosted a double-dip at Wrigley Field against the Los Angeles Dodgers.

In the opener, the Cubs opened the scoring with a single tally in the fourth. The Dodgers were still down 1–0 with two out and nobody on in the top of the ninth. Up to the plate stepped left fielder Lou Johnson, an ex-Leaf. Johnson walloped a Rich Nye pitch over the fence, tying the score.

The game went into extra innings. Nye was relieved by Chuck Hartenstein, who went on to lead the '67 Cubs with eleven saves. Hartenstein pitched a scoreless tenth. In the eleventh, Ron Fairly pinch-hit for the Dodgers. Hartenstein retired Fairly. Los Angeles failed to score. Ernie Banks led off the twelfth frame with a homer and the game was over. Chuck Hartenstein got the win, improving his win–loss record to 8–4.

In the nightcap, Hartenstein came into the game in the top of the ninth with the Cubs ahead 5–2. He gave up four hits and four runs without recording so much as a single out. Hartenstein was charged with the loss as the Cubs fell 8–6.

Ron Fairly of the Dodgers was sent up as a pinch-hitter in both games of the doubleheader. He failed to reach base both times.

• • •

Steve Hargan, four days shy of his twenty-fifth birthday, started on the mound for Cleveland on Labour Day of 1967. The Indians were visiting Minnesota. Hargan was in his second full season in the majors.

The Twins took a 1–0 lead in the bottom of the second inning. Cleveland tied it in the top of the sixth, only to see Minnesota inch ahead with a run in the home half of the frame. The Twins knocked Hargan out of the box in the process. Minnesota scored twice in the eighth and won 4–1. The loss dropped Hargan's record to 14–12.

• • •

Tom Murphy, twenty-one, was the starting pitcher for the El Paso Sun Kings on Labour Day of 1967. The Sun Kings were visiting the Albuquerque Dodgers, who were in first place in the AA Texas League standings. Murphy, a righty, had already pitched as high as AAA. He had not yet pitched in the majors. The Sun Kings were an affiliate of the California Angels.

Murphy surrendered three runs, all earned, in seven innings. He took the loss as the Dodgers prevailed 6–2. It was the last day of the Texas League regular season.

• • •

Héctor Torres was the starting shortstop for the Seattle Angels when they hosted the Hawaii Islanders on Labour Day of 1967. It was the final day of the AAA Pacific Coast League (PCL) regular season.

Torres, a native of Monterrey, Mexico, was just sixteen years old when he played his first pro game back in 1962. He reached AAA in 1966.

The Angels won the game 5–3. Torres went one-for-three and scored a run.

• • •

Roy Hartsfield, manager of the Spokane Indians of the Pacific Coast League, was gambling on Labour Day of 1967. Hartsfield had chosen twenty-year-old Alan Foster as his starting pitcher in this crucial home game against the Vancouver Canadians on this, the last day of the regular season.

Foster had thrown a pair of no-hitters for Hartsfield in 1967. The second had taken place just three days earlier. Was he up to the task of holding Vancouver at bay on three days' rest?

It was a so-called must-win for Spokane. Going into the day's games, they had a half-game lead over the Portland Beavers in the PCL Western Division. Portland had a doubleheader against Tacoma, while Spokane had just one game against Vancouver. If Portland swept and Spokane lost, the Beavers would claim first place.

Portland took both games from Tacoma.

Hartsfield was forced to yank his starting hurler in the top of the third inning with two out. Foster was done for the day, but the game was still close. Spokane was behind 2–1.

Pulling Foster out of the game proved a wise decision. The Spokane bullpen threw six and a third shutout innings and won the game 5–2.

With the win, Spokane tied Portland for first place in their division. A one-game playoff was scheduled for the next day, in Portland. The Indians won that game 6–1 to earn themselves a berth in the best-of-seven PCL finals against the Eastern Division champs, the San Diego Padres.

Spokane lost the series four games to two. San Diego won the first three games of the series at home. The Indians then notched a pair of victories in Spokane. The Padres then wrapped up the series with a road win.

• • •

What, then, do Phil Roof, Chuck Hartenstein, Ron Fairly, Steve Hargan, Tom Murphy, Héctor Torres, and Roy Hartsfield have in common?

The answer, if a bit obscure, is this: all were playing (or managing, in Hartsfield's case) while the Toronto Maple Leafs were playing their last ever game, on Labour Day of 1967, and all were members of the Toronto Blue Jays during their inaugural season, 1977.

Three additional 1977 Blue Jays were active on Labour Day of 1967 but did not play: pitchers Bill Singer and Jerry Johnson, and third baseman Doug Rader.

• • •

Phil Roof is part of the answer to a similar question: Who suited up for both the Maple Leafs and the Blue Jays?

Roof and Rico Carty are the only two to play for the Leafs and the Jays. Galen Cisco and Jackie Moore played for the Leafs and coached for the Jays.

Acknowledgements

Thank you so much to the individuals who permitted me to interview them for this book: Ron Stead, John Bukowski, Bill Park, Bob Hunter, Frank Repchik, Doug Beckett, Sparky Anderson, and Dr. Ron Taylor. My heartfelt apologies to anyone I have forgotten.

Thank you also to Bill Humber, Richard Prentice, Pat Tuero, and Len Parisi.

Sadly, some of the people listed above are no longer with us.

Staff helped me out at the Toronto Reference Library, York University, Toronto Archives, and the Archives of Ontario.

Robert Jones and Martin Tilk proofread this book for me. Any remaining errors are my own.

Many thanks to my editor, Allister Thompson, to freelance proofreader Ashley Hisson, and to the fine folks at Dundurn Press: Elena Radic, Laura Boyle, Janna Green, Eden Boudreau, and Meghan Macdonald.

Most of all, thank you to Eva Rosenstock, my wife, for loving me as I am.

Notes

1 *The Globe*, May 5, 1914.
2 *The Globe*, May 5, 1914.
3 *The Globe*, May 5, 1914.
4 Toronto *World,* May 11, 1911.
5 Akron *Beacon Journal*, July 10, 1899.
6 Toronto *Daily Star*, July 26, 1924.
7 Toronto *Daily Star*, July 24, 1918.
8 Toronto *World*, May 26, 1887.
9 Toronto *Telegram*, June 20, 1932.
10 David Shoalts, "Drive to Put Carnegie in Hall," *The Globe and Mail*, March 17, 2001.
11 *The Globe and Mail*, October 22, 1945.
12 *The Globe and Mail*, May 2, 1946.
13 *The Globe and Mail*, May 2, 1946.
14 Author's interview with Ron Stead.
15 *The Globe and Mail*, May 8, 1946.
16 *The Globe and Mail*, May 8, 1946.
17 Author's interview with Ellis Ferguson "Cot" Deal.
18 *The Globe and Mail*, May 18, 1946.
19 Gordon Walker, Toronto *Daily Star*, May 18, 1946.

20 Ted Reeve, Toronto *Telegram*, May 18, 1946.
21 Toronto *Daily Star*, May 18, 1946.
22 Ted Reeve, Toronto *Telegram*, May 18, 1946.
23 Toronto *Daily Star*, May 18, 1946.
24 Toronto *Daily Star*, May 17, 1946.
25 Author's interview with Ron Stead.
26 Rex MacLeod, *The Globe and Mail*, October 4, 1960.
27 Al Nickleson, *The Globe and Mail*, January 7, 1955.
28 Jim Coleman, *The Globe and Mail*, January 17, 1959.
29 Jim Coleman, *The Globe and Mail*, July 13, 1946.
30 *The Globe and Mail*, March 30, 1968.
31 *The Globe and Mail*, March 30, 1968.
32 Al Nickleson, *The Globe and Mail*, January 4, 1951.
33 Milt Dunnell, Toronto *Daily Star*, September 17, 1952.
34 Milt Dunnell, Toronto *Daily Star*, September 17, 1952.
35 Jim Vipond, *The Globe and Mail*, November 14, 1947.
36 Joe Perlove, Toronto *Daily Star*, October 22, 1945.
37 Vern DeGeer, *The Globe and Mail*, May 10, 1944.
38 Jim Proudfoot, *The Globe and Mail*, August 31, 1957.
39 Al Nickleson, *The Globe and Mail*, September 26, 1950.
40 Jim Coleman, *The Globe and Mail*, August 10, 1948.
41 Jim Coleman, *The Globe and Mail*, July 14, 1942.
42 *The Globe and Mail*, July 4, 1942.
43 Milt Dunnell, Toronto *Daily Star*, September 18, 1952.
44 Milt Dunnell, Toronto *Daily Star*, May 11, 1950.
45 Jim Coleman, *The Globe and Mail*, July 14, 1942.
46 Jim Vipond, *The Globe and Mail*, October 28, 1947.
47 Joe Reichler, Casper *Star-Tribune*, September 10, 1945.
48 Scranton *Times-Tribune*, September 10, 1945.
49 Lancaster *New Era*, September 10, 1945.
50 Stan Baumgartner, Philadelphia *Inquirer*, September 10, 1945.
51 Pittsburgh *Press*, September 10, 1945.
52 Stan Baumgartner, Philadelphia *Inquirer*, September 10, 1945.
53 Buffalo *Morning Express*, May 9, 1881.

54 Buffalo *Morning Express*, May 9, 1881.
55 Buffalo *Commercial*, May 16, 1881.
56 Chicago *Inter Ocean*, May 26, 1881.
57 Boston *Globe*, June 16, 1881.
58 Chicago *Inter Ocean*, July 5, 1881.
59 Toronto *World*, September 7, 1885.
60 Toronto *World*, September 7, 1885.
61 *The Globe*, July 19, 1897.
62 Brantford *Expositor*, May 22, 1905.
63 *The Globe*, August 4, 1906.
64 *The Globe*, July 6, 1928.
65 Toronto *Daily Star*, December 19, 1928.
66 Toronto *Daily Star*, November 1, 1932.
67 Toronto *World*, August 16, 1882.
68 Hamilton *Spectator*, May 28, 1885.
69 *The Globe*, June 25, 1885.
70 Boston *Globe*, July 11, 1886.
71 Hamilton *Spectator*, April 8, 1880.
72 Kingston *Daily News*, August 26, 1901.
73 *The Globe*, July 23, 1902.
74 *The Globe*, January 25, 1901.
75 *The Globe*, March 25, 1931.
76 Montreal *Star*, June 17, 1931.
77 Neil MacCarl, Toronto *Daily Star*, May 23, 1956.
78 Jack Dulmage, Windsor *Star*, March 17, 1970.
79 Jack Dulmage, Windsor *Star*, March 17, 1970.
80 Jack Dulmage, Windsor *Star*, March 17, 1970.
81 *Star Weekly*, September 18, 1937.
82 Jim Proudfoot, Toronto *Star*, April 7, 1994.
83 Al Sokol, Toronto *Star*, February 2, 1974.
84 Al Sokol, Toronto *Star*, February 2, 1974.
85 Milt Dunnell, Toronto *Star*, January 3, 1993.
86 Eddie Storin, Miami *Herald*, March 9, 1959.
87 Eddie Storin, Miami *Herald*, March 9, 1959.

88 Eddie Storin, Miami *Herald*, March 9, 1959.
89 Brantford *Expositor*, March 12, 1966.
90 F.C. Lane, *Baseball Magazine*, August 1914.
91 St. Louis *Dispatch*, April 3, 1910.
92 St. Louis *Dispatch*, April 3, 1910.
93 F.C. Lane, *Baseball Magazine*, August 1914.
94 *Baseball Magazine*, September 1917.
95 Buffalo *Courier*, December 27, 1909.
96 Buffalo *Courier*, December 27, 1909.
97 F.C. Lane, *Baseball Magazine*, August 1914.
98 F.C. Lane, *Baseball Magazine*, January 1916.
99 Harry Grayson, Kingston *Whig-Standard*, June 29, 1943.
100 Author's interview with Doug Beckett.
101 Neil MacCarl, Toronto *Star*, August 8, 1966.
102 Nancy Randle, "Their Time at Bat: A Women's Professional League That Made Baseball Herstory," Chicago *Tribune Magazine*, July 5, 1992.
103 Shelley Rolfe, Richmond *Times-Dispatch*, April 23, 1951.
104 Shelley Rolfe, Richmond *Times-Dispatch*, April 23, 1951.
105 Flint *Journal*, July 24, 1967.
106 Jim Hawkins, Detroit *Free Press*, July 9, 1972.
107 Halsey Hall, Minneapolis *Star*, July 3, 1958.
108 Minneapolis *Star*, January 31, 1958.
109 Kingston *Whig-Standard*, June 4, 1888.
110 Kingston *Whig-Standard*, June 13, 1888.
111 Neil MacCarl, Toronto *Star*, August 1, 1962.
112 Neal Russo, St. Louis *Post-Dispatch*, October 12, 1964.
113 Shreveport *Times*, July 10, 1930.
114 Shreveport *Times*, July 10, 1930.
115 Shreveport *Times*, July 10, 1930.
116 John Steadman, Baltimore *Sun*, May 2, 1999.
117 John Steadman, Baltimore *Sun*, May 2, 1999.
118 Ottawa *Daily Citizen*, January 13, 1897.
119 *The Globe*, March 31, 1887.
120 Pittsburgh *Press*, September 23, 1890.

121 *The Globe*, November 9, 1893.
122 Emmett Wilson, Seattle *Star*, April 19, 1946.
123 Shawnee *News-Star*, July 24, 1945.
124 Ed Terrell, Marshall *News Messenger*, July 4, 1948.
125 Frank McGowan, Birmingham *News*, March 16, 1949.
126 Toronto *Daily Star*, September 17, 1935.
127 *The Globe and Mail*, September 18, 1935.
128 Toronto *Daily Star*, September 17, 1935.
129 Brooklyn *Daily Eagle*, September 17, 1935.
130 Toronto *Daily Star*, September 20, 1935.

Bibliography

BOOKS

Carnegie, Herb. *A Fly in a Pail of Milk*. Mosaic Press, 1997.

Cauz, Louis. *Baseball's Back in Town*. Controlled Media, 1977.

Freedman, Lew. *Baseball's Funnymen*. McFarland, 2017.

Gairey, Harry. *A Black Man's Toronto, 1914–1980: The Reminiscences of Harry Gairey*. Multicultural History Society of Ontario, 1981.

Henry, Keith. *Black Politics in Toronto Since World War I*. Multicultural History Society of Ontario, 1981.

Holway, John. *Voices from the Great Black Baseball Leagues*. Dodd, Mead, 1975.

Johnson, Lloyd. *The Encyclopedia of Minor League Baseball*. Baseball America, 1993.

Marchildon, Phil. *Ace*. Penguin Books Canada, 1993.

Morris, Peter. *Catcher: How the Man Behind the Plate Became an American Folk Hero*. Ivan R. Dee, 2009.

Neft, David. *The Sports Encyclopedia: Baseball*. St. Martin's Griffin, 1999.

O'Neal, Bill. *The American Association*. Eakin Press, 1991.

O'Neal, Bill. *The International League*. Eakin Press, 1992.

Robinson, Jackie. *I Never Had It Made.* G.P. Putnam's Sons, 1972.
Shearon, Jim. *Canada's Baseball Legends.* Malin Head Press, 1994.
Stump, Al. *Cobb: A Biography.* Algonquin Books, 1994.
Utley, R.G., and Scott Verner. *The Independent Carolina Baseball League, 1936–1938.* McFarland, 1999.
Williams, Pat. *How to Be Like Jackie Robinson.* Health Communications, 2004.

NEWSPAPERS

Albany *Argus*
Altoona *Tribune*
Augusta *Journal*
Baseball Magazine
Bowmanville *Canadian Statesman*
Bristol *Herald Courier*
British *Whig* (Kingston, ON)
Brooklyn *Daily Eagle*
Buffalo *Commercial*
Buffalo *Courier*
Buffalo *Courier Express*
Buffalo *Morning Express*
Buffalo *News*
Buffalo *Times*
Carlisle *Evening Herald*
Chattanooga *Daily Times*
Chicago *Chronicle*
Chicago *Tribune*
Cincinnati *Enquirer*
Courier (Waterloo, IA)
Courier-Journal (Louisville, KY)
The Day Book
Dayton *Herald*
Democrat and Chronicle (Rochester, NY)
Detroit *Free Press*
Elizabethton *Star*

The Expositor (Brantford, ON)
Fort Worth *Star-Telegram*
The Globe (Toronto, ON)
Green Bay *Press-Gazette*
Hamilton *Spectator*
Herald and Review (Decatur, IL)
The Inter Ocean
Johnson City *Press*
Kenosha *News*
Kingston *Daily News*
Kingston *Whig-Standard*
Marion County *Herald*
Marshall *News Messenger*
Milwaukee *Journal*
Minneapolis *Star Tribune*
Mobile *Daily Item*
Montreal *Gazette*
Morning Journal-Courier (New Haven, CT)
Muskegon *Chronicle*
New Orleans *Republican*
New York *Daily News*
The News (Frederick, MD)
Northern Advance (Barrie, ON)
Ottawa *Citizen*
Ottawa *Journal*
Ottawa *Times*
Philadelphia *Inquirer*
Philadelphia *Times*
Pittsburgh *Daily Post*
Pittsburgh *Press*
The Plaine Dealer (Hazleton, PA)
Richmond *Times-Dispatch*
Rock Island *Argus*
Rockford *Morning Star*

Rockford *Register-Republic*
St. Louis *Globe-Democrat*
St. Louis *Post-Dispatch*
Scranton *Times-Tribune*
Seattle *Star*
Sheboygan *Press*
Sporting Life
Springfield *Union* (Springfield, MA)
Star Weekly (Toronto, ON)
The Tennessean
Toronto *Globe and Mail*
Toronto *Star*
Toronto *Sunday World*
Toronto *Telegram*
The Varsity
Washington *Times*
Wilkes-Barre *Times Leader*
Windsor *Star*
The World (New York, NY)
The World (Toronto, ON)

MISCELLANEOUS SOURCES

Sporting News Player Contract Cards

LINK TO HARRY DECKER'S PATENT

patentimages.storage.googleapis.com/51/c5/df/c6117918cb8805/US812921.pdf

Image Credits

6 (*top*) *Globe*, June 27, 1914; (*bottom*) Toronto *Daily Star*, April 24, 1914
10 Hennepin County Library
15 City of Toronto Archives, *Globe and Mail* fonds, Fonds 1266, Item 13401
21 *Globe*, July 4, 1903
23 New York Public Library
27 Library of Congress
29 Library of Congress
34 Library of Congress
43 Library of Congress
46 Toronto *Star*
51 U.S. National Archives
67 City of Toronto Archives, *Globe and Mail* fonds, Fonds 1266, Item 14854
71 City of Toronto Archives, *Globe and Mail* fonds, Fonds 1266, Item 6161
72 City of Toronto Archives, *Globe and Mail* fonds, Fonds 1266, Item 7698
91 City of Toronto Archives, Fonds 1257, Series 1057, Item 4275
124 Chicago History Museum, Chicago *Daily News* collection, SDN-001354
143 Private collection
151 Library of Congress
161 Library of Congress
162 Library of Congress

169 Richard Prentice
174 Frank Repchik
190 Library of Congress
223 Hennepin County Library
225 Library of Congress
261 Library of Congress
265 Library of Congress
267 IFI Claims Patent Services

Index